Pencil Dancing

MARI MESSER

new ways to free your creative spirit

WALKING STICK PRESS
Cincinnati, Ohio

www.writersdigest.com

Visit our Web site at www.writersdigest.com for information on more resources for writers.

To receive a free weekly e-mail newsletter delivering tips and updates about writing and about Writer's Digest products, register directly at our Web site at http://newsletters.fwpublications.com.

05 04 03 02 01   5 4 3 2

Library of Congress Cataloging-in-Publication Data

Messer, Mari, 1933-
    Pencil dancing : new ways to free your creative spirit / Mari Messer.
            p. cm.
    Includes index.
    ISBN 1-58297-077-7 (hc : alk. paper) — ISBN 1-58297-005-X (pbk.)
    1. Creation (Literary, artistic, etc.) I. Title.

NX165 .M475 2001
701'.15   2001026016
                                                                         CIP

Edited by Jack Heffron, Meg Leder and Donya Dickerson
Cover and Interior Designed by Stephanie Strang
Cover Photography by Frank P. Walsh, Naoyuki Fukamachi, Junshi Nakamichi/Photonica
Interior Photography by Photodisc
Production coordinated by Mark Griffin

*A tip of the hat, a deep bow and
a word of enormous, heartfelt thanks to*

Mary Crosset for her patience and tenacity in typing this book into life Jack Heffron and Meg Leder, editors, for believing in the idea and helping it take form Jen Haller at Joseph-Beth and Mary Ellen Camelle at Grailville Art & Bookstore for their "good steers" Suzanne Fisher, former director of community education and the Art Academy of Cincinnati, for taking a chance on a new approach to creativity The folks at The Wellness Community, a center for cancer patients, for inspiring the idea for *Pencil Dancing.* Kirk Polking, writer and mountainous source of answers to all my confused questions, for all her invaluable advice Sr. Agatha Fitzgerald of Chatfield College for her beautifully rendered mandala drawings Mary Schickel, who taught me by example what it means to be a "life artist" The Public Library of Cincinnati and Hamilton County, especially the Literature Department, for tracking information Cincinnati Nature Center for peaceful woods walks between chapters Jane Heimlich, Linda Walker, Gordon Baer, Lynn Robins, Karen Souhrada, Isabelle Healy, Mary Cox, Bill Wexler, Alan Bayowski and Jean Fredette for their input and encouragement

And special thanks to the creative spirit in each of us.

Mari Messer is a writer and creative consultant who has contributed columns and articles to local and national publications including *The Wall Street Journal's National Business Employment Weekly, Artist's & Graphic Designer's Market, Liguorian, Women's World News* and the journal of The University of Texas Medical Branch at Galveston. Her poetry has appeared in regional literary journals. Previously, the author served for ten years as director of communications for a nonprofit organization. She has a B.S. degree in Art Education from the University of Wisconsin at Madison.

For over fifteen years, Mari Messer has designed and led workshops on creativity, writing, and art for groups and organizations including GE Career Center, Hospice of Southwest Ohio, Widowed Person's Service, The Wellness Community for cancer patients, Universiy of Cincinnati College of Nursing, Mercy Hospital, College of Mount St. Joseph, Mariemont City Schools, The Art Academy of Cincinnati and many others.

what's inside

1

Creativity 101: Practicing the Basic Steps

2

Polishing Your Powers of Observation

3

Creating With Your Whole Self

4
Losing Your Logical Mind

5
Freeing Your Creative Elves

6
Befriending Your Beasts

7
Creating From the Inside Out

8
Dancing With Your Creative Spirit

An Invitation to Dance

I can't dance. Never could. Except for closed-curtain midnight whirls around the living room, accompanied by recorded piano music, I've never had fewer than two left feet on the dance floor. But I think I know dance. I know that life is a dance. I've discovered, if only by coincidence, that creative expression, in whatever form it takes, is a dance. This dance between conscious and unconscious, creator and critic, left brain and right brain results in something original and often surprising. This idea is not a theory. It's a process I've observed first-hand in my own practice of writing and art.

The connection between creativity and dance came to me by accident years ago. A newspaper article about one of my workshops led to an invitation to do a class for The Wellness Community, a center for cancer patients. "Come up with a title that's upbeat and sounds like fun," the director asked. I brainstormed, pored through books, and picked the brains of other writers and creative people. Nothing clicked.

Then I found these lines—which to this day I carry around on crumpled paper—from Alexander Pope:

> True ease in writing comes
> from *Art*, not chance, as
> those move easiest who
> have learned to dance.

Bingo! That was it. You can substitute your own art form for the word *writing*, and Pope's words become a creative anthem. Isn't that what creativity in any of its forms is all about? A dance between innovation and logic—flowing, exuberant, expressive, joyful. I called my class "Pencil Dancing" and continue to use the same name for many other classes and lectures for writers, artists and other creatives. People seem to know instinctively what the course is about. They say they're attracted by the suggestion of flow and ease. They come because they're curious, blocked and needful of encouragement and inspiration. Most of all, they come because the course sounds like fun.

Fun, it took me a long time to discover, is a central element in creativity. At first, fear drove me to try to become creative. Many years ago, when I was attending the University of Wisconsin, I met a med student who wanted to give me a Rorschach ink blot test to practice for his launch into psychiatry. Intrigued, I agreed. What the results showed, he said, was that I was either creative or crazy. I opted for creative. From that day on, I aimed to be creative, though at the time I wasn't sure what creativity really was or how to go about becoming that way. Least of all did I realize that creativity is fun.

In my search for clues on how to be more creative, I discovered that people talk about creativity as if they know exactly what it is. Yet even researchers, scientists and other creative authorities can't agree. Over time, I've come to think it's mostly a mystery. It's as if someone were to give you an exotic pet. The animal is so unique that no one can advise you on its care and feeding. What then? You are, you soon discover, caught in the middle of a mystery.

The difference between people who are able to draw on their creativity and go freely in and out of the mystery and those who can't or don't depends on how much this ability has been protected, loved, fed and exercised. This book explores ways to develop creative abilities and keep them healthy, bright eyed and bushy tailed.

Books on creativity often talk exclusively about creative genius, an unattainable state for most of us ordinary folk. When we don't measure up to Mozart or Rembrandt or Shakespeare, we're tempted to give up on our own gifts. But failing to win medals for creative genius doesn't mean you can't benefit from being innovative. Abraham Maslow found that the high-functioning people he studied were similar in almost every respect to creative people. In other words, becoming more creative can help you function better and increase the quality of your life. The direction that creativity takes doesn't matter. Inventing a creative way to fix a broken bicycle or garnish a poached sea bass or become a better parent is just as valid as writing a great novel or painting a great work of art. There are almost as many kinds of creativity as there are creative people, and some kinds overlap. Here are some examples of different kinds of creativity:

- **VERBAL**: writing, acting
- **VISUAL**: painting, sculpture, dance, movie making, interior design, fashion design
- **SCIENTIFIC**: research, scientific innovation and discovery
- **AUDITORY**: music, theatre, film, poetry read aloud or silently
- **PHYSICAL**: sports, dance, body therapies, medical practice
- **MECHANICAL/STRUCTURAL**: architecture, machine and tool design, sculpture
- **RELATIONAL**: parenting, teaching, human resource work
- **INNOVATIVE**: inventing, problem solving, idea production

Creativity can be expressed in all these ways and more. Yet there's disagreement among researchers about whether you can do anything to become more creative. One study I read showed that if you do a creative exercise before performing a task, you'll do a better job. In my experience, when people loosen up, give themselves permission to innovate, give up on goal mania and stop comparing their work to others', they become more creative. Many authorities say creativity is not so much an inborn talent as a habit of mind. Like any good habit, creativity can be learned—or at least released from confinement.

We begin in chapter one to explore ways to release the genie by unlearning what you've been taught. Whatever people have told you about creativity, chances are you haven't heard the whole story. What you *have* heard may give you a skewed idea of what innovation is all about. Your mental computer may be clogged with statements like

- "Creative people are only involved in the arts."
- "Creativity demands extremely high intelligence."
- "Only a few people are creative."
- "Creativity is the next-door neighbor of madness." (Well, maybe just a little.)
- "Creative ideas are airy-fairy, fanciful and useless."
- "Surgeons, homemakers, truck drivers, librarians and farmers can't be creative."

In this book, we'll explode the myths of creativity. First, we'll begin to lay the groundwork by examining how we look at time, creative space and the innovative self in each of us. Then we'll explore methods for polishing our seeing powers and for creating with the whole self through our feelings, memories, senses and both sides of the brain. Later, we'll investigate ways to lose the nagging, logical mind and free creative elves so they can spin straw into gold. Finally, we'll gingerly approach our fears and other gremlins. We'll discover how to enlist their help in hacking through the underbrush of uncertainty to emerge in a new place: the home country of the creative spirit.

Each chapter ends with a "Seed Thought." Plant it in the garden of your reverie, and let it sprout in all the ways it wants to. Write it on a slip of paper, and carry it with you. Read it, and mull it over during your coffee break or while you're waiting in line at the supermarket. Discuss it with friends. Watch it bloom.

What you will read in this book is sometimes diffuse, overlapping and seemingly contradictory. That's as it should be. Creativity can't be grasped directly and tied in neat bundles—that's why people often call it "sideways thinking." There are no step-by-step directions.

You can only capture the flavor of creativity by listening to stories, seeing creativity operate in other people's lives and, most important, learning how it works in your own experience. That's why you'll find at the end of each chapter explorations and other exercises that will help you blaze a trail through your creative homeland. Do the ones that intrigue you and that you have time for. Don't feel obliged to complete the whole roster unless you have a lot of time on your hands, need something positive to do or really want to!

HOW TO USE THIS BOOK

Pencil Dancing is a tool. It can be used in countless creative ways, just as a screwdriver can be used not only to tighten screws but to make holes for planting seedlings or to wedge a stuck window. You can read each page, front to back. Or you can skim the chapter titles and start with one that leaps out and grabs you. There's no one right way.

Read a chapter like you'd take an aspirin: whenever you need to cure a creative headache. Use it to jolt your innovative muscles into action. Do a couple of explorations at the end of the chapter to crystallize what you've read. Jump into the explorations right away or later or not at all—it's up to you. Don't push. Enjoy. Do whatever feels comfortable. Use the book to draw a protective circle around yourself, to create some delicious solitude. Set aside time in your date book every week to explore a chapter and do a few of the explorations at the end.

If you're a "people person," try using the book with a group. Have everyone read a chapter, do some of the activities at the end of the chapter and share their thoughts at a get-together. You can use the book at work, too. Read a chapter aloud before a meeting or do some of the exercises as a warm-up to promote team spirit, get creative brains clicking and start your staff off on the right foot (or the left brain, as the case may be). If your work happens to involve teaching, you can use the book's ideas to ignite students' enthusiasm for writing, art and other subjects.

Have fun. Let your creative mind *dance*!

creativity 101: practicing the
basic steps

ch 1. Raffia in the Doorway

Strands of raffia hang in the doorway of the classroom where I teach writing and art. To get into the classroom, you have to part these long strips of palm leaves. It's a reminder. One woman said she ought to be wearing a long, slinky gown and smoky eye makeup since she felt like a star of silent movies threading her way through a beaded curtain. "Good!" I said. "You got the message: Leave everything you've learned outside the door. Come in prepared to become somebody new."

So on our journey through this book, I invite you to step through the raffia curtain. Leave all your preconceptions about creativity behind. Think of our time together as an undoing. Think of creativity as a seagoing vessel encrusted, over the years, with barnacles. From time to time you have to chip away the barnacles that slow down your vessel.

What are the barnacles? You probably began to accumulate them as early as grade school, maybe before. You were told to color inside the lines, to paint all trees green and the sky blue. Like the little boy in Antoine de Saint-Exupery's *The Little Prince*, you may have drawn a boa constrictor that swallowed an elephant and had adults tell you it looked like a hat.

Through your school years, you were taught that a test question has only one right answer. You memorized answers so you could spew them out on demand. So today, if your kid mind entertains any divergent thoughts, your adult mind tosses them aside as useless, maybe even dangerous.

Over the years, barnacle layers continue to grow. You learn the shortest route to work, to the shopping mall, to your friend's house. From then on you don't deviate. Media hype tells you what deodorant to use, what toothbrush to buy, what frozen slab of dinner to nuke in the microwave. You comply. The barnacles thicken. You take on more responsibility. You become busier and busier. After all, you only go round once, and you have to pack everything possible into the time you have, right? The barnacles have covered your hull; they slow your vessel and weigh you down. You don't have the time or energy to scrape the crud off. Sadly, most of us are in that same boat.

Let me give you a case in point of the fix we're in. In a workshop a few years back, I tried to get participants to peel down to their hulls—to expose their inborn creative resources. I said, "What if you were suddenly whisked away to another planet? You have to leave everything behind: your family, friends, pets, home, car, job, possessions, *everything*. What would you have left?" They had ten minutes to make a list.

The group looked stunned. They stared into space, pens poised above blank paper. No one said a word. I had a sinking feeling like I'd stepped into quicksand, and it was already up to my nose.

A scowling man in a denim shirt blurted, "I'd have nothing! What else is there?" No one responded. Silence hung thickly in the room. The clock ticked. Fingers twiddled with pens. I considered never asking such a question again.

Then, from the back of the room a pudgy redhead piped, "Oh, I'd have *lots* of things!"

"Name *one*," the man challenged. The redhead grinned as she read her list. "I'd still have my sense of humor and my memories, talents, spiritual faith, love for those who'd been close to me, everything I've learned in my lifetime. . . ." She named thirteen things, ending with a poignant zinger: "and most important in a situation like this, I'd still have my ability to start over!"

Others picked up on her optimism. "I'd have my health," said a sprightly gray-haired woman. Someone else added, "I'd have my flexibility—it's helped me through tough times before." "I'd have my creativity," offered a guy in a sweatshirt with "motivate!" imprinted on the front. They became animated and filled with ideas. They had discovered new resources.

More Than We Realize

"We're made of more than we realize," said Christopher Reeve, in a recent TV interview. The movie star we knew as Superman was paralyzed in an accident during an equestrian competition. He spoke as he exhaled, aided by a ventilator, his head supported by a cushioned brace attached to a motorized wheelchair. If, in such an extreme condition, he can discover this "more" that we're made of, why can't the rest of us?

Part of this "more than we realize" is our barnacled creativity that can be exposed and expanded once we've peeled away old habits of thinking, perceiving and experiencing. The first step to being exposed is to empty out, to return to unknowing, to reinstate our amateur status and to look at the world with fresh eyes.

You don't have to be a genius to see in new ways. Everybody has this ability. You don't have to be Albert Einstein or Pablo Picasso or Emily Dickinson or Thomas Wolfe. You don't have to invent Post-its or Ivory soap or Apple computers. Your innovation can be as simple as blocking a leaky window by stuffing a plastic bag in the crack.

I once asked workshop participants to bring in something to share with the class that they created. As you might expect, they brought poems and paintings. One also came with a fragrant loaf of freshly baked bread cut in cubes for us to taste. Another brought an oriental arrangement of several large mums in a shallow ceramic dish. And another proudly displayed a photo of her five children—she had created not only the photo but the children, too, she said.

SEED THOUGHT

"One of the first things you will find as you begin to share with the world this beautiful, wild-hearted, lovingly developed gift of your personal creativity is that the world wants no part of it."

Jim Borgman
Cartoonist

We often think of creative people as writers and artists, musicians and actors. But a creative person can be anyone. There are creative surgeons and creative waitresses. I even know a creative engineer; John works for a large corporation by day and builds model railroads after hours. If you think model railroading isn't creative, picture this: John has made miniature trees of dried goldenrod sprinkled with ground-up foam and sprayed with green paint. The track ballast, the gravelly stuff used to line both sides of a railroad track, is cat litter, fresh from the bag. (When the model train whizzes by, you get a whiff of the litter's fragrant dust.) His telephone wires are fishing line. He cut tiny water tank roof shingles from fine sandpaper. His chain link fence is made from a window screen. Billboards, both freestanding and mounted on miniature buildings, were once part of junk mail that most of us throw in the trash.

We tend to think we need the staggering intellect of a rocket scientist to be creative. We forget that people with little formal education can come up with ideas the experts never thought of. In fact, being an expert can actually stunt creativity. Experts can know so much about what *has* worked and what *should* work, based on calculations, that they can't approach a problem in a new way.

My Uncle Len didn't finish grade school, but he was one of the most creative people I've known. He was able to set aside accepted knowledge and to think upside down. Faced with the common problem of squirrels raiding his bird feeder, he came up with an uncommon solution. Most deterrents involve a barrier to keep squirrels from climbing the feeder pole or descending its cord. Uncle Len's solution used *sound*. He rigged the bird feeder with a buzzer that was triggered by the squirrel's weight. When bushy-tailed thieves approached the bird's banquet table, BZZZ! The buzzer startled them away.

Creativity is an attitude, a way of being, in life. You begin by forgetting what you know. Leave behind the baggage of everything you've been taught about the way things are. Question everything. Here are a few examples of statements that seem like "eternal truths," but if you think about them in a different way, you'll find they have some exceptions.

- Snow is white. (At dusk, it's often blue or purple.)
- Yellow fire hydrants are more visible than red ones. (This may not be true if they're viewed against a background of dried yellow grass.)
- Water is runny. (If you put it in the freezer, it isn't.)

Begin to think sideways. Scrape away the resistant barnacles impeding your creativity. Take a deep breath, part the raffia curtain and come on in.

EIGHT TRAITS OF A CREATIVE PERSON

Courage
You're not afraid to fail.
You think independently; you're not overly influenced by others' opinions.
You have confidence in your own abilities and insights.

Tenacity
You possess unwaning energy and enthusiasm.
You persevere despite difficulties.
You finish what you start.

Sensitivity
You're open and receptive to new ways and ideas.
You're sensitive to a need or opportunity.
You have a keen awareness of your surroundings and of other people.

Flexibility
You're not locked into doing things a certain way.
You're quick to compromise and willing to try a new approach.
You're eager to broaden experience by listening to other people's ideas.

Originality

You have the ability to generate many unique answers to a single question, problem or situation.

Your creativity is a true expression of your real self.

You don't strive to be original, but you naturally are.

Good Judgment

You can recognize a good idea or a bad one.

You show realistic insight.

You're willing to test ideas in the real world.

Broad Experience and Skills

You show competence in at least one chosen field.

You have many interests.

You're an articulate and persuasive communicator.

Playfulness

Your sense of humor is infectious and not harmful to others.

You honor the spirit of exploration and curiosity.

You're not ashamed of your ability to fantasize, dream and imagine.

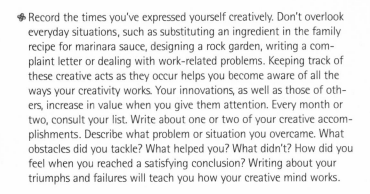

Explorations

✿ Record the times you've expressed yourself creatively. Don't overlook everyday situations, such as substituting an ingredient in the family recipe for marinara sauce, designing a rock garden, writing a complaint letter or dealing with work-related problems. Keeping track of these creative acts as they occur helps you become aware of all the ways your creativity works. Your innovations, as well as those of others, increase in value when you give them attention. Every month or two, consult your list. Write about one or two of your creative accomplishments. Describe what problem or situation you overcame. What obstacles did you tackle? What helped you? What didn't? How did you feel when you reached a satisfying conclusion? Writing about your triumphs and failures will teach you how your creative mind works.

✿ What "barnacles," imposed from outside yourself or from within, are the most stubborn obstacles to your creative expression? What ideas do you have for reducing or eliminating some of them? What do you most want to let go of? Write your thoughts.

✿ Write down the "Eight Traits of a Creative Person" from page 12. Underline in one color the traits that describe your current creative self. Underline with a second color traits you'd like to nurture and further develop. Hang the list on your bulletin board or refrigerator—someplace where you'll see it every day. Keep a log of your progress and the obstacles you encounter. From time to time, redraw your chart to reflect your current creative profile.

ch 2. *Going Into Your Egg*

Around Easter you can often find large plastic eggs with a hole in
one end that you can look through. Inside, you see a whole environment—a meadow with trees and flowers and animals or a tiny room
with Lilliputian furniture and people. In your imagination, you enter
this egg, just as you might go into your creative space: a particular
room or studio or private corner where your innovative process begins
to cook.

The voluntary seclusion that writing or any other creative act
requires can be described as "going into your egg"—your private place
of fruitful potential—with the goal of hatching something new. The
places creative people choose as refuges in which to incubate ideas or
to do their work are as unique and varied as the people themselves.
Here are a couple of examples.

Annie Dillard, in her book *Holy the Firm*, describes how she
secluded herself in a tent in the Blue Ridge Mountains, where she had

HOW TO

FIND YOUR OWN

INSPIRATIONAL

SPACE

gone to read and to write: "I read, lost, every day, sitting under a tree by my tent, while warblers swung in the leaves overhead and bristle worms trailed their inches over the twiggy dirt at my feet." You can almost smell the campfire smoke. You can hear the warblers chortle. You share Dillard's creative space as you read.

Others have sought sanctuary in enclosed and sheltering places. In his book *The Way of St. Francis*, Murray Bodo tells about Saint Francis's continual return to the caves of Umbria where "he discovered as soon as he left the feather beds and velvet curtains of home that life is a journey not so much outward and away as inward toward the core of the heart and that caves are best for that kind of journey."

Many writers and creative people have found their own equivalents of Saint Francis's cave, enclosures that protect and feed the creative process. Artist Meinrad Craighead writes of a childhood experience "lying with my dog beneath the blue hydrangeas in my grandmother's garden, shaded against a hot Arkansas afternoon." Memories of this and other familiar spaces are re-created in the rich colors and textures of Craighead's paintings. Author Jessamyn West, too, enjoyed in her youth the security of an enclosed creative space. She wrote inside an old bathtub in her backyard. It was her "egg" place.

My own cave experiences began at age seven with a hideout under the back porch that smelled of pungent decaying grass clippings put down to cover the dirt. Among these clippings and sheltered by the underbelly of the porch, I plotted endless dramas, acted out in the round by movie star paper dolls. Creativity grew like corn in the night. Were the grass stains worth it? Of course. The back porch plays paved the way for other cave experiences. When I was nine, I mulled and wrote while I sat on a campstool inside a wooden crate that had once housed a sofa from my dad's furniture store. The crate stood on end beside the very porch where the dramas had unfolded.

More recently, and for varying reasons, I've written in a bathroom, on a fire escape outside a third-floor walk-up in downtown Baltimore, paddling in an aluminum rowboat around southwestern Ohio's Lake Isabella and on a second-story porch overlooking a monsoon-flooded courtyard in Pakistan.

Many other creative people share my devotion to enclosed

creative spaces. Karl Lagerfeld, a designer at Chanel, says he thinks best—gets most of his design ideas—while soaking in a bathtub. J.D. Salinger wrote in a cement bunker behind his house. And, of course, Annie Dillard had her tent.

Writers and creative people have told me about other places where they go to invoke the muse:

- A string hammock under tall maples in the backyard.
- In my car on the drive to work. I don't have a cell phone or radio or CD player—on purpose.
- Beneath tall pines on a path in the woods.
- In a corner of my basement where I make tiles on the Ping-Pong table.
- Tilted back in a disgustingly ratty recliner.
- In my office, with my door closed and the phone on hold. I can only get away with this for short stretches, but even ten minutes can be productive.

These places trigger the creative response by temporarily shutting out the world so you can dive down into your creative unconscious. This space is like a walled garden. Private. Contained. Interestingly, the word *paradise* is derived from a Persian word meaning "walled garden." This walled space contains creative energy and keeps it from seeping away.

Often, we mislead ourselves into thinking we need a special atmosphere to be creative. Usually the atmosphere we think we need is someplace other than where we are: "If I lived in a garret in Paris, I could write like Baudelaire." You envision yourself lounging in a café sipping absinthe. You wear arty black clothes and speak flawless French. This is the dream you hold in your mind: When the garret magically materializes, *then* you will write, *then* you will create.

When I get ideas like that (and I do), I remember the painting of van Gogh's bedroom. The room in the painting is spartan and simple, but you get the idea the artist felt at home there. His paintings were tacked up on the walls. He had made the place his own.

I once visited an artist's studio that reminded me of van Gogh's bedroom. Jack painted in one room of a tiny Victorian house in a small

Kentucky river town. He lived in the other room; a hook on the back of the door was his closet. While we had tea, my feet were numb with cold, but I had an overwhelming feeling of being at home. This was a place where creativity happened. You could feel it in the air. You could see it in the colorful splatters of oil paint on the floor where his easel stood.

A creative space may be spartan, even derelict, but it should be familiar and comfortable. Most important, your creative space must be uniquely *yours*. What artifacts, items from nature, furnishings, colors do you like to live with? How have you put your own stamp on your space? Your space is your miniature creative universe. Let it house meaningful things.

Writers and other creative people have told me they like to surround themselves with things that speak to them. A writer I know cites an antique desk as being important to her creative space. The desk's past inspires her to write with a sense of who she is and where she came from. An artist friend keeps a small sand tray in her studio. In it, she arranges and rearranges a number of tiny objects until they suggest a theme for a painting. In my own place hangs a giant four-foot grapevine wreath strung like a Native American dream catcher. It holds a pinecone from Wendell Berry's hometown, a miniature birch bark canoe, a chunk of alexandrite and a papier mâché wren in a nest. The piece is suspended over the sofa where I often write. I use it to reinforce confidence and a sense of place.

Even if you have little space, a few meaningful objects can personalize that space. I know a businessman who travels frequently and stays in austere commercial hotels. He always takes a framed photo of his family and some of his kid's drawings and school projects to decorate the room and make him feel at home in an unfamiliar place.

I once had to share a small room at the Sina Hotel in downtown Teheran, Iran, with three children and a peace corps worker. Lack of laundry facilities meant that wet clothes were constantly strung across lines that bisected the room. Clutter was everywhere. An odd shoe, a camera, a stray fork from dinner littered the floor. But we washed out a yogurt bottle and filled it with blossoms from the hotel garden. I won't say this was a very creative environment, but it had at least this one focal point of beauty and order.

We can use such a focal point to personalize an environment where many of us spend a considerable amount of time: our cars. I haven't seen many cars decorated as creative space. My own turquoise Honda contains mainly junk and clutter, although at one time it did have a beaded Indian necklace hanging from the mirror. A copywriter I once knew was better at automobile interior decorating. She stuck putty onto pinecones and seashells, and stood them under her speedometer. Of course, her car was orderly to begin with.

The most dramatic example of creative space on wheels that I've ever seen was inside a gray Toyota, rusted and mud splashed, parked by the curb around the corner from my place. I spotted it on one of my regular patrols around the neighborhood. Inside, on the ledge above the dash, was a whole farm! Can you imagine? The ledge was covered with green Astroturf, cut out in several places to expose a mirror pond or two. Tiny toy horses and cows grazed in the green turf. A miniature fence surrounded the serene setting and presumably kept the toy cows and horses from wandering over the edge.

Many times I walked by the same place, hoping to catch the perpetrator—no luck. Still, every time I pass the spot where the car was parked, I remember the startling sight of the miniature farm. And I'm inspired again.

Decorating a space with meaningful objects makes it real. Spending time in such a space reinforces who you are as a unique creative person. The place where you regularly create becomes, over time, a stimulus to your work. It's as if the space could speak: "Oh. Here she is in her favorite chair (or desk or studio). Time to crank up the old idea maker."

To enter the creative process, be prepared to go into your egg—or tent or bathtub or cave or packing crate. But first, make it yours. Mark it with congenial colors and meaningful objects. Let your innovative process begin to cook in the very space that surrounds you.

SEED THOUGHT

"Build an inner place to protect your truth."

Richard Bach
Running From Safety

Explorations

❧ List all the creative spaces you've discovered or occupied that you can remember. Do they have any elements in common? What made them comfortable/uncomfortable, secluded/exposed, unique/ordinary? Write about a current refuge. What place inspires your creative energy most?

❧ Did you have a favorite creative space as a child? A tree house? A blanket-covered card table hideout? A snow fort? Write about the place and why you liked it.

❧ Write about ways you could change your work space into a more creative space. What could you do to make even a small space more uniquely yours? More private? More comfortable? More inviting?

Site Write

❧ Explore places near your home to find a creative space to write (or sketch). Consider spaces such as a park, a restaurant, a hill overlooking your town, the side of a stream, an ice cream parlor, a boat. Try a few sites and write about your experience in each one. Did the site inspire your creativity? Were there distractions? Did you feel at home in this space? Write your thoughts.

ch 3. Time...and Time, Again

You may have heard this story—I don't know if it's true—about a
ruckus in the Indiana statehouse over daylight saving time. All the
clocks in the state had been happily ticking away on standard time for
as long as anyone could remember. No one made a peep. But a few
years ago, the story has it, some politicians thought their state should
get in sync with other states and adopt daylight saving time in summer,
just as neighboring states do. The hitch: Indiana is heavily agricultural,
and the farmers objected to the time change. In the upset that fol-
lowed, one of the farmers was reported to have blurted, "The extra
hour of sunlight will burn our crops!"

      The misunderstanding may seem nonsensical to those of us
who are controlled by the clock, whatever time it runs on, and who
grumble only mildly at setting our clocks back or ahead (and never can
remember which). What we may not realize is that farmers live by natural time, not mechanical time. It's understandable that someone who

"HURRY

SICKNESS"

AND

CREATIVITY

plows before the spring rains and plants after the last winter frost could find mechanical time confusing.

Natural time depends, as its name implies, on *nature*. It's tied to phenomena such as the ripening of fruit, the changing seasons and the readiness of a creative idea to be harvested. There's not much use in trying to speed up a ripening kumquat. It's ready when it's ready, and no sooner. Natural time is slow as it needs to be.

Mechanical time is tied to clock and calendar. While it complies loosely with natural time, its divisions are artificial units: months, days, hours, minutes, seconds—even nanoseconds. Mechanical time can be troublesome because we feel like it is ticking away faster and faster.

Let's look at how time seems to speed up. Every time we add a new responsibility or activity to our day, we have to cut something else. When cutting more ceases to be an option, we simply speed ourselves up. We go faster. We hurry. But we can't catch up. We rush through the days and weeks and years of our lives without allowing our endeavors to ripen in their own natural time. Instead, we're driven by deadlines, hounded by overscheduling and drowned in a sea of busyness. Creativity suffers. Despite all our timesaving devices, we never seem to have enough of what the devices are supposed to save: time.

I once knew an editor who had trained herself to do two things at once to save time. She could be present at a meeting and write an article or edit a newsletter and talk on the phone at the same time. She walked fast. She talked fast. In the middle of a sentence, she already had one foot out the door. Before long, several others in the department had caught the "hurry disease."

As people attempt to do more and more in less and less time, they develop time urgency or "hurry sickness," according to Diane Ulmer, R.N., M.S. As clinical director at the Clinical Institute of Behavioral Medicine in Berkeley, California, she has seen firsthand how the hurried life can negatively affect creativity. As anyone who has ever tried to juggle a swarm of projects all at once knows, hurry frazzles the creative mind.

"You can't rush creativity," Ulmer says. "Hurry can become chronic. We all experience time pressure at times. Time urgency is when time pressure causes us to speed up how long it takes us to do something. We talk, walk, do everything faster. This can become a habit or a way of being and lead to 'hurry sickness.'" Ulmer cites four symptoms of hurry sickness that, once they take hold, can dull creativity and even take their toll on health:

1 **DETERIORATION OF THE PERSONALITY.** Interests become narrow. There's a preoccupation with getting things done. Life begins to be measured in terms of quantity, not quality, causing thoughts to become dry and uninteresting.

2 **RACING MIND.** Anxious thoughts and loss of ability to focus create stress, interfere with creativity and disrupt sleep.

3 **INABILITY TO RECOLLECT PLEASANT MEMORIES.** The mind is riveted on the future or stews about the past. The only things that can drag the person back into the present are crises and problems. Life is lived on the surface and not deeply entered into.

4 **INABILITY TO EXPERIENCE INNER CONTENTMENT.** In a headlong rush to get things done, the person has literally given up on savoring life's satisfying experiences. Chronic rushing, or what Ulmer calls "time urgency" or hurry sickness, has a negative impact on creativity, spiritual experience and quality of life.

Hurry sickness is like watching a video on fast-forward. You get to the end sooner, but you don't enjoy it much. Yet, a feeling of shame is often attached to slowing down. "I feel like I'm cheating if I'm not productive every minute," says my writer friend Linda, mother of three and captain of a large household that includes two cats and a garden. "It's the Puritan ethic, I guess, that drives me, even though I need some quiet time, and I'll get sick if I go without it."

Many of us have lost the balance between activity and rest. Our tapes need rewinding. This rewind time is essential to clarity and energy, two forces that power creativity, and it allows creativity to incubate in its own sweet time.

A Catholic priest who was an accomplished calligrapher once

SEED THOUGHT

"The trouble with being in the rat race is that even if you win, you're still a rat."

Lily Tomlin

told me that the empty space around the letters he so carefully puts down on parchment with a nibbed pen is just as important as the artfully drawn letters themselves. The deliberate design of open space to allow letters to snuggle together with just enough room for comfort and grace is a fitting metaphor for balancing natural and mechanical time, slow with fast.

One of the best antidotes to the hurried life is regular contact with nature. A leisurely stroll on a woodsy path or along a sandy strand can help you slow down so your creative energy can catch up with you. (Veto the urge to make this a fitness walk you can execute in half the time.) Just twenty minutes in the woods will put you back in your body. And it will put your body back on natural time. You'll feel like you just came back from a two-week vacation.

Exposure to nature is one way, but not the only way, to slow your life's pace. Some other ideas that writers and creative people I know put to use in their own lives are to

- grow a garden or care for a few windowsill plants
- stretch and bend to slow music
- take a short, fifteen-minute nap
- sing to themselves, or hum
- play or listen to music
- sketch or paint
- watch goldfish swimming in a tank

You may have your own special routine for balancing time. More suggestions on quieting your mind appear in chapter thirty-six. The common denominator in all these approaches is relaxation. Relaxation dissolves mechanical time. It slows your pace. It—well—relaxes you.

As the world becomes more and more dependent upon technology, we experience increasing difficulty in finding natural, creative time. Already, cell phones have invaded private time that was once used for creative mulling. Computers have accelerated thinking and communication. We feel out of step if we don't try to keep up with our machines.

There's a segment in an old *I Love Lucy* episode where Lucy and Ethel are working on an assembly line decorating cakes that move past on a conveyor belt. Suddenly the conveyor belt speeds up. The cakes whiz by faster and faster. We laugh at Lucy's antics as she tries to keep up, blurping frosting everywhere. In real life it's not so funny when you can't keep up with the cakes.

Do you have to keep up? It depends on what's important to you. Maybe you should ask yourself, Where does your life's meaning lie? What's important? How are you balancing your mechanical time and your natural time? (Or are you?)

Creativity has a foot in each time system. It's as if you stood at the state line with one foot in Indiana and the other foot in Ohio. Inspiration begins in the Indiana cornfields where the ears ripen in their own time and the creative "aha!" occurs when it's good and ready. Development—the process of honing a creative idea or expression—grows mostly out of mechanical time: deadlines, planning and evaluation.

The question is, What state are you in? Are you spending enough time in Indiana?

Explorations

❧ Set aside a half hour to do *nothing*. Resist the temptation to put the time to "good use" straightening up the room, reading a report or doing the wash. See how long you can last doing absolutely nothing. (This is practice with training wheels for the mind-clearing methods we'll discuss later in the book.) At the end of the half hour, write about your thoughts and feelings.

❧ Make a list of five of the most important things you give your time to. What's the most meaningful one? Why? Is anything missing from your list that could further your creative growth or add pleasure and dimension to your life? Write your thoughts.

Experiment

❧ Schedule time off. Write down the time in your appointment book, and keep the appointment just as diligently as if you'd made a date with a friend. What will you do with this hour or day to yourself that will contribute to nurturing your creativity? Where will you spend the time? Write about your experience.

Research

❧ For one week keep a notebook citing the times when you feel hurried or stressed. Did you build in some time for self-nourishing to compensate? (Even just a stroll around the parking lot where you work or the block where you live can be a respite.)

❧ For several days, record how you spend your time. What proportion of your time was spent in an activity that enriches life and creativity? What proportion was spent on unproductive busyness or unnecessary commitments?

ch 4. Lots of Butterfly Nets
Catch Lots of Butterflies

While on the island of Antigua, I saw an incredible sight along the water's edge. As I approached what appeared to be a bush covered with yellow flowers, the flowers suddenly dispersed into the air and were gone! My mind hit the wall. How could this happen? Flowers can't fly. Or can they?

In that instant, I realized that what I'd seen were not blossoms but yellow butterflies—hundreds of them—clustered on the bush's branches. And, like newly fledged ideas, they quickly vanished into the salt mist.

But this time I'd brought a net—a notebook where I could catch a thought and preserve it like a butterfly under glass. I rushed back to my room to grab the notebook and write.

You don't need a notebook. You can jot or draw your ideas on anything: a paper napkin, the back of a grocery list, your palm. I've used all three. I've written on the inside of a blue passenger satisfaction

CAPTURE

CREATIVE IDEAS

ON THE FLY

form on a Pakistani airliner, and I've scribbled on a scrap of paper from my coat pocket while walking in the woods. I've done this because my notebooks were always someplace else, someplace far from where butterfly thoughts show up for catching.

I've learned from experience that ideas, like butterflies, must be caught on the fly. If you miss them when they first appear, they're likely to evade your net and be gone forever. English essayist Francis Bacon advised carrying a pencil in your pocket to write down fleeting thoughts. He said, "Those that come uninvited are commonly the most valuable and should be secured because they seldom return."

If your mind is as holey as mine, you'll find it's a good idea to have idea-catching notebooks in places where ideas might pop up. Think of these notebooks as mousetraps. Put them where the mice are likely to come out. And wait.

Saving your thoughts through writing in a journal or notebook serves three important purposes:

- It keeps your creative juices flowing, even if all the creative time you have is a ten-minute snatch here and there.
- It preserves thoughts, ideas and experiences you might otherwise forget.
- It provides an ever ready source for ideas, writing starts and visual inspiration.

Since grade school, I've kept many kinds of journals. Perhaps you have, too. At age eleven, I drew cartoon strips of Superwoman. Years later, I wrote in a diary with a tab that locked away teenaged musings with a tiny silver key. Ultimately, the diary gave way to scrapbooks with flowery prose scribbled in the margins. Now I keep several kinds of notebooks, sometimes as many as seven at once. And I regularly steal from each of them for writing and other creative work.

The kind of journal you keep can influence the kind of creative work you do and vice versa. Try several different types to see which ones feel comfortable and work best for you. Here are a few ideas.

The Trash Can Notebook

Everything goes in here: hopes, fears, dreams, tentative meanderings. I use a stiff gray composition board folder with loose-leaf notebook paper inside. It's cheap and functional. Over the years, the outside has come to look like a trash can. Pencil smudges, doodles, quotations in red marker defaced the cover. But the grungy look is welcoming. Its appearance says, "You can write and scribble anything at all in my pages. I don't care. I'm here at 3 A.M. when you can't sleep, ready to take whatever you've got." At the end of a year, I put the pages in a manila folder and file it away. The trash can's cover lives on.

Try the trash can yourself. Its promise that you can throw away a page without disturbing the rest of the book helps you feel free to write whatever comes.

The trash can is the workhorse of notebooks. You can fill both sides of a page in less than an hour, and you don't have to care how the writing turns out. It's like talking to a friend. You're free to express all your embryo ideas. If you keep only one notebook, consider this one.

The Two-Line Journal

This is my favorite. I've been keeping one for over seven years. The two-line journal offers a way to focus on a single thought every day and record it for later use. The list below offers ideas of what to look for. While it takes just a few minutes to write your thought, you search all day long for that one thing that deserves saving in your journal. It keeps your creative antennae tuned. All you need is an appointment book with enough space to write a line or two. I keep mine in a Sierra Club spiral appointment book that has stunning nature photos on the left and seven days' worth of spaces on the right. In these spaces, I can write two lines—or up to six lines if I squish my writing small. You can use the two-line journal to hold

- brilliant ideas you'd otherwise forget
- short quotes and observations
- thumbnail sketches
- happenings of the day

- meaningful personal philosophies
- a short rhyme
- a grumble about the state of the world
- a crisp, descriptive phrase or two

Think of this book as your medicine chest: A line a day keeps creative block away. It has two other benefits. Knowing you'll need a line or two at the end of the day makes you more observant. Limited space makes you more succinct. The book inspires you to polish a line, turning it over and over in your mind and rewording it before you write it down.

Pocket Notebook

These small, spiral notebooks fit in your hand and can travel in your car, pocket or bag.

When I was writing poetry, poems would pop out, nearly whole, at inopportune times. I'd be swimming laps in the pool beside my place and suddenly, *pop*! An idea or a phrase or sometimes a whole fresh-baked poem would jump into my head unexpectedly. But its shelf life was short-lived. If I didn't write it down right away, it would be, like a startled butterfly, gone.

After I'd had to traipse dripping wet upstairs to get paper and pen, I learned to keep a notebook in my towel bag. If you're like most creative people, you've had the same experience with your spontaneous thoughts. Perhaps you're breezing along the interstate or standing in a supermarket line and an idea comes, *pop*! With a pocket-size notebook, you're ready to catch a thought when it sticks its head out. Think of this kind of notebook as a miniature net to catch your unpredictable ideas before they disappear.

Scratch Pads

I like to keep scratch pads all over my place. They're available at office supply stores in packs of a dozen. The small size is great for a quick notation, a fleeting phrase or the nucleus of an idea. A slightly larger size works well for more developed thoughts. Later, you can tear off the page and toss it into a file folder with related ideas and half-hatched thoughts. When you're ready to go to work, you'll have a whole arsenal of ammo to help you do battle with the blank page.

This book was pieced together largely from such notes made at all hours of the day and night. I set up a file box with each chapter on a color-keyed index card. (I used a file box which has "follower bars" to keep heaps of pages from flopping over. This kind of file system can be found in most office supply stores.) The system is handy because your outline emerges almost magically from the notes.

Do you like to work directly on a computer? The scratch pad note system can still be a helping hand. When you awake with an idea in the middle of the night and don't feel like dragging yourself to the computer, you can write down your thoughts without getting out of bed. Then, the next day, you can transcribe the notes into your PC.

The First-Draft Tablet

There's a lot to be said for writing by hand. Many writers and other creatives do it, even if they're proficient typists. They say handwriting slows the process and gives them a more intimate contact with the page. The movement of the hand itself seems to enhance the flow of ideas. It's like writing a letter to a friend—a task that, to many, is not as intimidating as facing the blank computer screen. Readers of the finished work can feel the connection.

Legal pads or regular-size, lined pads work well for this kind of writing. I buy mine by the dozen from an office supply store. I prefer the letter size that fits a standard file folder. When I'm finished scribbling a draft of an article or chapter, the draft can be conveniently filed away. When you're just doodling or scrambling around for ideas, you might want to try writing *across* the lines, with the pad turned sideways. Writing against the lines gives you a gleeful sense of rebellion; you don't let ruled lines or margins hem you in. It's like disobeying an unwritten law without getting caught. Such reckless abandon fosters creativity.

SEED THOUGHT

Eduardo Galeano writes that in the eighteenth century when the Chiriguano Indians were first exposed to paper, they called it "the skin of God." If you were to look at your own notebooks and writing paper in this way, how would your view of creative expression be influenced?

Sketchbook

There are sketchbooks for every kind of media from marking pen and colored pencil to watercolor and pastels. Whether you're an artist or not, you may want to try expressing your ideas visually. Sketchbooks with a blank space at the top of the page and lines on the bottom allow you to work with both words and images.

The only journals I don't recommend are the expensive overly fancy ones. I once took a bookbinding course where I made a hand-sewn tan leather-bound book with ivory deckle-edged pages. It was impressive—so impressive that, to this day, I've never written in it. The book effectively dampened my urge to write, especially the urge to write freely with ink blobs, mistakes and all.

So when you choose a notebook or journal, keep in mind what it's supposed to do: encourage you to create. It should invite spontaneous abandon and provide a place to capture ideas on the fly.

A fresh new blank notebook is a bare butterfly bush with the potential to become a home to battalions of butterflies. If you begin it, they will come.

♣ Scout stationery stores, bookstores, places that carry school supplies
(such as drug and grocery stores), office supply stores, and art and
craft stores that carry notebooks and paper products. Select a variety
of notebooks, including several pocket-size ones, to try. To provide
material for your notebook trials, write or draw a one-page life history. Use the smaller notebooks to make notes.

♣ Speak your thoughts about a day's happenings into a tape recorder.
Wait a day or two to play back what you've said. How does this kind
of "journal" affect your creativity?

♣ Begin a scrapbook that utilizes words, drawings, magazine clippings,
photographs, and colored and textured papers. Choose a theme or
subject to structure your book: a trip, trees, your garden, your family
history, your favorite quotations.

Project

♣ Choose a subject for a written journal (see ideas above). Decorate the
cover of a plain spiral notebook with a collage of related images—old
greeting cards, travel brochures, artwork or photos clipped from magazines—to express your theme.

ch 5. Rusty Water

The two-room pinewood cabin my grandfather, dad and uncle built by the lake for our summers in Wisconsin was a primitive structure. My mother cooked on a kerosene stove in the kitchen when she wasn't running in terror from its flames, which leapt sometimes nearly to the ceiling. Once the meal was cooked, someone had to take the garbage to the hole my dad had dug across the road. Garbage disposal was my brother's job. I was assigned to water fetching duty.

What water we needed came by way of a rusty red iron pump sunk into the sand just outside the kitchen door. Though I'd never pumped a drop before, it didn't take long to learn how. On my first try the pump handle made "squee-squaw" noises as the water gushed into a tin pail hanging on the pump's spout. Whee! I was making water come out! Then, to my surprise and consternation, I saw the water was as brown as mud. When I eventually hauled the bucket inside to show my mom, she said, "Keep pumping. It'll come clear."

So I kept pumping. Sure enough, the water began to flow more and more clearly. Finally I had a bucket of clear water we could drink, cook with or use for washing dishes. I had learned something. To this day when I'm struggling with a writing project or some other creative effort, I think of first attempts as "running off the rusty water." Thinking in this way gives me freedom to make mistakes, do a few trial runs and not be ashamed of rewriting the lead to an article a dozen times, finally finding a perfect lead hidden in the third paragraph.

When you read the polished work of Ernest Hemingway or Annie Dillard or Maya Angelou, you never see the misfires that ended up crumpled in the wastebasket. It's easy to get discouraged if you compare your work in progress to someone else's carefully honed piece. You can't see how much rusty water the writer had to pump before the piece came clear. Rusty water is the impure liquid from which creative expression is distilled.

IDEO, a product development company in Palo Alto, California, has a rusty water motto: "Fail often to succeed sooner." Can you imagine the sense of freedom you'd have if you could let yourself fail— on *purpose*?

My friend Karen told me she had purchased some expensive handmade Japanese washi (rice paper) to use for her sumi-e painting. The trouble was she couldn't paint on it; she was too concerned about messing up the expensive paper. I suggested using newspaper or a special kind of paper that you can paint on with plain water that darkens just like black ink where you brush it, but soon evaporates. She tried the special paper. After a few practice strokes, she'd run off the rusty water and was ready to tackle the expensive wash.

Sometimes to get a whole class through the rusty water stage, I invite them to scribble all over the first page of their notebooks. They approach the project with reckless abandon. They're energized. The energy carries over into their writing. Other times I've asked them to write in ways that express their present moods or moods that stick in their memories. What results is the jagged handwriting spawned by anger, the swirly script of joy, the tightly controlled writing of stress. Such exercises are a form of deliberate error.

The idea for deliberate error isn't mine. Instead, it grew out

SEED THOUGHT

"Be like the fox who makes more tracks than necessary, some in the wrong direction."

Wendell Berry
"Manifesto: The Mad Farmer Liberation Front"

of psychiatrist Viktor Frankl's logotherapy. His theory, the way I understand it, is to dive right into whatever bothers you. If you can't sleep, try staying awake as long as you can (trying to sleep is usually counterproductive, anyway). If you're afraid to begin to write, wreck the page, doodle, take dictation from stream of consciousness. Run off the rusty water.

I read that a Nevada strip mine had to process twenty-five tons of earth to produce one ounce of gold. Imagine that! You could be wearing twenty-five tons of earth around your neck in a flimsy, thin gold chain. This idea applies to creative expression, too. Twenty-five tons of effort—mistakes, blind alleys, false starts, rewrites, paintovers, redesigns—go into one successful ounce of finished creative product.

"An artist must not be afraid of error," says Betty Edwards in *Drawing on the Artist Within*. "Error can be useful if one keeps in mind the goal of the search, always trying each new bit of information for *fit* with the problem at hand. Errors can show you what doesn't work." The same is true for writing or any other creative process. Errors are the twenty-five tons of earth you have to dig up and sift through before you can produce one tiny, shiny nugget. And as Edwards suggests, the twenty-five tons of dirt are never completely wasted. You learn from it where the gold *isn't*. You get a better idea of what doesn't work.

A few years ago a graphic designer and I collaborated on a logo design that proved to be a struggle that stretched on for months. I had come up with the basic idea: a dove shaped like a heart and holding an olive sprig. Something about the design didn't work. We made it fatter, slimmer, taller, shorter. It still didn't work. It looked like a squirrel on a treadmill. The deadline was looming, so one afternoon we sequestered ourselves. More versions rolled out. They didn't work. Finally, we hit on an idea to add a tiny line no bigger than a hyphen to close off the outside edge of the heart shape. Viola! It worked. We had run off the rusty water. Later the finished artwork won the Art Directors' Club Silver Medal. No one saw the rust.

If it hadn't been for an image in my mind of a tin bucket filled with mud-colored water, we might not have gone beyond a dozen versions. The pump had communicated a valuable lesson. When you're up to your neck in the murk of creative confusion, remember this: Keep pumping; eventually it'll come clear.

Explorations

✤ Try, firsthand, a method for running off rusty water: Write for ten minutes about an object that has special meaning for you (a pocket-knife your dad gave you, your grandma's antique rocking chair, a trophy you've won, a shell you brought back from the shore). When you've written for ten minutes, start over and write from another angle for ten more minutes. Repeat two more times so you'll have four pieces of writing about the same object. Which version has the most life? Where is the rusty water you needed to run off? With a highlighter pen, mark the passages where you see the most life.

✤ Hold a writing marathon where you write continuously for an hour or more about anything that comes into your mind. Write fast. Don't stop. (It may help to do this project with a friend or with a group and share your writing afterward.) As above, highlight the passages with life, as well as the rusty water that led to greater clarity.

Case History

✤ Write a chronological description of a creative project or piece of writing, including how you slogged through the twenty-five tons of earth to find the nugget inside. Was the nugget something you expected to find, or was it a product of the culling process as you refined the work?

polishing your powers
of observation

ch 6. Wake Up and Notice
the Fuzz on the Rose Petals

Have you ever noticed the velvety down on a rose petal, as fine and soft as a baby's cheek? Have you ever stared transfixed, mystified by the way the rose petals fit together with such grace and beauty? You have? Then you're an exception. Most of us look, but we don't see. As Georgia O'Keeffe said, "No one sees a flower, really, because to see takes time." O'Keeffe painted flowers large so you couldn't ignore them. You *have* to look at the details of her flowers as they spread their petals across a canvas as big as a window. Viewing an O'Keeffe feels like looking through a giant magnifier. You can't miss the nuances.

There's another aid to observation in O'Keeffe's flower paintings. Each painting, almost without exception, features just one subject—a morning glory, for example. By singling out an object, by isolating it, by enlarging it, you are forced to see detail—maybe for the first time. The Japanese have been aware of this less-is-more philosophy for centuries. Their practice of arranging just a few blossoms, usu-

ally three or five, in a simple container invites you to pause and observe the detail: the texture of leaves, the varying lengths of stems, the
way one flower inclines its head and the other looks straight at you.

But our Western way of excess obscures detail. We're apt to
think that if one rose is beautiful, a bouquet of dozens of flowers of
every conceivable hue is even better. I once received from a co-worker
what I still think of as a funeral arrangement or a garland for a racehorse. The giver's thoughtfulness was heartfelt, but the huge popula-
tion of flowers was just too much to attend to. So I pulled out three
carnations and a sprig of fern and put them in a tall glass container.
The rest of the arrangement, seemingly undisturbed, I gave to a
neighbor. Now the bouquet was "O'Keeffed"—just three flowers
isolated in a vase. They had my full attention.

Details take time and patience to assimilate. Images that blip
past on a TV screen at a rate of sixty to a hundred a minute, as they
often do in commercials, leave little opportunity to focus on detail.
The effect is almost hypnotic. You see a headlight, a car careening up a
hill, a grill headed straight for you. You never really get a good look at
the car the commercial is selling.

A number of modern artists have produced "color field paintings" to slow us down and encourage us to search for details, no matter
how sparse. You've probably seen some of these. At first, the paintings
seem to resemble a rectangle sawed from a wall that a housepainter
just covered with a bucket of acrylic and a wide brush, framed and
hung in a show. But look closer. You'll begin to notice details: slight
variations in the overall color; subtle, almost subliminal textures.
Robert Rauschenberg's massive black paintings on scrunched newspaper reveal subtle shapes and textures that delight the eye. Looking
at these paintings teaches us that paying attention to detail is rewarded.

We rarely stretch our attentiveness to see what's right in front
of our eyes. Yet such attention to detail is important in creative work,
whether that work is writing, painting, music, dance or theater. A
single detail can trigger a creative idea. Close observation can provide
a solution to a seemingly unsolvable problem.

Lynn, a sensitive and deeply insightful poet I know, says that
detail can inspire a poem even when the finished poem doesn't have

much detail in it. She also says she sometimes writes a poem full of details that people typically overlook. "I often fix on ants, how leaves move, how sunlight grows hour after hour," she says. "These details are important to me. Imaginative detail in my poems springs from what I've observed in real life." She adds that her graphic art background has made her more aware of visual detail. "In a lot of my poems, I try to paint a picture. It may not be a tangible one, but it's composed of images. To be aware of all this, I make a conscious effort to stay wide open."

For a creative person, "staying wide open" means becoming litmus paper, sensitive to what's before your eyes. We tend to see stereotypically, according to the idea we already have of a thing. This idea often lacks detail or sometimes goes against reality itself.

I remember a man on a Florida beach who was sketching a palm tree. After an hour or so, when he had finished, he showed me his drawing. It was obvious he had worked hard; he had erased and repencilled. But he had missed some significant details. Instead of curving gracefully toward the sea, the palm's trunk in the drawing stood up as straight as a redwood. The leaves were identical in size and shape, like the ones on a plastic tree from a party store. And the artist had failed entirely to notice the strange burlapy fabric a coconut palm produces.

We all tend to see things with the details removed. Objects and events are easier to file in our mental computers if they can be classified according to their general kind and not singled out by unique detail. This is just the way our brains work.

We are born with only a rudimentary ability to observe. In the first months of life, not only do we miss seeing the fuzz on the rose petal, but we see the rose only in a general way. When we first pick up a paintbrush in early childhood, many of us draw a person as a circle— a lopsided circle maybe, sometimes with squared corners, but recognizably a circle. Later, as our brains develop and we begin to notice more detail, we add stick arms and legs. Still later, we observe eyes, mouth, nose, fingers and toes, and they become part of our creative expression. We're seeing detail!

When at last we learn to read and write, our brains are forced to sort things into abstract concepts and words. Few of us notice fingers and toes anymore. As adults, we tend to lose our ability to notice even those objects right in front of our noses every day.

I once asked a class to spend ten minutes a day trying to notice everything around them. The next week, when the class met, a man exclaimed in surprise, "I saw the hood ornament on my car for the very first time!" He had been driving that car for more than eight years.

Is it important to notice a hood ornament? Maybe. Maybe not. A writer could insert the hood ornament as a detail in a novel or as a clue in a murder mystery. The car owner could remove the ornament and use it to flip off pop bottle caps. In any case, whether an observation is useful or not generally can't be determined at the time it's made.

You never know when a particular detail will be just what you're looking for to inspire a creative work, and observing details is tedious work. Is the effort worth it? Let's look.

Details Give Depth, Richness, Groundedness and Life to Your Work

We've already discussed how detail could have enlivened a sketch of a palm tree. Writing, too, can be lit up by including observed nuances. One exercise I propose to people in my writing classes is to look carefully at a scene or object for ten minutes and then write about it, pressing into service all the significant details. Here's an example by Linda Walker, a student in one of the classes:

> The girl seated in front of me came in late. She is
> dressed like the others in shades of black. Her
> jacket proclaims "Feminism Lives!" She's cut
> holes into the ends of her sleeves so that her fin-
> gers jut through the fabric. Around her neck she's
> wound at least ten necklaces, all leather except for
> one circle of seashells. On her head is a large
> black beret cocked jauntily to the side. I can't see
> her feet, but I'm sure she's wearing clogs.

Now let's look at a rewrite of this paragraph without most of the details:

> The girl seated in front of me wears black clothes
> and a hat. She has necklaces around her neck. I
> can't see her shoes.

Can you see how the richness drains away as soon as details
are eliminated, leaving a boring corpse of writing? In the first piece,
you can *see* the young woman. You might predict whom she'd date,
what she'd choose from a restaurant menu, how she gets along with
her parents—you feel like you know her. Not so in the second example. The girl could be anyone. She could be in mourning or trying to
look sophisticated. The details aren't talking.

Details Give You a Sense of the Larger Whole

I once went to a shelter to interview three women for an article on
battered wives. While the details of the women's stories were different,
taken together, they revealed a pattern. The women said tension would
increase day after day, no matter what they did, until it resulted in the
inevitable explosion of abuse. Later, the husband would beg forgive-
ness, the wife would take him back, and the cycle would start all over
again. After the article ran, several women wrote to say that the details
of these women's lives helped them become aware of the pattern in
their own abuse. As a result, they were able to seek help before the
situation escalated.

In other instances, details can point to a larger truth by revealing a person's character, as they did in this journal notation:

> Inside a town house on Chestnut Street, an old
> woman moves a birdcage on a long-legged stand
> closer to the screen door, closer to the frail breath
> of air from the outside that brings an almost im-
> perceptible cooling. Peering out from the cage
> are the glass-bead eyes of a pale blue parakeet.

What conclusions can you draw from this passage? What kind
of woman would take the trouble to give her parakeet the benefit of

fresh air on a hot night? The details answer, or at least suggest. You can observe such small dramas and note the details that tell a larger story. Michelangelo said that it's by looking at fingernails that we can determine a person's character. Don't overlook details. Pay attention to fingernails.

Details Supply a Warehouse Full of Creative Tools

You never know what tool you'll need—or when. When I was starting out in my first, one-room apartment in Philadelphia, I needed to erect a room divider to hide the sink. As a low-paid PR assistant I couldn't afford to buy a divider, so I decided to make one from bamboo poles and a matchstick shade. The problem was how to make the poles stand upright and not fall over. They needed something flexible to hold them in place. I remembered playing paddleball as a kid, so I bought some of the balls at the five-and-dime and nailed them to the ceiling. Poles of just the right length could be wedged into place over the balls to provide support for the shades. Of course, a real carpenter would have done it differently and more professionally, but I am not a real carpenter. The point of this example is that observed details, such as paddleballs from a childhood game, can be useful in future creative problem solving.

There's no such thing as an insignificant detail, even though the words are often found in each other's company. Jack Kerourac says that details are the life of prose. They are also the life of poetry, and the inspiration of painting and other creative acts. To fuel your own creativity, train yourself to observe and remember details. Think of this training as mental push-ups: preparation for being able to see a rose all the way down to its fuzzy petals. We can't write or draw until we can see. And we can't see until we take time to notice.

Explorations

❧ Without looking at your shoes, write a paragraph or two about them. Then, while looking at them, write another paragraph or two. Do you see any difference between the first writing and the second? Repeat the process using as your subject a particular flower or plant, your vacuum cleaner, the inside of your car or your wallet.

❧ Go to a public place, such as a fast-food restaurant, an airport or a ballpark. Study the people. What are they wearing? What habits and mannerisms do you detect? Based on your observations, draw conclusions about one of the people. Write for twenty minutes at the site. After you leave, write from memory about several other people you saw.

Walkabout

❧ Walk around your neighborhood or a park for twenty minutes. Consciously observe as many details as you can. Afterward, write about what you remember. Practice this exercise at least once a week to improve both your powers of observation and your memory.

ch 7. The Principle of Devoted Attention

In at least one way, we're like jungle animals. We think continually about what we'll eat and worry continually about what will eat us. In other words, predatory vision rules our lives. We notice only what we *fear* and what we can *use*. Everything else falls through the cracks.

Creativity depends upon broader observation; narrow, two-track predatory vision won't work. Ordinary seeing is usually linked to assessment: Do I like it? Does it serve my need? Will it harm me? Anything not tied to fear or need is likely to go unnoticed.

For example, an apple tree stands in an alley behind my place. People do not see it because they buy their apples from the neatly stacked and uniformly sized fruit display at grocery stores such as Kroger. I know this is true because all summer long the pungent smell of rotting apples dominates the alley. The ripe, red fruit goes unpicked. Nobody notices.

Advertisers claim that people are only interested in the WIFM factor: "*What's in It For Me?*" WIFM leads to predatory seeing. Let's

LEARN TO SEE BEYOND PREDATORY VISION

say you're in the market for new wheels and a commercial for a Cadillac that zigs flashes on the TV screen. If the car, zigging or not, is out of your price range, your attention shuts off. But if you've just come into an inheritance from Great Aunt Ethel, you might watch with interest and even try to read the small print.

Predatory vision and the WIFM factor are at one end of the vision spectrum—the noncreative end. At the other end is an entirely different way of seeing: devoted attention. Devoted attention is similar to "aesthetic arrest." It's an absolute "becoming one with" that engulfs the whole person and seems to make time stand still. Distractions are ignored or overcome through concentration on the object. When you practice devoted attention, you are like a toddler first noticing the lower branches of a brightly lit Christmas tree. You look up and up and up until finally you fall backward, entranced.

Noticing is a form of devotion. We pay attention to what we love, and we come to love what we pay attention to. What is not worthy of devotion? Devoted attention causes us to see a thing just as it is so it can speak to us from its own being.

A few years back, I had an experience with an Idaho potato. It began, innocently enough, after I read Peter Bishop's essay in *Spring Journal*, "The Vegetable Soul." Bishop wrote that he wasn't going to talk about flowers or trees or exotic plants or things that grow in the sea. They could too easily become spiritual symbols. What interested him were vegetables, such as cabbage and potatoes. They had soul.

I wasn't sure about cabbage, but potatoes had held magic from as far back as I could remember. When I was six, my dad began a large garden and drafted the whole family into service, hoeing and planting. We stood with the dark, loamy peat to our ankles, the sun pressing our backs with its hot hand, the musty scent of earth drifting up from the holes we dug. One day we were to plant potatoes. My dad showed me how to cut a potato into pieces containing at least one eye and to plant the slivers in the ground. The eyes, he pointed out, were what made the potato grow. If there was proof of potato magic, this was it.

So Bishop's conclusion that potatoes had soul was not altogether beyond belief. I wanted to put it to the test. At the supermarket I bought the largest Idaho they had and brought it to work the next day where it rested upright in a scissored-off paper cup on my desk. The vegetable's endearing pudginess won me over right away. It reminded me of a manatee.

I'd read that in early days in France no one would eat potatoes because everyone thought they looked like lepers and could cause leprosy. To me, my Idaho looked like a lumpy head, too friendly to cause any ill. But I planned to keep an eye on it.

As the days went on, potato man began to take on a personality. I drew a face on it to help it along. A few days later, someone added a pointy paper cap with the words *The Wiz* lettered in red. People began to come into the office to have a look. These same people had piles of potatoes in their vegetable bins at home.

I don't remember how long the vegetable ruled over my desk from its paper cup perch, but to this day—after having practiced devoted attention, even unintentionally—peeling a potato feels like taking a life.

The potato and I had formed a bond of sorts. And it had happened without my wanting to eat it or it wanting to eat me. From this contact, I came to better understand potatoness. Devoted attention does that. You learn something that facts themselves can't teach: a thing's core or essence. This lesson comes slowly; devoted attention requires patience.

When I teach writing and art classes, I ask students to write about or draw the same object many times. The intent is for them to learn by attentive observation. A seventeen-year-old boy in one of the art classes rendered an apple over fifty times using many mediums. Each rendering was unique, beautiful and competently drawn. The boy basked in praise from the rest of the class, answering questions, describing his work. Thinking that he must have enjoyed the project, I asked him what he thought of the exercise. "It was *boring*!" he exclaimed, patience perhaps not an outstanding virtue of teenagers. In a society bent on moving faster and faster, as we discussed earlier, devoted attention is seldom practiced. We haven't time for it. We also lack the patience required to pay attention to something that's not sensational—something that, by this seventeen-year-old's judgments may not even be mildly interesting.

SEED THOUGHT

"How little observed are the fruits we do not use."

Henry David Thoreau
Faith in a Seed

But that's the point: *Anything* can be interesting if you pay attention to it. Eastern cultures have made sacred rituals of such attention. Consider the simple act of drinking tea. In the West, we might drain the cup in a single slurp, like our role models on TV drain a can of Pepsi. In Japan, not only is the actual drinking of a cup of tea worthy of care and attention, but so is the whole tea process. Three volumes in the *Ch'a Ching* describe every detail from cultivating the plant to the serving and drinking of the tea. Similar attention is paid to painting, flower arranging, poetry and food preparation, to name just a few of the Japanese arts.

Creativity depends in no small part upon subtleties that hover at the edge of awareness. Practicing devoted attention will put you in touch with them. Such a practice can, as the Japanese say, "polish the mirror" of your observation. Here are some things to keep in mind:

- Be open to whatever comes, just as it is. Don't try to change it or hold on to it or make it useful.
- Be deeply affected by each experience. Practice devotion.
- Pay attention as often as possible. (This one is not as easy as it sounds.)
- Treat everything as worthy of your notice.

I never thought much about Canada geese, except that their "wacka-wacka" honking sounded like a rusty screen door. On a site write by a pond, this passage resulted:

> Round-bellied geese preen their feathers in the
> rain. They waddle down the boardwalk on
> spindly legs, their wings folded behind their
> backs, like Churchill.

I'd learned a thing or two about geese by attentive looking. If you train yourself to see without predatory vision, everything will reveal itself to you. You'll see potatoes and apples and Canada geese as if for the first time. Your creative muse will hug you in jubilation.

✤ What's the most boring object you can think of? A lightbulb? A clothespin? A potato? Spend ten minutes just paying attention to that object. Then write for twenty minutes about your impressions. Repeat with a different object each day for a week.

✤ Write about the same object each day for a week. Devote ten minutes to looking and ten minutes to writing. How does your impression of the object change with each writing?

Site Write

✤ Choose a site, indoors or out, and plant yourself there for at least a half hour. Observe closely the objects or people you encounter. Focus on no more than one object in five minutes. Write your experiences.

Research

✤ Keep a notebook of your encounters with objects or other people. How many of these encounters involve predatory vision (fear or desire)? How many involve devoted attention (for the subject's own sake)?

ch 8. Think Like an Alien

HOW TO

CLARIFY YOUR

VISION

Imagine how you'd feel if you'd never before seen the sun fall off the edge of the horizon. Suddenly, there you are in the dark. Are you terrified? Curious? Despondent? Imagine, then, that you've survived that first dark night, perhaps even worried yourself into sleep. How would you feel when the sun miraculously reappeared the next morning? Amazed? Jubilant? Awestruck?

We have come to know that the sun will rise and set at certain times, depending on the season. We're rather cavalier about the whole affair. But if you were the first person on earth, as Mark Twain charmingly describes in *The Diary of Adam and Eve*, you might not be so complacent. At first, Eve tries to knock down the stars by throwing clods of earth at them. None fall. She then tries to prove that a rock can swim; it can't. Later that night, she sees some stars "melt," and fears that all of them will run down the sky in the same way. So she stays awake all night, looking. She tries to "impress those sparkling fields on my memory, so that by and by when they are taken away I can by my fancy restore those lovely myriads to the black sky and make them sparkle again, and double them by the blur of my tears."

We smile at Eve's misplaced concern. After all, we know that if even a hundred stars should melt on a given night, there are whole universes of stars to take their place. We know volumes of other things, too; this knowledge allows us to take most everything for granted. As Wordsworth wrote, "The world is too much with us, late and soon." We've forgotten how to think like an alien.

I once began to keep notes for what I had envisioned would ultimately become a story about an alien visit to Earth. As somewhat of a lifelong alien myself, I thought I was uniquely qualified. The idea was that an alien rockets to Earth from another planet to check us out and report back what he sees. I admit that this plot sounds like the TV epic *Mork & Mindy*. The echo of series past may be why the notes ended up in the waste can. Although this project did not survive, the idea seemed sound at the time, and I learned a lot from the failed project. It taught me to see like an alien.

Much of what I noted when looking through alien eyes contradicted what I'd been taught I was supposed to see. I'd never noticed the contradiction.

- We exterminate naturally occurring wildflowers—violets, spring beauties, dandelions—in our yards, and we plant flats of petunias, pansies and geraniums we buy at the garden store.
- A machine that makes "white" noise for people who are bothered by noise is for sale in catalogs.
- The side of a landscaper's truck proclaims, "We care about your trees." The bed of the truck holds the broken body of a chainsawed maple.

Being an alien is frustrating work. Eventually I got distressed and quit keeping notes. But once you start to think like an alien, it gets into your cells. You begin to see all life's contradictions, humor and wonders. Like an alien, you and your fresh-washed mind meet another world that often tries to fool itself or just doesn't think about what it's doing and saying. Sometimes what you learn by thinking like an alien is side-splittingly funny. Sometimes, as in war and politics, it's terrifying.

However disturbing or laughable, such clarity of mind is essential to creativity. The creative act requires flexibility and the ability to see through the skin of sacred cows. You can achieve all this by learning to think like an alien.

The alien mind shone bright in a creative workshop I attended a while back. Facilitators had divided us into groups of five or six and supplied each group with an assortment of Tinkertoys: disks and cylinders with holes and sticks to connect the pieces. In twenty minutes, we were to build a tower, and the group with the highest tower would win. To make the project more interesting, the facilitators circulated among us, taking away pieces we planned to use and giving us other pieces we hadn't planned for.

The two engineers in our group immediately set about drawing a structurally sound design for the construction. They overruled all of our more casual suggestions—after all, they were the experts. So we gave in and watched while they measured and planned. Our construction was only half completed when we idle watchers looked around to see a neighboring group had finished. Its tower was a pyramid, only a foot tall. We snickered silently.

At the end of the twenty minutes, our group's tower was still in progress: the engineers arguing about the best way to proceed, the rest of us looking on. When the bell rang, each group presented its project. The group with the foot-high pyramid went last. We snickered, this time out loud. Then a dark-haired fellow who was more than six feet tall put the pyramid on his head like a hat and stepped onto the table. The group's tower was now over nine feet tall! We all laughed in amazement. The experts had been bested, but good! How could this be, when we had the experts on our side? There must be more to creativity than meets the eye. The nine-foot tower proved it. The alien mind had won out.

HOW TO THINK LIKE AN ALIEN

UNWRITTEN RULE 1: Never Become an Expert
Approach each task as if you're meeting it for the first time. If you
are an expert by training and already impaired, consult a novice for
advice.

You may have heard the story of the stuck truck. It's a good il-
lustration. An optimistic truck driver tried to muscle his rig through
the opening under a low bridge that spanned the highway. The rig
got stuck. Within minutes, traffic had backed up for miles—horns
blaring, drivers cursing. Also within minutes, experts converged on
the truck like flies on raw meat. They offered crowbars and cranes
and tried to pull and push. The truck stayed wedged. Then a small
boy wandered over and suggested that the driver let some air out of
the truck's tires. He did, and the truck was immediately freed—
thanks to the advice of a child.

**UNWRITTEN RULE 2: Don't Unnecessarily Limit Yourself by
Rules—Written, Spoken or Merely Assumed**
Often, the first thing we look for when confronted by a situation is
the accepted way to solve the problem. What are we expected to
do? We don't start with, What's the best way to go about this?
What *is* the problem?

In a workshop I facilitated, aimed at expanding imagination, I
invited participants to picture themselves as rosebushes. One
woman asked if she could be a palm tree because she was fond of
palm trees. No one else thought about *not* being a rosebush. It
never crossed their minds. An alien would likely have asked, "Do I
have to be a rosebush?" just like the woman did. Or the alien
might have imagined he was a palm tree or a feather or a spaceship
without asking.

UNWRITTEN RULE 3: Be Flexible
When the facilitator kept taking away our Tinkertoys and giving
us ones that were shaped differently, we had to continually rethink
our plan. The engineers balked. They stubbornly clung to their

original concept, inflexibly shutting out any new, perhaps better, approach.

UNWRITTEN RULE 4: Don't Be Afraid to Expose Sacred Cows
Engineers know more. We were so certain of that, we gave them full say in designing the Tinkertoy project. Even after we began to see how far off track we were, none of us spoke up to say, "Hey, this approach is going nowhere. Let's try something new." We were goaded by a sacred cow into giving up our own ideas. It's not uncommon for that to happen in a group.

Some researchers conducted a study to see whether a subject would speak up when the rest of the group had another opinion. The researchers placed two pencils, one shorter than the other, on a table in front of the group and asked each person to point to the shorter pencil. The subject didn't know that the rest of the group had been instructed to point to the longer pencil. As this experiment was repeated with different people, the response was nearly always the same. The subject caved in to the group's opinion and pointed to the long pencil, just as we gave in to the expertise of the engineers.

You've probably heard the story of the emperor who paraded through the village dressed only in his bare skin. The emperor's subjects, afraid to tell him the truth, praised his beautiful clothes. A child finally proclaimed the emperor's nakedness, just as a child suggested lowering the stuck truck to release it.

Clear seeing depends on your ability to maintain your own sense of what's true, at least until you're proven wrong or you begin to see in a different way. It's easy to hatch a creative idea. Sticking to it, faithfully, to bring it to life requires a steadfast commitment to your own truth.

UNWRITTEN RULE 5: Look at Everything As If You've Never Seen It Before
Observe like an alien. Ask, "What is this? What's it made of? What are its properties? What else is it like?" The Alien Method is harder than it sounds. It takes practice to see what's really there.

The walls in my home are white. When they were painted a few months ago, I was given six colors of paint to choose from, all white. Colonial White, Whisper White, Cloud White—their differences were so subtle, I couldn't always tell one from another. What's more, now that the paint is on the wall, it continues to change. Right now, under the lamp, it looks pale yellow. The far wall looks gray-blue, interrupted by a swath of pale peach from reflected sunlight. I see blue-mauve shadows behind picture frames and in the grid cast by a brass pie stand.

The alien mind sees colors on the wall even if it *knows* the wall is supposed to be white. The ordinary mind sees only white—the limited view of our Tinkertoy engineers who suffered a whiteout when they rejected any new ideas. The ordinary mind stops short, limits options, gets stuck in old ways of doing things. It doesn't venture into uncharted territory to bring back a profusion of new ideas. To do that, you have to become an alien.

Becoming an alien takes practice. You have to unlearn, little by little, most of what you know. Only then can you shed a tear because the stars are melting.

Explorations

❧ Pretend you have just arrived from another planet. Keep a list of events, actions, customs and practices that you find unusual or contradictory. Do this for a week and then write about your findings.

❧ Describe in writing an object from a dream or from a catalog without naming the object. Have a person who has never seen the object before read your description. Then show her a picture of the object or name the object in your dream. How close did your description come to what the person imagined?

❧ How would you describe the colors of a rainbow to a blind person? The sound of the sea to a person who can't hear? Write your description. (Naturally, you'll have to use another way to describe color other than by naming it "blue" or "red." So, too, with sea sounds that are usually described as "booming" or "hissing." You might try capturing colors through sound description and sound through color description.) Be creative!

Experiment

❧ Experience, as if for the first time, a hot bath with bubbles, something chocolate, waking up in the morning. Write about it for twenty minutes. How was this experience different from or the same as previous ones?

Walkabout

❧ Return to a place you've visited often: a shopping mall, the library, the dentist's office, a grocery store. Visit it as if you've never seen it before. Observe like an alien. Write for twenty minutes about your observations.

ch 9. Up to Your Neck in Swamp Water

Writers and other creative people are, as the Noel Coward song goes, like mad dogs and Englishmen. We go out in the noonday sun. We go out in rain and snow, and we may even dream, as Thoreau did, of spending a day submerged in swamp water. "Would it not be a luxury," Thoreau wrote in June 1840, "to stand up to one's chin in some retired swamp for a whole summer's day, scenting the sweet-fern and bilberry blows and lulled by the minstrelsy of gnats and mosquitoes?"

No doubt the swamp he had in mind was Beck Stow's Swamp near Concord, Massachusetts, an area he knew like a favorite pair of shoes. Here he did his walkabouts in gray predawn mists, in pelting winter blizzards, in the silvery cast of moonlight and in the heat of midsummer afternoons. Why? Why would anyone seek a frog's-eye view of a swamp in midsummer?

I was curious. Thoreau was a writer—the kind of writer I aspire to be. If he thought it would be a luxury to stand to one's chin in

EXPERIENCING

THE CREATIVE

POINT OF VIEW

swamp water or to observe the world in all its season's weathers, there must be value in his point of view. I wasn't ready to venture into swamp water, but I was willing to try rain.

Armed with umbrella, pencil and pad, I went to the woods one rainy summer afternoon to sit on a damp bench by the pond and watch the goose parents and their newly fledged offspring. It's true: Geese by the pond behave differently in the rain. They tromped through puddles like mischievous kids getting their shoes wet. Their goose parade passed close to my bench, trustingly close to where I sat under my umbrella like a large blue mushroom, still as a stone. Rain had surrounded us in its curtain of intimacy. I was just another goose watching my kin with no human beings around. Despite my increasing discomfort as a trickle off the umbrella dampened the back of my shirt, I could see that Thoreau was right. Being with an animal, an object or a place under varying conditions can expand your creative point of view.

Maybe you've fallen into a different point of view by accident, like when you visit your old grade school and are surprised to see how the classrooms have shrunk. Or you've been forced into a new outlook when your usual route to work is closed off by road construction and you go through a neighborhood you've never seen before. I had a point of view redo one winter when my car was laid up for two months waiting for a part. If you've never sat on a cold bench in a snowstorm waiting for a bus, you can't really empathize with anyone who does. A half hour in the cold opens your eyes. I'll never pass a bus stop again without a twinge of recognition.

Seeing from many points of view polishes powers of observation and keeps thinking muscles flexed. Whether a little or a lot, we all tend to repeat the Narcissus myth. We look into the pond and fall in love with our own reflection—with our own view of things and our own habitual ways of operating. It's as if we wore glasses with red or blue or green lenses. We see the world colored by the lens of our own experience. That lens necessarily obscures what's true and narrows our ability to see. Because creativity depends on wide, flexible vision, seeing in this limited way constricts creativity. Our downfall is not to have narrow vision but to fall in love with that vision so we can't see a situation from any other point of view.

I once did a creative workshop for a group of technical staff who had lost their jobs through a Fortune 500 company's downsizing. They were intent on pursuing jobs exactly like the ones they had lost and were unable to envision any other option. Many had been out of work for nearly a year. To make matters worse, their tunnel vision had kept them from dealing with feelings of grief and loss, feelings that were beginning to show up in illness and accident. Flexible thinking that could have helped them find other solutions to their job problems was so foreign to their usual way of operating that creative ideas were likely of little help. Flexible thinking has to be exercised or, like a couch potato's body, its muscles atrophy and it drifts off to sleep.

Fortunately, life often provides us with plenty of wake-up exercise. A writer I know was walking in the woods after a rainstorm and was about to take a path that was usually soggy after a downpour. She saw a woman with only one leg approaching on crutches. "Is the path muddy up ahead?" the writer asked. "No," the woman answered. "I just came through there, and it's fine." The writer headed on down the path where the woman on crutches had just come. Soon she was muttering under her breath as her Reeboks began to sink into the ooze. Then she saw imprints in the mud of the tips of crutches and between each pair a single footprint. Her point of view changed immediately.

Changing your point of view can help solve problems creatively, as it did when some fund-raisers faced a dilemma. Their information packet, to be sent to thousands of would-be donors, was a hair heavier than planned. The additional postage for the unanticipated extra weight would double the mailing cost and put them over budget. Funds were tight. They knew their boss's reaction to the extra expense would not be kind. Then they looked at the problem from another viewpoint. They saw the mailing piece as not *overweight* but *oversize*. A slight trim off one end of the return card did the trick and rescued the budget.

To jolt people into thinking from another point of view, I often bring a thumbless garden glove to a workshop and ask, "What's the first thing you notice about this glove?" Naturally, everyone says, as I would have, too, if the roles were reversed, "The thumb is missing." When I ask why they didn't notice that there were four fingers

SEED THOUGHT

"Solutions to problems often depend upon how they're defined."

Mary Catherine Bateson
Composing a Life

still intact, they are forced to think. They experience a viewpoint switch. Zap! Just like that.

You don't have to wait for experiences to reorient your point of view. You can keep a toned and flexible point of view by exercising your creative imagination. Imagination has an edge over experience: It's always handy, and you don't have to worry about getting soggy in swamp water or being bothered by what other people will think of your responses. You can use anything at all to trigger your imagination.

One of my first experiences with imagination triggers is the beginning of a house, actually just a cemented-over basement, in a lot a few blocks from where my aunt and uncle used to live. Every time we drove by it, I tried to imagine what it would be like to live in a house that ended at ground level. Think about it. How would you feel when you woke up in the morning and looked out the window at a wall of dirt? Would you even have a window to look out of? During a tornado warning, would your neighbors pound on your cellar door, yelling to come in? How would you give directions to someone trying to find your house? Would you say, "It's the empty lot between the white frame and the red brick"? Just this one switch in imaginative viewpoint led to hours of creative wonderings.

Like a puppy, point of view needs frequent exercise to stay flexible and healthy and to prevent hardening of the arteries of insight. Here are a few ways to keep yours in shape:

- Get to know as many people who are vastly different from you as you can. Imagine yourself in their place. Dialogue with people you wouldn't ordinarily talk to: the mail carrier, bank teller, baby-sitter, neighborhood children, grocery checker or the person seated next to you in a waiting room or on a plane. Aim for a variety of ages, cultures, ethnic origins. Check out museum exhibits or read depictions in historical novels and books to put yourself in another time and place.
- See the world differently, as Thoreau did, by walking before dawn or after dark (if your neighborhood is safe) and visiting new places, even if those places are just down the street.

- Expand your experience by learning a new skill or reading biographies about people who interest you.
- Continue to develop your own individual point of view. What's your opinion on issues you see on the evening news? Whom do you admire? Why? What's the single most important thing to you?

If you're a writer, expanding your point of view can help you see into your fictional characters or give you ideas to fuel your article, book or poetry writing. Other creatives can use altered points of view to gain insight into expression in art, dance, drama or music. Lao-tzu said that you have to *become* the thing in order to understand it. How many conflicts could be prevented if we could learn to walk in another person's shoes?

A newly designed wheelchair enables people without use of their legs to elevate themselves nearly to standing height so they'll be at eye level with other people who aren't wheelchair confined. Have you ever wondered how you'd feel if you were sitting down—only four feet tall—and surrounded by a forest of standing people? Would your neck ache from always having to look up? I'd never thought from a wheelchair point of view 'til I saw this new wheelchair on TV.

Whether fate hands you a ticket to a new point of view or you invite one through deliberate change or refocusing, the experience can be broadening. You can learn a lot by standing up to your neck in swamp water—even if you do it only in your imagination.

Explorations

✤ Cut out photos from magazines of people's faces as different as possible from one another with regard to gender, race, background, occupation. Paste them on index cards. Draw one at random from the stack. Jot down a focus question: a decision you need to make, a problem you want to solve or a subject you want to consider. Write for ten minutes from the point of view of the person in the photograph. Repeat with another photo. Use the person's presumed vocabulary and manner of speaking. Try putting several of the photo characters into a story. Try sketching or painting or dancing as if this person were expressing his own thoughts and feelings.

✤ Write like your cat or dog or goldfish would talk.

✤ Write the names of body parts on small cards, such as the back of business cards. Use parts such as elbow, foot, intestines, fingernail, navel, cell, shoulder, nose, armpit or strand of hair. Pick one card at random, and write for ten minutes as if the body part you selected could speak. What would it see? What questions would it ask? What would its complaints and pleasures be?

Site Write

✤ Write about the same place for ten minutes a day for seven days. Change your point of view or the time of day each time you write. For example, write at a river and look upstream, downstream, close-up and across its wide expanse; write in early morning and late evening, in rain and shine.

✤ What would a scene in the woods look like if you viewed it from the top of the tallest tree, an insect-eye view from the tip of a blade of grass, a bee's view from inside a flower, a mole's view from inside its hole? Write your impressions.

10. Pencil Dancing With Talking Rocks

Sitting on my closet shelf is a rumpled brown paper bag with the words "Famous Talking Rocks" hand-lettered on the outside. The bag contains a collection of orphan rocks—holey, weather sculpted, bleached by sun and sea—that I picked up on a Florida beach. They are not your usual collector's shells. In fact, when the UPS agent saw that I intended to ship ten pounds of these lumpy gray beach refugees back to Ohio, he was stunned.

I didn't try to explain, but these were special rocks. Each had a history. They could talk. One looked like a bear fetish with a hole in its forehead and left flank. An amoeba-shaped rock was porous and black with a pearly something imbedded in its hollow. I even had a clinker piece of broken coral in a cactus form with roughly calcified skin embossed with pimply blips shaded from cocoa brown to buff. Each rock had a voice. Each was unique, and therefore, valuable—worth the fifteen dollars it cost to ship them to Ohio.

DRAWING

AS A WAY

OF SEEING

I intended to use the rocks in writing and art classes and creative workshops. They would be commissioned to "speak," one-on-one, about how to become more observant. I had been using creek stones before these. But they were rounder and didn't speak quite so eloquently. The sea rocks were different. They had been tossed together and stormed upon by an enormous power. It was written all over their surfaces and deep into them. They had character.

In class, I pass around the talking rocks in their brown paper bag. Each person, eyes closed, reaches in to get one. For the first few minutes they get to know their rocks through touch, the way a mother comes to know a newborn. Then they take a few minutes just to observe, to look at the humps and hollows and holes. Finally, they pick up their pencils and do focus sketches of the objects' outlines without looking at their papers.

The process is slow and deliberate. Pencils inch along the large sheets of newsprint, making studied lines that attempt to duplicate the rocks' contours. Often the lines crisscross or ramble off the pages. It doesn't matter. It doesn't matter, in fact, that the drawings look more like scribbles than artful renderings. What *is* important is simply concentrating on the rocks themselves. Sketching is incidental. The intent is to listen while the rocks talk.

Sometimes the group repeats the exercise using their other hands but still not looking at the emerging drawing. After several sketches with each hand, they write about their experiences. The whole process takes only twenty to thirty minutes, but afterward they find they've developed a deep attachment to their rocks, a devotion inspired by careful looking. When I ask what they've learned, they say,

- "This is the first time I've looked at anything for more than a few seconds. It's almost like a meditation."
- "I began to see more than the rock. In some ways, after a while, I began to see into myself."
- "When you take time to really look at something, you begin to see in a new way."
- "It reminded me of looking at the ocean. You're not trying to see anything in particular, you're just looking—just filling your eyes."

Careful looking, whether you're sketching or not, polishes
and increases powers of observation that are crucial to creativity.
Concentration on an object you're drawing inspires two kinds of seeing: actual observation of the object and imaginatively seeing into the
object's essential character. Each feeds creativity in a different way.

Outer seeing, as you draw the contours of an object, helps you
focus on the object's color, texture, shape, natural properties. If you
don't have a talking rock, you can substitute a talking philodendron or
a talking wrought iron gate—anything that will sit still long enough to
pose for a focus sketch. It doesn't matter whether you can draw or not.
The object is to pay attention to what's there and use your pencil to
keep your mind from wandering off into its own field of daisies. Drawing, I have come to believe, helps you see better, write better, comprehend better. Try it. You'll be surprised what you'll discover.

Seeing into an object is perhaps an even more useful benefit of
focus drawing. By concentrating on a rock's contours and carefully
putting down what you see, you lull your naggingly chatty analytical
mind to sleep. It gets bored and dozes off. It leaves you alone, like a
ferocious beast temporarily anesthetized, so you can discover how to
switch from logical thinking to creative thinking.

When I feel stuck in my writing, I often take out colored
markers and draw or just doodle aimlessly. The bright colors attract
the inner mind like a spinning mobile draws the attention of a child.
Other images come. When they do, they can be written about, danced,
whistled, drummed or molded. You don't need lessons. When the images arise, just approach them in a spirit of discovery. Art can be your
bridge between imagination and creative expression. Try different
media for your sketching, experiencing the strengths and limitations of
each one. Some suggestions:

- colored pencil, soft black pencil
- crayon
- pastel, charcoal, sidewalk chalk
- marker, fountain pen
- oil bars, oil pastels

While you experiment with sketching mediums, you may also want to try different colors, kinds and sizes of paper. Whether or not you look at your work as you sketch, the tools you use will influence the way you see. If, for example, you're sketching with a fine-point pen, you're likely to see and draw fine details and textures. Working with a fat stick of pastel? You'll probably notice an object's general shape. Maybe you'll blend colors to suggest a dimensional quality. Whatever your drawing tools, by making an object visible on the page, you etch it into your mind.

I observe differently when I draw than when I write. Drawing requires attentiveness. If you've ever watched a group of sketchers, you know what I mean. They look at the object, look down at their paper and make a few lines, look back at the object, then return to their paper. There's a dialogue, a dance, going on between observing and recording. When I write, I usually have much less back-and-forth attentiveness to the subject, even when I write on-site at the corner park or on the banks of the Ohio River. I tend to catch the action, register a few details, and then write several paragraphs before checking back. By drawing every now and then, I remember how to see attentively.

True seeing requires energy and concentration. Seeing attentively with concentrated focus is difficult even for short periods of time. Our powers of observation are like a flashlight that can focus only on one small area at a time, leaving everything else in the shadows. Without concentration, the flashlight flits from here to here to here to here. We look. We don't see.

The difference between looking and seeing is like the difference between reading a menu and tasting the food. By giving your attention to an object as you draw, you learn to see, not just to look. You contact what Frederick Franck calls "the Sanity of our core." Practice focus drawing, along with other drawing and creative expression to help you lose your mind and regain your sanity.

✤ Draw a patch of grass from memory, then draw while looking at the real thing (bring a clump inside or draw on the spot). What is different about each experience? Write your thoughts.

✤ Draw an object—a flower in a vase, a still-life arrangement of fruit, a rattan footstool—with the hand you don't normally use to write. Then draw the same object with your writing hand. (Don't worry, in either case, whether the result looks like fine art.) Write about the difference between these two ways of drawing.

✤ Slightly crumple a piece of foil or stiff plain paper, and draw it as carefully as you can with pencil or pen. Write what you learned about eye-hand coordination. About *seeing*.

✤ Draw the spaces surrounding an object, not the object itself. Choose an object with open spaces, such as a flower with its stem and leaves or a bentwood rocker. Write about the difference between observing the background and looking at the object itself.

Creative Recess

✤ Play music that suits your mood: lively, serene, explosive, somber. Make lines or shapes to express what you observe inwardly. Use a broad-tip marker or paint and a large brush. Don't try to make the lines or shapes look like anything in particular. Be free. Experiment. Play. Write about what you observed in your inner experience.

Practice

✤ Draw an object without looking at your drawing hand or the page. Take your time. Repeat several times. Write about the effect of this practice on your eye-hand coordination and on your ability to observe closely.

Walkabout

✤ Observe the bare branches of trees as if they were a sketch or the trees' leaves as if they were a painting. What do you see in the intricate patterns of branches or leaves? Let your imagination dance. Write about what you see.

✤ Visit an art museum to see how artists have expressed their own seeing. Do their paintings depict inner or outer seeing? Compare several artists' paintings by writing about what you think they saw as they worked.

creating with your
whole self

11. Lessons From the Velveteen Rabbit

On rainy Saturdays I sometimes drop by Ferguson's Antique Mall. The sprawling one-story building shares the neighborhood with fenced graveyards for dismembered auto bodies and with Western diners advertising steer-sized steaks. I go there to relive someone else's past. Other people's histories are written on the yellowing hand-embroidered dresser scarves, the dusty mandolins and the moth-eaten moose heads. They inhabit the wooden ironing boards and carpenter's toolboxes, and even the Log Cabin syrup cans no one realized would become valuable. Everywhere amid the haze of cigar smoke and the maze of crisscrossed electrical cords, there are mementos of someone's life. Each relic has its own story.

This particular rainy Saturday, I spot on a shelf, between a toy fire engine and a tin soldier painted blue, a worn gray velveteen rabbit, sitting splay legged and forlorn among the other toys. One of his eyes is missing. His fur is grimy from handling. I almost have to look away because I see too clearly how much the rabbit was loved by some phantom child, now disappeared into adulthood or long ago dead of old age.

The toy reminds me of a passage from Margery Williams's book *The Velveteen Rabbit or How Toys Become Real*. "Generally by the time you become Real most of your hair has been loved off—your eyes drop out and you get loose in the joints and very shabby." The velveteen rabbit in her story became real over time by having his fur loved off, by being left out in the rain and by being clutched too closely by a small child.

Creative expression becomes real in much the same way. Realness comes when we experience the unpleasantness of rubbing up against the prickly world, both inner and outer. It can be a dismembering process, requiring that we re-form the broken pieces of ourselves over and over, gradually becoming more wise, more clear, more real. In Williams's story, Rabbit wishes he could become real without uncomfortable things happening. We do, too.

Often those times that have abraded your fur and left it salt stained and faded have honed your creativity without you knowing it. I often ask a class to write about the worst things that ever happened to them. They always moan, "Why do we have to revisit that old stuff? We put it out of our minds long ago." But they write anyway. And they always discover something unexpected. They come back bursting with talk:

- "For me, I was surprised to find the worst of times was the best of times. I unexpectedly lost my job and the whole family was devastated. But we worked through it. We had to reorient our priorities and count our pennies. I found my writing at the time was crisper and more genuine. It had greater depth. In the end, it was the job loss that convinced me to do writing full-time."
- "I never liked to think about the time when our house was destroyed by a tornado. But when I began to write about it, I realized it was a time when our family and our neighbors became very close. We relied on each other for emotional

support, and we helped each other clean up the mess and salvage what we could. We'd cry over finding some high school graduation picture or one of the kid's sports trophies. My painting was different after that. I could paint my feelings."

- "Writing about my daughter's attempted suicide helped me see this traumatic time more clearly. I can empathize with her pain and with other people's pain, regardless of the cause. The experience has deepened me."

Realness implies close contact with thoughts, feelings, experiences, other people. Writing is a contact sport. So is painting. So is any creative act. The contact happens between you and your subject and between you and your audience and between you and your work. It's how your fur gets rubbed off. The rubbing peels away all the separating layers, all the bundled fluff that keeps you and your world from being in close touch. The peeling away makes you real.

Think of realness as a kind of dance. Not the faraway kind where you can't tell whose partner is whose, but the close-up, moving-as-one kind of dance where you couldn't slip tissue paper between you and your creative ground. This close contact, this dancing as one, keeps you in touch with your own creative reality.

In a film, artist Jackson Pollock demonstrated what happens when you lose contact with your creative work. It goes awry. He threw away paintings that resulted from this loss of contact. I think he would have been wise to struggle with them for a while longer to see if they could be brought to some resolution. As a closet painter, I'm often tempted to give up on work in progress that's gotten up and walked away, refusing to cooperate. But I know if I quit in the difficult place, I'll never finish, and the unfinished painting will haunt me because I won't be able to throw it away. Finishing a work reestablishes contact. It keeps your feet on the ground.

Because creativity seems to come from some unknowable place, we often think of it as pie in the sky, unconnected with everyday reality. In truth, creativity demands professional-strength, hard-nosed realism. Without at least one foot on solid ground, creativity evaporates like fog in the noonday sun.

SEED THOUGHT

"A snake without a skin might make a fair job of crawling into another snake's shedding, but I guess no snake would be fool enough to bother with it."

Robert Henri
The Art Spirit

"Stay on the ground," Mother Teresa once said. Grounded-ness is a prerequisite for authenticity. It keeps pie out of the sky and on your plate where it belongs. We used to know how to stay on the ground without thinking about it—without going to a grounding workshop, without catching ourselves every time we discover we're floating in close company with clouds.

Almost nothing in our world today encourages us to be groundedly comfortable with our own realities. We're bombarded at every turn by relentless attempts to get us to fit the cultural mold. Becoming part of the crowd makes us more predictable, easier to sell to, a marketer's dream. By succumbing to advertised urgings to reshape ourselves through plastic surgery, hair dye, wrinkle cream, weight-loss pills and muscle-building machines and to have the socially approved car, house and neighborhood, we sacrifice physical authenticity. By succumbing to urgings to reshape our thinking to fit advertising and people's opinions, we sacrifice mental authenticity. Most often we don't realize how much ground we're giving up. We've been brainwashed. Creativity loses its voice.

When I give talks to large audiences about creativity I often bring along a very tall giraffe. Not a real giraffe, of course, but an orange and black one painted on a long scroll rolled up on a wooden dowel rod. The scroll gets hung center stage so that when it unrolls like a window shade, people suddenly see this huge giraffe. I ask them, "What is this?" They invariably answer, "A giraffe." I ask again; they respond the same way. I say, "No, it's not a giraffe. It's a *picture* of a giraffe!" They groan.

The giraffe—whose name, by the way, is George—is meant to show, visually and dramatically, the difference between *virtual* reality and *real* reality. It demonstrates how our concepts separate us from our ground. We're so well traveled on the information highway and in the media and in our mind's fabrications that we forget that "knowing about" is not the same as Knowing.

When I was in high school, I liked to paint posters for student council elections and homecoming. One evening I was painting away, completely wrapped up in what I was doing, when my mother placed a glass of lemonade on the card table next to my paint water. Without looking, I reached for the glass and took a big swig. AAAACK! It was paint water! What a difference between my idea of lemonade and the reality of that awful tasting brown sludge. A concept is not the thing itself. Being real is the ability to know the difference.

Being open to your authentic lemonade-tasting experience can be a struggle. The thinking mind with all its preconceived (and often wrong) notions keeps sneaking in. You have to be constantly on guard. It's a lot like trying to keep crabgrass from taking over your front lawn. You're never finished. Whenever you're not looking, it pops up again.

In a recent interview on PBS, a young man described his job at a computer consulting firm. He spoke glibly of seventeen-hour workdays and taking his laptop on a trip to Aruba so he could work on the beach. The company had virtually taken over his waking life. "I *am* the company!" he said. "I've been totally assimilated!" You could almost hear the crabgrass grow.

Creativity depends upon a multifaceted, authentic self—one that hasn't been assimilated by a company or anything else. Even if your fur gets worn and faded, if you create from your Authentic Self, you don't have to try to be original. Whatever you do will have vitality and originality. It will grow, organically, from who you are.

❧ List ten endings to "I am _____." (I am friendly. I am sometimes messy. I am a writer. I am an adventurer. I am a walker.) Write for ten minutes on what you like or don't like about one or two of these descriptions. Repeat weekly or monthly, without looking at former lists, until you have four to six sets. Set aside an hour or two to review the lists and your writing about specific items. Are any of the listings repeated? What's missing? Which are roles? Which are personality traits? What have you learned about your *real* self?

❧ Write a letter of encouragement to your creative self. Recognize what that side of you has accomplished and the obstacles it has overcome. Mention large and small acts alike: varying an old recipe, designing a scrapbook, writing an article, decorating a room, building a workbench. Mail the letter to yourself.

❧ Who or what has been the catalyst for your creativity? Who has offered encouragement? Write about your experiences.

Recollection

❧ When have you felt most like your real self? What was that self like? What circumstances existed at the time? What gave you support at the time? Can you express yourself without such support? For twenty minutes, write your thoughts and feelings.

❧ Write about the worst thing that ever happened to you. How has the experience shaped you, made you different? What did it teach you? How did it make you more real?

12. The Cow and the Racehorse

Have you ever made a decision you later regretted? Have you ever been of two minds about something? It was probably your nonlogical self who regretted or thought twice about something your thinking mind decided on its own.

This other self is called a doppelgänger, which translates from German as "double walker." Inside the skin of each of us there are two selves. Generally, we try to keep one of them in the closet. Psychologists and researchers sometimes call these two elements right brain and left brain, though these people argue over which is which exactly and what function, specifically, each side has.

I like to think of the two modes of thinking as Racehorse Mind and Cow Mind. This idea grew out of a conversation with a Kentucky farmer I met when I was on my way to a retreat center and lost on a narrow road miles from even a half-horse town. There were no humans in sight in the vast landscape of green hills and corn and

GET YOUR

TWO MINDS

TO DANCE

TOGETHER

tobacco fields. Finally, I saw a farmer on a tractor in one of those
fields. I waved him over to ask directions, and we began to chat about
farming and fields and horses and cows as we watched the horses run
exuberantly and the cows graze almost somnambulantly in their pastures. The farmer said he sometimes thinks like a horse and sometimes
like a cow. The two, he said, are opposites, but complementary. The
cow is hardest to comprehend because it isn't so much "out there."

Those thoughts stuck with me the rest of the trip and for
months, even years, afterward. I began to recognize the two modes as
they played out in creative life. Cow Mind, for all her awkward slow-
ness, gradually meanders into meaning. Grazing through sweet grass,
standing in brackish water to her haunches, she's in no hurry to get to
the finish line and may not even know it exists. The creative process
begins with the right-brained cow randomly grazing, munching from
one tuft to another. Her wanderings turn up something important
from time to time: a bright idea ("Oh, a daisy!") or a potential problem
("Oh, a barbed wire fence!").

This way of thinking (what Betty Edwards, author of *Drawing
on the Right Side of the Brain*, calls the R-mode) is difficult to understand because it's amorphous and nonverbal. It's often called the
"moon mind," based on its ability to perceive more broadly, but also
more diffusely, than the conscious mind. You can get an idea how this
works. First focus your eyes on an object just a few feet away. Notice
how everything around it blurs. Now broaden your vision. Notice how
everything, even the object, is indistinct, but how much wider your
viewpoint becomes. Cow Mind sees broadly like that, but her vision is
often unclear. It takes Racehorse Mind to clarify.

Racehorse Mind is as different from Cow Mind as a steam-
roller is from a rose. If not controlled, this left-brained way of thinking
can take over, crushing the juice out of creative expression. We don't
usually realize how deeply we've bought into this rational approach
(what Betty Edwards calls L-mode) until creativity dries up. Racehorse
Mind is like a laser beam. He can zero in on a particular element, but
he can't see the big picture. And he can't hold two opposing ideas at
once. Racehorse Mind doesn't want to be bothered with Cow Mind's
messy paradoxes and contradictions. At the sound of the starting horn,

he wants to dash flat out to reach the finish line. He doesn't fool around. Racehorse Mind is only capable of revisiting what he already knows. He can only organize, categorize and clarify. He can't create.

This doesn't mean that Racehorse Mind plays no role in creativity. The focused, logical, differentiating skills of this way of thinking are essential to shaping and evaluating a creative idea once it's unearthed. Without shaping and evaluating, a creative idea remains a diamond in the rough—unpolished and unusable in its natural form.

The trick is to get the two minds to work together like a team of draft animals to pull your wagon. When this happens, you get whole brain creative thinking in a back-and-forth communication where each part of your brain knows its role and stays on its own side of the fence. You are the farmer, the mediator. When the racehorse tries to run away with everything and not let the cow have her input, you have to pull back on the reins. When the cow is content just to graze and meander, you sometimes have to jolt her with a prod.

How does all this racehorse and cow stuff work out in real-life creativity? Let's say you're writing a poem. Who's doing it? If it's just Racehorse Mind, you're bent on a lot of logical constructing. You've read up on how poetry is done. You set your mind to it. You do it. The result is usually contrived and stiff. If just Cow Mind writes it, you let the poem develop organically in its own time. You don't force it. You wait. You write down what comes, but the result may be raw, messy, unfinished. Cow Mind gives the work its creative spark, but you can't see that because it's obscured by too much junk. It takes Racehorse Mind to do the refining. Cow creates; Racehorse shapes. When the two work together, you create from the inside out, naturally. To write a natural poem, you have to begin by milking a natural cow. Later, you pour the milk into a separating machine and let the cream rise. This is where the racehorse comes in: separating, organizing, arranging.

A poem created in the natural way has a certain juiciness that the reader can sense. You can usually tell which side of the poet's brain a poem was born in. When the poem speaks to you at many levels and has a certain magic you can't quite put your finger on, it most likely originated in a mind not disinclined to wander. When the whole thing fits together like a finely tuned timepiece, you know a mind with judgment and focus was brought in later to complete the finished work. It's a cooperative effort. The two ways of thinking balance each other.

It helps to visualize how these two sides work together. The ancient Chinese yin yang symbol vividly shows the relationship between such opposites. The symbol looks like a flattened tennis ball, one half white, the other black. Each half has a tiny dot of the opposite in itself—a dot of white in the black; black in the white—to show that no element is completely pure and that both are constantly changing. The dark half is said to be feminine; the light half, masculine.

Yin is the creative source, the dark bin out of which creative ideas come. Yang is the shaper of those ideas into useable form. Both are equally important, but yin has to be on top—to come *first*. You can't shape something unless there's something there to shape. If the yang shaper steps in too soon, before the yin source has had time to weave her magic, the work will unravel. You may have experienced this effect if you tried to write and the editor stepped in too soon. Yin has to be allowed to have her whole say. Then yang can have his turn.

Students always ask, "Why can't you lead with a left, like they do in boxing? After all, isn't the left-brained yang more logical, better able to differentiate?" Yes. Precisely. That's its handicap. It can know only narrowly, through abstract intellect and words. Right brain, on the other hand, draws from broad experience, both inner and outer. As Swiss psychiatrist Carl Jung said, "The creation of something new is not accomplished by the intellect, but by the play of instinct [right-brained yin; Cow Mind] acting from inner necessity."

To get your two sides to dance together, to become a balanced double walker, isn't easy. You start out like the farmers who joined the army and couldn't remember which foot was left and which was right. Instead of commanding, "Left, right, left," as the new troops marched, the drill sergeant yelled, "Hay foot, straw foot." Get acquainted with the list of traits in this chapter to help you know your hay foot from your straw foot, your Racehorse Mind from your Cow Mind.

Once you begin to recognize the two functions and the parts they play in your creative life, you'll be able to get them to march together, walk together, and finally dance together—not back-to-back, but face-to-face.

SEED THOUGHT

"...we have a cultural bias which nurtures the separation of the rational and metaphoric minds. Further, the culture in which we live is prejudiced against one of them."

Bob Samples
The Metaphoric Mind

BALANCING THE TWO SIDES OF YOUR BRAIN

Racehorse Mind	**Cow Mind**
QUALITIES	*QUALITIES*
doing	being
fast	slow
extroverted	introverted
logical	creative, artistic
competitive	cooperative
goal oriented	process oriented
deliberate	spontaneous
differentiating	wholistic
linear time	organic unfolding
concrete reality	amorphous mystery
verbal	visual
thinking	feeling
way of the head	way of the heart
conceptual	experiential
focused	diffuse
HYPER HORSE	*HYPER COW*
steamroller expediency	neglect own needs
workaholism	sloth
driven	lacks motivation
compulsive organization	confusion
FEEDING YOUR RACEHORSE	*FEEDING YOUR COW*
follow planned strategy	follow your curiosity
work hard	play
organize (meetings, spaces, ideas)	spend time doing nothing
insure survival, success	insure meaning, relationships
do brain things	do creative things
(calculate, compute)	(paint, write, garden, cook, build)

Explorations

✤ Write a dialogue between your Cow Mind and your Racehorse Mind. Let each express the difficulties it has with the other, as well as the help it gets from having the other cover its blind side. How could the two sides understand each other better? Work together more effectively? How is each one a helpful asset? A detrimental burden? (They can be both at different times.)

✤ Recall a particular creative activity, such as writing an article or poem, creating a painting, playing an instrument, acting in a play, dancing to music. Write about the part Racehorse and Cow Minds played in the activity. Repeat with several different pursuits.

Project

✤ Based on your findings in the assessment above, design a plan for expanding your less-developed mode of operating, whether Racehorse Mind or Cow Mind. Use the trait chart to suggest ideas. Schedule time to fulfill your plan. Write a monthly update on how you're doing.

13. The Roots of the Lotus Are in the Mud

MESSY FEELINGS

SPEAK YOUR

CREATIVE TRUTH

There's a lotus pond in the woods at the Cincinnati Nature Center where frogs snooze through warm days on floating lily pads and their snores resound like the *thrung* of loosely strung banjos. Here and there above the water, pale faces of lotus blossoms glow on their slender stalks, broadcasting a subtle scent. The lotus flowers seem aloof from heat, from froggy noise and from the primal ooze below. After several weeks of dry weather have cleared the water and the debris has settled, you can see where the plants have their root. It's hard to believe that these most pristine of flowers could have emerged from this brown guck. As the Vaipulya, an old Indian sutra, says: "The lotus arises from the mud, but it is not dyed therewith."

In this way, feelings are like lotuses. Their roots nest in messiness, but from these roots spring amazing bursts of unsullied honesty and truth upon which creativity depends. Creativity is at least partly a means of translating feelings into experiences—into something tangible that can make the feeling life knowable to others. Without feelings, said Joanna Field in *On Not Being Able to Paint*, "life would be only blindly lived." Real feeling destroys illusion, clarifies personal values and gives insight into the inner world where creative inspiration lives.

Feelings are messy. They can be smothered but not controlled. They're illogical and sometimes downright painful, but they are our truth. Paying attention to feelings is a way to take your mental temperature to see what you really think. Feelings, if you're in touch with them, will tell you how things actually are with you. You may not always want to hear what they have to say.

In classes where we talk about feelings as they relate to creativity, I hand out the list that appears later in this chapter so people can see the whole colorful range in one place. Invariably the response is mixed. One man in a class said, "There are things on this list that we shouldn't feel. We're not supposed to feel suspicious or smug. And we certainly aren't supposed to feel angry." His feelings had been selectively caged.

How often have you been told not to feel angry or sad or jealous or guilty? As a child, when you showed an emotion, were you told to squelch it? "Big kids don't cry." "I don't care how you feel." "Wipe that smile off your face." "You want to pout? I'll give you something to pout about." "Don't feel guilty; it wasn't your fault." Do these voices still echo in your cranium? Is it any wonder that we often hide feelings, even from ourselves?

"I never realized how often I swallowed my feelings," a woman in a writing class said, "because I never told my husband or friends if I was angry or sad. Pretty soon *I* didn't even know what I was feeling. A certain numbness set in that cast a shadow over everything, even my writing. The characters in my short stories were dull as dust. Like puppets, they acted but they had no real life in them. They had disowned their feelings, too."

Disowned feelings don't just go away. They often get projected onto someone else who isn't remotely responsible for inspiring them. A man I know told me of just such an instance. He and his wife were taking their only daughter to college for her freshman year. When the last of her clothes and belongings had been lugged up the

SEED THOUGHT

"When we close the door to our feelings, we close the door to vital currents that energize and activate our thoughts and actions."

Gary Zukov
The Seat of the Soul

stairs to her dorm room and he and his wife were about to leave, he felt a sudden surge of anger. "I yelled at my wife as we drove away in the car. All the way home I could feel this smoldering anger. At the time, I thought it must have been caused by something she had done. Later, embarrassingly, I realized the anger covered up the sadness I was feeling at seeing my daughter leave home, a sadness I couldn't admit even to myself."

Undeniably, feelings can be painful, but they are your body's internal radar. They tell you what's good and what needs to change. Sometimes we'd rather keep our illusions. "I really hated my job," a former advertising copywriter told me. "What I really wanted to do was to write full-time, create this novel I had in my head. But it was too scary to think about winging it, so I told myself the job offered security, a good pension, weekly paychecks. I couldn't face my real feelings, because if I did I'd have to make a change."

Feelings are like stepchildren. If you want them to be part of your family, you have to take them in—totally, in all their unwashed grubbiness. Taking your feelings in can be a distasteful medicine to swallow, but without the swallowing there's no transformation and feelings won't be available for use in the creative process. I wonder if this idea of facing uncomfortable feelings bravely and directly is what's behind an initiation practice of an African bush tribe. In order to be considered adult, their young people have to drink a poison that is harmless if consumed quickly and without hesitation, but lethal otherwise. Trying to smother painful feelings is like drinking slow poison. It can hurt you.

If you don't recognize feelings, they control you. Your creativity is skewed because you're not in charge. Blocking certain feelings, even if they're painfully negative, is like tying down some of the keys on a piano. You can't play a song without all of the notes. Yet even with complete willingness on your part, feelings aren't always easy to recognize. Three things intervene:

1. **FEELINGS AREN'T THOUGHTS, EVEN IF WE SOMETIMES THINK SO.** To say, "I *feel like* I really ought to go to the meeting," express-es a *thought*, not a feeling. The word *like* is a clue. Saying, "I *feel*

like having a Big Mac," or, "I *feel like* an idiot when I can't remember someone's name," aren't expressions of feelings. Saying, "I feel hungry," or, "I feel embarrassed" are.

2 **FEELINGS ARE SPECIFIC, BUT SOMETIMES THEY'RE HARD TO RECOGNIZE BECAUSE THEY COMBINE AND OVERLAP.** Maybe that's what we mean when we say we're "in a stew." Our feelings are all mixed up like beef cubes and chopped vegetables in a pot. They've been cooking together, and we can't sort them out. We feel angry, frustrated, impatient, upset all at once.

Because feelings are difficult to sort out, we often globalize them. "I feel wonderful!" (Excited? Inspired? Healthy? Energetic?) "I feel terrible!" (Disappointed? Depressed? Sick? Regretful?) If you don't know specifically what your feelings are telling you, it's easy to become programmed into someone else's reality. You can lose your personal authenticity and sacrifice creativity.

An editor told me she hadn't realized how deeply she had denied her feelings and bought into her company's propaganda. "I didn't see it until I cleaned out my files after several years with the company. Reading over the work I'd done was like descending through geological strata. I could see how brainwashed I'd become so that I couldn't see that our newsletter glowed with stories of how helpful we were to customers when in reality they were complaining all the time about quality and service. I hadn't stopped to consider how I felt about this, I just caved in to the company line."

3 **FEELINGS ARE SLOW.** Feelings come from a deep, nonverbal, instinctual place. They have to be translated from feeling to thought to expressive language. It's like wanting to talk to an Italian who speaks no English but does speak French, so you find a Frenchman who speaks English and Italian to be the go-between. The translation enables you to communicate, but it's tedious and slow.

"Don't ask me right now how I feel about something," a teacher told me. "If you do, I'm likely to tell you what I think at the moment, but tomorrow I'll change my mind because, by then, I'll know how I really feel. It takes time for my feelings to surface.

They work about as fast as a ten-year-old computer with an over-burdened hard drive."

With all these obstacles hindering our efforts to get in touch with our feelings, isn't there a less frustrating, more direct way to let feelings have their say? One way is to let feelings communicate in their own language: metaphor. You don't have to name a feeling to experience it consciously. You can meet a feeling on its own muddy ground by creating a metaphor that uses a figure of speech to describe it:

- My body is a wet noodle. (I'm depressed, exhausted or maybe just relaxed.)
- I'm walking on land mines. (I feel anxious, fearful, cautious.)
- I've been steamrollered. (I feel overwhelmed.)
- Someone just took a weight off my shoulders. (I feel relieved.)
- The walls are closing in. (I feel trapped.)

Metaphor preserves and explores your feelings without turning them into a concept. Metaphor eliminates the middleman from your translation queue so the flavors of your feelings are not filtered. It gets you out of the mind-set that you have to know everything in an intellectual way. You don't. In fact, scientist and writer Rachel Carson said, "It's not half so important to know as to feel."

You may have to engage in some mud wrestling before you can grab a feeling by its roots. But feelings that are allowed to blossom form the basis for creative expression by connecting you with your authentic voice, your real truth. It all begins in the mud.

I'M FEELING

Close your eyes and point to a feeling in the list, or pick a number and count down the list to a particular feeling. Recall a time when you felt that way. Reenter the experience and write for ten minutes. Don't use the word itself in your writing.

relaxed	ashamed	shocked
confident	cautious	astonished
confused	depressed	smug
suspicious	overwhelmed	exhausted
guilty	optimistic	enthusiastic
angry	lonely	nostalgic
frustrated	loving/loved	rushed
sad	jealous	uncomfortable
embarrassed	bored	energetic
disgusted	mischievous	adventurous
fearful	fragmented	threatened
happy	curious	

Explorations

♻ Construct a "Feeling History." Fold a letter-size piece of paper in half lengthwise. In the left-hand column list turning points from your earliest memory forward. You might list milestones such as early years, school, first job, marriage, etc. Leave some space between transition listings. In the right-hand column, opposite each turning point, list the feelings these turning points inspired at the time. For example:

Early years:	dependent, cared for, adventurous
School years:	curious, confused, energetic
First job:	cautious, optimistic, enthusiastic

Write about one of the turning points and the feelings it inspired.

Project

♻ Collect images that make you feel disturbed, peaceful, energized, nostalgic, etc. Sources for your images can be old photos, magazine or book illustrations, travel brochures, your own drawings, junk mail. Keep the images in a file folder, and pick one at random. Write about the feelings the image inspires, recalling any experiences in which these feelings were present.

Research

♻ Visit an art exhibit or review, a work of fiction. List the underlying feelings you detect in the work itself. Write about your findings.

14. Drawing Inspiration From Your Past

Consider: Your whole life, up to the second you read these words, is *memory*. And now even that second is memory. No matter how long or short your life has been until now, all but the "present moment" is recorded in the archives of your mind. This giant mental iceberg contains only a thumb-sized tip of experience that's going on right now. The rest, the whole submerged mountain of backlog, is memory. What are those memories? How do they influence your creative life?

Your memory is you. Without it you would lose yourself and your sense of the unique person you are. Just as your body is composed of cells, your sense of self is composed of experiences: what you've learned, people you've encountered, mistakes you've made, adventures you've braved, losses you've suffered. These are the raw materials that fuel the engine of creative expression. You draw on memories whenever you create, whether you work with words, images, voice, instrument or test tubes.

**MEMORIES,
DARK AND LIGHT,
AID CREATIVITY**

Creative people are like mental pack rats. They save memories like some people collect first-issue stamps. Our trouble is that we have difficulty locating and processing the experiences that hide in the cobwebby corners of our minds. In our mental attics, everything is jumbled together in amorphous confusion. Unless a memory is pulled, struggling, from the jumble, it tends to settle more and more deeply into the dust of the inaccessible unconscious.

Search and Rescue: Step One

Value your memories—pleasant and not so pleasant alike. A good place to start is where you grew up. This place had more to do with who you are than you might care to think. And because you create from the person you are, home has an impact on your creative life, too.

I grew up in Elgin, a town of fifty thousand, in northern Illinois. It was not a town I wanted to be from. I'd read about other, more exciting towns in books I borrowed from the kids' section of the stone castle of a downtown library. There were books about how the West was won that made me want to live in Cheyenne or Flagstaff. Even the funny sounding cities like Pocatello and Albuquerque and Chattanooga sounded more exciting than Elgin.

All Elgin had was the pokey Fox River meandering through downtown, where two blocks of shops were connected by a town square that every Christmas housed a live tree, freshly cut from a local farm's woods. Punctuating the square was the Tower Building with its always slow clock jutting from the pinnacle and a Walgreen's soda fountain on the ground floor. What else could you say about Elgin? Oh, yes, it claimed the rambling, potentially flammable wooden sprawl of the Elgin Watch Company as its own resident source of employment, a place where I actually worked one summer.

It took years for me to appreciate the town's endearing ordinariness. This denial of roots kept me from owning a big corner of my own attic's memories. It left a hole where beginnings ought to have been. I learned that unvalued memories tend to slink away like shamefaced ragamuffins. Memories have to be valued if you want them to stick around.

Jane, a friend of mine who has written a couple of successful books, is embarking on a third: her memoirs. It's not that she doesn't have enough interesting tales to tell. She does—tales we all share, if only vicariously, of adventures in Hollywood and New York, life passages from student to wife to mother.

Where she runs into difficulty is that she sometimes forgets how important her story is. I remind her, as I often have to remind myself, that our commonly shared root experiences are what people most want to read about.

The test is to imagine yourself at the end of your life looking back. What will you see as important? Most likely all the outward ornaments of fame and fortune will fade. It won't matter much whether you had an exalted job title or drove a Mercedes or got your name in a volume of *Who's Who*. What will remain will most likely be earthy and small: an awkward first date with a boy named Lyle whose Adam's apple bobbed when he talked; how you cried when a peach tree in your backyard split in half during a storm; the smudge of flour your mother had on her forehead when she was baking almond bread. Small memories will become big. You will feel like an archaeologist in an excavation project who has unearthed a precious shard with your bruised digger's hands.

These memories are the kind you can reach out and grab. They have a tactile feel. "Memory is sensual, not logical," Laurie Colwin says in *Shine On, Bright & Dangerous Object*. A memory of substance is not a recitation of multiplication tables or so-and-so's theorem. It's a living, breathing thing. It has the power to inspire a creative act.

Search and Rescue: Step Two

This step involves the capture or recapture of those precious shards. If you've ever tried to write directly about, say, your first red two-wheeler bicycle, you've probably come up with a description that's thin and lacking in substance. But if you put yourself back into the experience by reliving, in your imagination, what you felt during that heady time, you'll be able to put meat on the memory's bones. You'll remember the day you dressed in your favorite blue shirt to go with your dad to the bike shop. The sun was shining. You could still taste the syrup from the French toast your mom had made for breakfast. As you saw your brother ride out on his own bike, you felt a surge of pride to think that today *you* would be a rider, too.

Another way to capture memories is to write them down as they resurface. Maybe you're washing your car and a totally unrelated memory shows up. You suddenly think about the time you first went fishing with your uncle Harry. As you stand in puddles of soapy car wash water, you remember standing, barefoot, in the stream. That little finny thing you jerked out of the rushing stream becomes clear again. The thing shimmers in the light. You feel like you've caught a whale. If you write down such memories when they come, eventually you'll build a body of recollections. You can put this body to work.

Search and Rescue: Step Three

Use your memories, distant or current, in your creative process. Start to see your memory as a resource. We all walk around with this huge warehouse of experience. By valuing and retaining our experience, we keep our granaries stocked. By using our internal wealth in creative work, we pay it the highest honor possible. Our respect assures the continued bountifulness of the warehouse.

My friend Radha, who was born in India and has lived in the U.S. for ten years, honors childhood memories of her native country by turning them into colorful prints from her press. She uses photographs of family gatherings, symbols from meditational practices and figures from Hindu mythology as part of her art. Her memories take on real life. Even unhappy memories are changed through the alchemy of ink on paper.

Many creative people have directly used dark memories in their writing and art. One woman has used painful memories of an abusive childhood as the basis for creative expression in poetry. By writing poems, she reconnects with her injured child self and nurtures it toward healing. By reentering the experiences through memory and using what she finds to build a poem, the experiences are transformed—and even the reader benefits from the transmutation.

Facing one's own crushing memories parallels the ancient myth of the dark goddess Kali, whose fanged fearsomeness kept all but the most courageous from approaching. If, as the myth goes, you're not put off by the string of human skulls around her neck or by her dark, terrifying expression—and you have the pluck to venture closer and closer—you will see her blackness turn to gold. The key to the transformation lies in having the courage to meet her face-to-face.

Many writers, painters and others have had the courage to go into the dark mines of their memories and extract the creative gold that becomes a glittering thread in their work. A middle-aged man has used writing to sort through recent marriage problems. A woman in her sixties has folded the loss of her spouse into the yeasty dough of a first novel. Anne Frank produced a hopeful memoir from the small moments of everyday experience set against the background of unfathomable tragedy.

Memories, both dark and light, can be used as building blocks in creative expression. Keeping track of memories of all colors and shades, valuing them and putting them to use in creative work provides a rich source of inspiration. Think back. What was funny, curious, sad, terrifying, yucky, stupid, exultant, perilous, victorious about your past—distant and recent? What do you remember? Where did you come from, and how did this place and its people make you who you are? Live the questions. Let them sit at your table, ride on your shoulder, sleep beside you in your bed. When they speak, listen.

SEED THOUGHT

"Nothing or nobody can deprive and rob us of what we have safely delivered and deposited in the past....Usually...people see only the stubblefield of transitoriness—they do not see the full granaries into which they have brought the harvest of their lives: the deeds done, the works created, the loves loved, the suffering courageously gone through."

Viktor Frankl
Psychologist who spent time in a World War II concentration camp

Explorations

❧ Close your eyes and mentally scan your life from beginning to present, jotting down the life-changing events you recall. Write several of these events across the top of a page. In columns under each memory, list the people, places and events that played a role at the time. Use your notes from one of the columns as memory triggers to write for twenty minutes. How have your past experiences changed your life? What dreams have you realized? What challenges have you met?

❧ Take an arm's length of adding machine tape or a large sheet of paper, and write the names of as many people you've known as you can think of. If you don't remember a person's name, write "the plumber," "the school bus driver from second grade," etc. Point at random to one of the names or fold the paper and note the name in its crease. Write about this person for ten minutes. If you don't know much about the person, invent. Continue adding names to the list, and periodically write about one of them.

Project

❧ Write a family history as far back as you can remember. If you can, get help from relatives and record their memories. Where did you, your parents and grandparents come from? What customs have been handed down from generation to generation? What stories? Go through old photos if you have them. How did the people in your family dress? What activities do the photos show? How has your background molded you and your creativity? Who in your family was creative? How did they express their creativity?

Recollection

❧ Do you remember a time when you took one last look at a place you were leaving and would most likely never see again? It might be a place where you've lived, a school, a vacation spot, a building where you worked. Write about seeing the place for the last time: your feelings, memories, anxieties, regrets or sense of relief.

❧ Write your thoughts and feelings about your hometown. What did you like about it? Dislike? How did the town make you who you are? Who were the town's characters? What were your town's unique places or common ones?

ch15: Coming to Your Senses

Senses. They're our feelers, our antennae that connect us to
the world, both inner and outer. Together with our thinking and
feeling apparatus, our senses give us feedback about how things are.
They are the body's radar, and that body radar informs creativity.

"The body, as it turns out, is central to the whole issue, for
creativity is a somatic process," says Morris Berman in *Coming to Our
Senses*. "You go into your body to discover its truth, and you write,
paint, dance, act or play your instrument from *that*." When creativity
comes from the inside out, it becomes embodied. It has substance.

When Josephine Johnson in *The Inland Island* describes a
toad as a lump of fudge hopping down the road, you can see it. You
can feel it. Maybe you can even taste it. Likewise when you see a
van Gogh painting, you want to reach out and touch those raised
swirls of paint. You feel his bodily movement in the dancing brush-
strokes. They make you want to dance, too. Creativity in the arts is

THE BODY

AS CREATIVE

INSTRUMENT

the ability to cause other people to experience what you saw, heard, tasted and felt.

In a sense, all creative people are safecrackers. We sandpaper our fingertips so we can feel the tumblers fall and we can break into where the wealth is. Sharpening senses is like sharpening pencils before starting to write or sketch. Senses provide information and a connection that feed the creative process. At times, the work of the senses seems almost automatic. We may not even notice when we're in danger of jeopardizing our sense connections through sensory overload.

In the 1980s, Marilyn Ferguson warned in *The Aquarian Conspiracy* that "Sociologists calculated that a person in Western Society receives 65,000 more pieces of stimuli each day than did our forebears 100 years ago." What would that figure be today, with the Internet becoming more commonly used, and information and experiences available at the click of a mouse? With well over a hundred TV channels to surf? With sound blasting our ears from speakers in restaurants, stores, rest rooms? Even in our cars we have one eye on the road and the other on a cell phone keypad as we plunk in a CD to stimulate our ears and gulp lukewarm coffee to jazz our taste buds. And there's probably a perfumed stick-on deodorizer somewhere in the car to disguise Fido's lingering scent.

We're overwhelmed by the noise of lawn mowers and vacuum cleaners and ambulance sirens. We're inundated by junk mail and phone solicitations and exhaust smells. To get our attention, the media have jacked up the volume and sensationalism of their offerings. Loud noise, fiery explosions and shock are tools to get us to tune in. But, ultimately, the result of such overstimulation is deadening. It leads to sensory disconnection.

Sensory disconnection involves the numbing or deliberate shutting down of body messages. This disconnection was evident in a local craft store one Halloween. Customers entering the store stepped on a mat that activated a recording of loud, raucous laughter. After just a few minutes of such intrusive noise people said they wanted to plug their ears. I asked a clerk how she could stand it for eight hours straight. "At first it drove me nuts, but now I don't even hear it anymore," she said. Overload had caused her to fall into sensory disconnection.

We can also lose contact with sensory input in a much more subtle way—inattention. "Of all the stimuli that impinge on the sensory receptors of sight, hearing, touch, smell and taste, only a small portion ever reach our conscious experience awareness," writes Willis Harman, Ph.D., in *Higher Creativity*. It's as if you're trying to crack that safe while wearing thick mittens. You can't tell when you've got the right combination because your senses are muffled. To unmuffle them, you have to pay attention. This paying attention is especially true for what I call the "orphan" senses—smell, touch and taste—that we ordinarily tend to ignore.

Smell

A sense often numbed by overload, smell commonly escapes notice unless it triggers a blatant reaction. Subtle scents are smothered by perfumes and deodorizers—sprays, underarm products, scented candles, household cleaners that are touted as smelling like spring rain or mountain wildflower. We are a society in terror of naturally occurring smells.

And yet German poet Johann von Schiller kept rotting apples in a drawer to put himself in a writing mood, and English poet Dr. Samuel Johnson was inspired by the smell of orange peel. Smell can be a powerful sense. It can bodily drag an entire experience from the past into awareness. Not little by little, but—shazam!—all at once. Have you ever smelled pine and been immediately transported back to that cabin in the woods when you were ten? Have you ever smelled a particular aftershave and felt the presence of another person who wears that brand?

This morning I took down my *Roget's Thesaurus* to look up a word, and out fell a small, pressed bouquet of fragrant sage, basil and lavender, tied with blue ribbon and anchored by a pearl-headed pin. The scent immediately transported me back, several months ago, to a friend's eightieth birthday celebration where we had made these herb corsages. Scents can do that. Our noses know.

I feel hopeful about our orphan sense of smell when I hear that thousands have lined up to see—or rather to smell—a rare "corpse flower" on display in San Marino, California. What tickles me most is that these people come to smell a flower that has a disgustingly putrid scent. Some say the smell is midway between dead dog and rotten fish. This gives me hope that one day we will grow to appreciate natural smells in the same way we value all the notes in the musical scale.

Touch

The second orphan sense is touch. I think it's become orphaned by our overdependence on the favored senses of hearing and sight. Or maybe our Puritan and Victorian heritage just keeps us "out of touch." Whether or not we're aware of it, this need to touch and be touched keeps up connected with our experience and thus with our own creative potential. Touch tells us what really is: the actual, dimensional, earthy presence, not what we imagine or think. The virtual reality of computers and TV doesn't include touch.

I discovered many years ago that what you learn by touch can be surprisingly different from what you think you know. My teacher was a kangaroo who was, amazingly, the guest of honor at a cocktail party in a suite of a downtown Philadelphia hotel. A New York couple had loaned the kangaroo, a wombat and other animals to a Broadway stage production, and the department store PR department where I worked asked them to bring the kangaroo to the party to publicize a new line of stuffed toys the store carried. At the press conference the kangaroo was extremely well behaved, except it snitched a stuffed olive or a canapé from the buffet table now and then. When the owner noticed my fascination with the haunch-sitting guest, she asked if I wanted to feel the inside of its pouch. I'd always imagined that a pouch where baby roos grew would be soft, but it felt like the down on a dandelion! Delicate. Soft. Warm. Touch is an experience you never forget.

Taste

Taste is the third orphan sense. Despite our cultural preoccupation with eating and imbibing, we seldom pay enough attention to appreciate what we're consuming. We're in a hurry. We're trying to read or watch TV or talk at the same time. We don't savor. Sometimes we don't even know when we're eating something whose shelf life has expired.

SEED THOUGHT

"...whenever I am offered a hard candy, whenever a woman varnishes her nails near me, whenever I inhale a certain smell of disinfectant in the toilet of a provincial hotel, whenever I see the violet bulb in the ceiling of a night train, my eyes, nostrils and tongue recapture the lights and odors of those bygone halls..."

Jean-Paul Sartre
The Words

In *One Hundred Years of Solitude*, Gabriel García Márquez jolts us back into our sense of taste by relating a particularly revolting habit of the novel's adolescent Rebeca: She ate dirt. Putting handfuls of earth in her pockets, she ate them bit by bit in what the writer describes as a "mineral savor that left a harsh aftertaste in her mouth." Whether we want to or not, as we read we can taste that same "mineral savor."

Taste, even a description of taste—pleasant or not—has an immediate, visceral effect. Maybe that's why we use taste allusions in everyday speech: He could *taste* victory. She wanted that job so badly she could *taste* it. He *tasted* bitter defeat.

Like smell, taste has a strong associative value. A friend says the taste of A&W root beer takes him back to high school days when he'd have a frosty mug of root beer on his way home from school. In their ceremonies, Native Americans sometimes put strawberry juice on the tongues of participants so they will associate the ritual with the sweet taste. A woman I know says she puts a whole clove in her mouth as she drives to the place where a group practices sitting meditation once a week. The clove taste is a reminder to her sense brain that she's about to take part in a spiritual exercise.

Sight and Sound

The remaining two major senses, sight and sound, are the ones most commonly relied upon for orientation. They're also the most likely to be burdened with sensory overload.

We've discussed at length in the chapters on sharpening your sense of observation how you can use sight to gather input for creative expression, so we don't need to cover the same ground here. But be aware that overload can fog your lens. Take time to see—as Thoreau says, to "let the object come to you by a true sauntering of the eye."

You could say the same about your sound sense. Let your ears *saunter*. Put margins of silence around your listening. Hear not just the obvious loud noises that you may already have switched off through sensory disconnection, but the beauty of subtle sounds.

We've often heard the hum of our car tires as we drive over a bridge, but composer Michael Robert Barnhart actually *listens*. He records the sounds from a suspension bridge in his town nicknamed the Singing Bridge—the sounds of cars rumbling over steel grids, of horns blaring, of wind humming in the cables. Then he puts the sounds into a computer and composes a symphony with them, using them as if they were musical instruments. Sound is his creative medium, a medium he found by paying attention to what he heard.

Senses are like instruments in an orchestra. When all the instruments play together, they overlap and meld. Different senses dominate, depending on the creative medium, but all play into the creative act. We may think the visual arts draw on sight alone, but even a flat painting can evoke the urge to touch. Just so, gourmet cooking depends on sight and smell nearly as much as taste. You can describe the experience of one sense in terms of another. For instance, country singer Bonnie Raitt said her guitar *sounds* like smoky bacon *smells*.

Writing, which expresses reality through a sort of verbal shorthand, depends on sense impressions to bring it to life. Looking at printed squiggles and blips on a page gives no direct sensory experience as does, say, looking at a painting or touching a piece of sculpture. Words have to overcome secondhand experience and make you see in your mind's eye, hear in your imagination's ear, touch with phantom fingers, smell with a nose that detects the ghosts of recollected scents, and taste with the tongue of memory (even if that tongue tastes dirt). Words have to be translated into experience. Poetry, where words trigger a sensual response, is as close as a writer can come to rendering direct experience. Writing that draws from the senses feels more real.

There are, of course, more senses than the five we've discussed. You were most likely in touch with all of them when you were a child, but now overload may have caused you to tune them out. You don't hear your tires sing on the suspension bridge or pay attention to smell unless it overwhelms you like a corpse flower. To the degree that you are victim to what Bob Samples, author of *The Metaphoric Mind*, calls "aloof detachment" of the average adult, you will be out of touch with your body and thus with your creative resources.

Pay attention, not only to loud sounds and dramatic images, but also to soft murmurs and ephemeral shadows. Sharpen your senses. Make your own bridge music.

Explorations

❧ Listen to the TV for five minutes with the picture turned off. Then watch for five minutes with the sound turned off. Write about the difference between the two experiences. What did you learn about your sense of hearing and your sense of sight?

❧ Go on a sense safari: Walk in the woods or around your neighborhood (take a pocket notebook and pencil with you). Focus on each of four senses (sight, sound, smell and touch), one at a time for five minutes each. Jot down notes from this experience. Later, write for twenty minutes what your senses told you.

Recollection

❧ Remember a time when you smelled one of the following:

frying bacon
gasoline
garbage
leather
an animal (horse, dog, skunk)
smoke (bonfire, burning building, incense)
strawberries
pine

Put yourself back into the experience, literally or in your imagination, and write for fifteen minutes.

❧ Write about a place you loved or hated. Incorporate all the senses in your description.

Visual Push-Up

❧ What if your left toe could hear? Your elbow could taste? Your tongue could see? Your hair could smell? Write for twenty minutes about what you'd experience.

❧ Write six ways to describe the smell of fallen leaves (comparison to other scents, effect on sense organs, etc.).

losing your
losing your
logical mind

16. A Kid's-Eye View of Creativity

Up and down the halls of Terrace Park Elementary School the walls are abloom with colorful paintings and crayon drawings. Each is a slice of child life. The paintings of people and houses and fantastic animals express humor, passion, optimism and vivid imagination un-contaminated by adult judgment. These youngsters' high-spirited cre-ativity hasn't been trained out—yet.

Besides making art, many of these same students have con-tributed their maxims and philosophies to a spiral-bound, school-published book not much bigger than a note cube. The book purports to be about friendship. In reality, it's saturated with quirky creativity that can instruct all of us who said good-bye to childhood long ago. In some of the quips you can hear the wheels of imagination turn as you read. The children expand on the small elements many of us would overlook and make connections many of us would never see. They write:

- "A friend is someone who will paint themselves and dress up as a flower and will stand in the dirt in the front yard when you trampled over your mom's new flowers."
- "A friend is someone who will go on as many roller coaster rides that you want to at Kings Island, even though they want to jump off and throw up."
- "A friend is someone who will eat your mother's healthy dinners and not complain until after she has left the table."

Creative expression by children, uncorrupted by adult rationality and reserve, can remind us grown-ups that we were all creative once upon a time. Creativity came as naturally as breathing. No one had to teach us. "The reason kids don't have to be taught to be creative is that creativity is essential for human survival," writes Daniel Goleman with Paul Kaufman and Michael Ray in *The Creative Spirit*. In other words, creativity is *built in* to human function. So how does it get lost? What happened to that creative child each of us once was?

The likely answer is that the adults around us lost patience. Creative kids can be disruptive at home and in the classroom. According to Glenn Ray, executive director of the Association for the Advancement of Arts Education (AAAE), "Creative kids are often not well behaved. They're curious and rambunctious." Adults feel duty bound to quell the insurrection and tame the wild child. Is it any wonder we sacrifice our creativity little by little as we grow?

Ray says, "One thing adults have difficulty with is that the creative resides in the intuitive side. Some feel intimidated with exploring creativity. It creates a problem for people who are prone to 'follow the rules.' Adults have a lot of baggage and ought to take notice of kids' attitudes and try to apply them in their own lives."

Some adults can do that without prompting; maybe it's because they never lost their childlike creative ability. One of those adults, Leo Buscaglia, who was a practicing child and the author of *Living, Loving & Learning* and many other titles, once wrote about playing in piles of newly raked leaves with his students. When neighbors insisted he clean up his lawn, he and the students hauled the leaves into his living room where they played to their hearts' content and didn't dispose of the leaves 'til they'd had their playful romps. Maybe it was this experience that inspired Buscaglia to write *The Fall of Freddie the Leaf.* In any case, unlike most adults, he didn't worry that the neighbors would think he had lost his mind. "I like to be called crazy," he said. "It gives you a lot of leeway for behavior."

Most of us don't feel we can afford such a label. We're too intent on paying taxes, balancing the checkbook and keeping a job in a culture that almost always demands a rational, no-nonsense, noncreative approach no matter how much it pays lip service to the opposite. We can, of course, haul our leaves into the house to entertain our childlike creativity in secret. And perhaps we have to do that to get along in the world. But by doing so we keep secret the fact that at least a sprinkling of childlikeness can add savor to life and work. We set no example. We perpetuate the myth of relentlessly logical practicality. To do otherwise takes courage, something uncorrupted children have in abundance. Here are some of the qualities creative kids have that we can learn from:

1 **THE COURAGE TO RISK.** "Children are more likely (than adults) to try new things and to experiment and explore," says Dr. Jerry Sasson, psychologist and elementary school principal. "They want to discover hands-on. As we get older, we tend to lose that courageousness." Without the courage to explore and to take risks in our work, creative expression stagnates. We're stuck, like Johnny One Note, playing the same thing over and over.

2 **A SPIRIT OF PASSIONATE CURIOSITY AND DEEP CONNECTEDNESS.** Glenn Ray describes this state as "a rich innocence." To kids, each experience is a new experience. They make up their actions as they go along, doing things for their own sake, with energy, passion and intense concentration. Curiosity and compulsion to learn for learning's sake motivate children in their explorations. Energy and concentration emerge naturally from whole-body involvement with their surroundings. Can we do this in our creative work? We can try.

3 **A YEN FOR HIJINKS AND HUMOR.** Watch kids stuff French fries
up their noses to look like walruses, slurp spaghetti or play with
green goo. Would an adult do any of that? Not on your life! But
an adult can learn to appreciate funny experiences. An adult can
laugh at the ridiculous. In Bombay, India, people get together just
to laugh. The people who do it call themselves "The Bombay
Chuckle Club." They gather. One person starts to laugh. Soon all
of them are laughing uproariously, holding their sides, tears
streaming down their cheeks. We may not be able to laugh on cue,
but we can learn to notice life's ridiculous, and therefore funny,
situations. Laughing will keep us from taking our creative work
and ourselves too seriously.

4 **ABUNDANT IMAGINATION.** Kids learn through imaginative play.
I came across an "Our Gang" of neighborhood preschoolers a few
days ago playing store on the sidewalk. They had denuded a bush
of its berries and leaves, gathered stones and twigs and set up shop
with their produce, offering me a leaf plate of squashed berries for
which I paid a couple of strands of dried grass, counted out in
their palms. The pretend experience was a way for them to re-
hearse, to practice interactions, to overcome fear of the unknown.
We can use imagination in the same way. I once heard of an indus-
trial designer who created the design for a complicated piece of
machinery completely in his imagination. We can use imagination
as a way to practice creative expression—to play with an idea
before committing it to static form.

5 **SPONTANEOUS UNADULTERATED HONESTY.** If you know a kid
or two, you're probably acquainted with their honesty—abrupt,
sometimes brutal, sometimes embarrassing. They tell it the way
they see it. Glenn Ray says he admires this natural ability to "cut
to the chase." Children also have the ability to notice the obvious,
which adults either don't see or don't want to, and to comment
on their observations loudly and clearly. My neighbor Anne tells
the story of taking her six-year-old twin granddaughters to a
movie about Egypt. In the middle of the movie, having paid rapt

SEED THOUGHT

"My source
[of creative
inspiration]
is following the intu-
itions I had as a
child, and those
were based on the
wonder of creation."

Meinrad Craighead
Artist and writer, in an interview

attention to every inch of footage with images of Egyptian people inscribed inside the pyramids, one of the twins blurted loudly, "Egyptians don't smile!" Grandmother blushed, and the audience chuckled. An adult would not have spoken out about Egyptian deadpan. An adult most likely wouldn't even have noticed. It took a child to cut to the chase. It takes a child to teach us the value of honesty, even brutal honesty, in producing an authentic creative product, whatever medium we work with.

There are, of course, more ways that we can learn from kids. To learn more, simply observe. Watch the way a kid eats spaghetti, for example. She doesn't cut it into neat lengths that will fit on a fork or wind it Italian style into a mouth-size swirl. If an adult doesn't stop her, she picks it up a strand at a time and slurps one after another noisily into her mouth. The act shows an eagerness to experiment, a sensuality, and an inventiveness and concentration that involve every cell and sinew. She doesn't worry about whether other people approve or whether she might get sauce on her shirt.

I'm not advocating that you slurp spaghetti, although, come to think of it, that might be fun. Nor do I encourage deliberate disruptiveness and complete unconcern for other people's sensibilities. What I do urge is a lowering of barriers. Kids can teach us how.

I've learned a lot about creativity from kids. Not just from those I know well, but from the ones I've met by chance and some I've never met at all.

If I'm on a walk or at a mall or shopping for groceries, I always talk to the kids I see. It's a good opportunity to tap into their minds. Once, on a walk in the woods, I came upon two little girls with their father. I commented on the girls' ponytails and the father explained, "They're not ponytails." The two girls chimed together, "They're our fountains!" These two tykes—I don't even know their names—hadn't been coerced into seeing things the same way everyone else does. They had their own ideas about ponytails, and Dad encouraged them to speak up.

Some of the kids I've learned from but have never met are our neighborhood's sidewalk artists. With colored chalk they've drawn a whiskered blue walrus with a fish in its fin, a pink plaid turtle and a blue-striped cat. I never know what I'll find. Sometimes there's just a long, wiggly green chalk line that trails all around the block. One Easter Sunday I nearly stepped on a drawing of a yellow-haired angel emerging from a pink tulip. Who would have imagined an angel could come out of a tulip? Only a kid.

So search out some of the little people—let their imaginative ways inspire you. Watch them. Follow them around. Talk to them. You may suddenly be possessed by the desire to write about angels in tulips or to haul a couple of bushels of leaves inside, just for the fun of it.

Explorations

🌱 Do something a kid would do: Walk in the rain and splash through puddles, play with bubbles in the bathtub, leap into a pile of leaves, run on the dewy grass in your bare feet. Write about how this experience felt.

🌱 Get a book by SARK at your bookstore or library, and follow the directions. (For instance, swing on a swing set in the moonlight or lie on your stomach to watch snails, as she describes in *Inspiration Sandwich*.)

Field Trip

🌱 Go to the kids' section of your local library. Squeeze into a small seat. Read about what causes rain, how salt is made, what kinds of shells you can find at the seashore. Watch what the kids there do, what they read, how they sit, what they say. Write for twenty minutes.

🌱 Find a hill in a public park and lie on your back in the grass. Watch the clouds for a half hour. Write.

Creative Recess

🌱 Remember some ways you used to play as a kid (building a fort, finger painting, playing in a sandbox). Can you reenact or imagine the experience to release your creative genie? Write about what you did or what you remembered.

🌱 Cut random shapes from paper of at least three different colors. Play with arranging the shapes in different ways on a larger paper or posterboard. Write about what you learned.

🌱 Set aside a couple of hours or a weekend. Write about what you used to love as a kid. Write about your ideal Saturday at age nine. Write about your childhood dreams. Are any still viable? Is there a thread that connects them with today's dreams?

17. Play As a Way
To Fire Creativity

A dozen of us sit around a long wooden table in the library at
Chatfield College, a small pastoral campus plunked down in the midst of
broad green farm fields. We are here for a workshop on drawing ancient
circular designs called mandalas. It's mid-July. The room is warm. Books
stacked high on the shelves around us muffle the mesmerizing sounds of
a Gregorian chant emitting from a shoe box–size tape player. A wall clock
ticks. We are each intent on our drawing, on creating circular designs
with compass, pen and colored markers. Mandala designs, our teacher
Sr. Agatha tells us, are everywhere. A daisy is a mandala; so is a rose window or a cross section of a tree. Navajo healers make a circular drawing on
the ground and place a person in the center to "pull them into harmony,"
she says. We, too, are being pulled into harmony by our play with pen and
paper, each of us as intent on our work as a child building a sand castle.

Sr. Agatha urges us to be playful, to be relaxed, to enter into
the drawing. One woman is having a hard time concentrating. She says

TWO SETS
OF TENNIS
DON'T COUNT

she keeps thinking she should be doing something more productive. "It is important to have something to do that has no purpose," our teacher pipes in her soft voice, looking up over her glasses. She says she has been drawing mandalas every day for as long as she can remember. It is her practice.

We mull her words. Silence closes around us as we work. It gathers around the young mother who had to get a sitter in order to come, around the truck driver who took the day off, around the retired business manager, around the middle-aged secretary and around the art student in black biker shorts. Sr. Agatha's words continue to echo in our minds: "It is important to have something to do that has no purpose."

Ever since that workshop over five years ago, I have encouraged students in my writing and art classes to have a "practice without purpose." After delivering my spiel at a recent Saturday class, one woman blurted, "Well, what would be the purpose of *that*?" Silence. Then a smile began to spread across her face and she said, "Oh, I get it! The purpose is to have no purpose. You want us to remember how to *play*!"

Yes. To remember how to play. That's it exactly. We have forgotten how, getting our idea of play mixed up with competitiveness and passive entertainment. Neither of these do much to promote creativity.

When play is handcuffed to competition, creativity is restricted. We're too intent on winning to risk a mistake, be inventive or even have fun. We play tennis to win. We want to win at the game of work and the game of life just as we do at Monopoly or chess. There's no room for real play. Even kids who used to get together a game of sandlot baseball just for the fun of it—all ages and both genders included—now play Little League ball, where the emphasis is more often on competition than on the pleasures and values of playing.

Sometimes we get play mixed up with passive entertainment. When we kick back to watch a golf game or theater drama or sitcom on TV, that's relaxation. The kind of play I'm talking about isn't spaced-out inactivity. It's active, even intense, participation: what you might call "purposeful purposelessness" or concentrated play.

"So?" I can almost hear the woman from the Saturday class chiming. "And what would be the purpose of *that*?" Why should we recover our ability to play? What does play have to do with creativity?

In my experience, having a practice without purpose helps you
drop down into the intuitive mind where creative insight occurs. This
state of mind isn't usually available to everyday consciousness. You
have to squeeze yourself into your spelunking gear and plop on your
headlamp and prepare to go below.

Play puts you closer to your intuitive mind by loosening the
knot that constricts the right-brained creative side, providing an opening that allows creative insights to enter. Play is a ballet dancer working
out at the bar before the big performance. Play is a jogger flexing muscles before the twenty-mile race. Play is a warm-up, a way of centering.

Carol, an artist I know, plays with dried navy beans on a piece
of black velvet before she starts to paint. Arranging and rearranging
the white beans on the black background, like placing stars in a con-
stellation, she brings up images from her mind. She moves the beans
around until images come. After this warm-up, she's ready to paint.

An artistic warm-up is like lighting a log fire. You can't just
strike a match and light the log directly. You have to prepare a fire with
layers of crunched newspaper and kindling so the logs will catch fire.
Play is the crunched paper and kindling for your creative fire.

"Playfulness allows experimentation and change," says Joan
Erikson in *Wisdom and the Senses*. When we're intent on carrying out a
successful project, our constricted attitude keeps us from achieving the
very thing we're so set on. It's as if we're tightly bound and still expecting to be able to get up and run. Playfulness bursts the strictures.

Playfulness is the ability to

- toy with an idea or thing without coming to premature
  conclusions, to see it from many angles, to reconfigure, to
  redefine
- do something just for the fun of it—without thinking about
  practicality or usefulness—and get fired up over simple things
- approach a project with the innocence of a child and the
  dedication of an adult, and be able to alternate between the
  logical mind and the creative mind
- appreciate and generate humor, to take things lightly
- exercise imagination and cultivate a rich inner life

SEED THOUGHT

*"Life must be
lived as play."*

Plato

You won't find these definitions in a dictionary or thesaurus, even though one dictionary I checked gave sixty-seven meanings for the word *play*. These volumes used words such as *amusement, diversion, recreation, competition* and even included, as synonyms, the words *romp, frolic* and *cavort*. While these are good solid definitions—and I'm especially enchanted with *romp, frolic* and *cavort*—none of these words adequately captures the elusive idea of creative playfulness.

Instead, I like a word my dad used so often I thought he invented it—an impression heightened by the fact that I never heard anyone else use it. The word is *putzing*. My dad was an expert putzer. In retirement he pursued a multitude of art projects for which he had only minimal talent. He created awful looking bookends and plaques using a technique he called "de-coop-age" (actually decoupage). It didn't bother him that the orange and olive paint flecked with metallic gold and silver offended aesthetic sensibilities. He loved this new form of putzing that he'd never had time for in his six-day work weeks. Putzing was fun.

Even the word sounds like fun. It doesn't take itself seriously. Could you tell someone you're putzing and still keep a straight face? The word *putz* is Yiddish for "fool." So when we putz, we're just fooling around, experimenting to see what happens, taking part in a practice without purpose.

Such a practice, whatever you call it, helps you remember how to play. It reduces or entirely eliminates the intimidation of

- what other people think of my efforts
- how I compare to other people
- whether what I achieve will be "good enough"

Practice without purpose allows you to discover things you couldn't discover in any other way. Creativity can't be forced. Playing around—putzing, practicing without purpose—invites the muse. Your practice can be anything from writing what Julia Cameron, author of *The Artist's Way*, calls "daily pages" to drawing one of Sr. Agatha's mandalas. Use these five criteria to keep you on the right track when you choose and participate in a practice.

Be Alone

I recommend doing your practice without purpose by yourself so you're not tempted to compete or compare the results of your practice to another person's. It's also easier to get into a creative trance, an intense working mood, if you're not distracted by other people's presence.

Be Regular

Set aside at least one hour once a week or so. Write the appointment in your date book, and respect it as you would any other commitment. Do not give up your practice time except for terminal illness or impending death. Perhaps not even then.

Be Without Purpose

Focus on deepening exploration, experimentation, play and fun, instead of on a result or goal. If you're not used to putzing, it can be difficult at first. Try to have a "let's see what happens" attitude. Once you've become proficient at your practice, you may be tempted to put it to practical use, like turning your writing into a book. If this happens, devote additional time to purposelessness or choose a different practice where you won't be lured into having a goal.

Be Intense

Purposelessness is not the same as aimlessness. Childlike playfulness is not the same as childish drifting. The heat and fire that you bring to the process is what anneals and tempers your practice. Attention, devotion and concentration provide the heat that accomplishes magic in a creative expression.

Be Spontaneous

Telling someone to be spontaneous is a lot like yelling at that person to relax. Trying to be spontaneous defeats the purpose. Think instead of allowing—merely allowing—yourself to take risks, make mistakes, play and have fun. Let your creative mind take over. If you're new to such a practice and it's giving you trouble, read chapter thirty-six and practice the suggestions on quieting your mind as a warm-up.

Invent your own practice, or try some of the practices suggested in the list in this chapter. The practice you choose doesn't have to be related to your professional field. Sometimes it's better if it isn't. Creative forms cross-pollinate. For instance, when I've been writing all day, I like to draw to rewind my inner tape and refresh inspiration. You can do different practices at different times. Experiment to see what works for you. But I'd suggest getting well acquainted with one type of activity before trying something else. The important thing is to do the practice following the five guidelines we just discussed so you can get into your creative mind and out of your rational one. As Sr. Agatha says, "The rational is rewarded, but creativity and imagination come out of the nonrational." A practice without purpose may not lead to fame and fortune, but I think I can say with some authority that if you commit yourself to such a practice, your creativity will be nourished. And yes, Sr. Agatha will be proud of you.

SUGGESTIONS FOR BEGINNING A PRACTICE WITHOUT PURPOSE

Ten Ways to Rev Your Creativity

1·Go to a lumberyard and ask if you can have its small wood scraps, or buy a set of child's blocks. Build and rebuild with these.

2·Keep a notebook in which you write daily for at least a half hour about anything that crosses your mind (see chapter four for suggestions on capturing ideas on the fly). Let this be a visit with yourself and not an assignment. Try site writing to inspire your practice.

3·Buy an inexpensive sketchbook, colored markers and a compass to draw circles. (If you don't have a compass, you can trace around a saucer.) Beginning in the center of a small-sized circle, draw a simple symbol such as a star, flower or butterfly. Keep expanding the drawing outward into larger and larger rings by inventing other forms to fit the space. You can get help from books on mandala drawing at your library or local bookstore. To add drama to your drawings, experiment with pastel gel roller pens on dark paper.

4· Play recorded music and invent a dance or do motions that suit your mood and the music. (If you still feel shy, you may want to do this in private with your shades drawn.) Write or draw the dance.

5· Assemble a box of interesting objects. Keep adding to your collection. Write for a half hour each day about one of them.

6· Sing out loud when you're alone in your car. Turn on your radio if that helps. Make up words as you go along.

7· Turn an ordinary activity—swimming, walking, exercising on a rowing machine or stationary bike—into a practice without purpose. Do it for no reason. Forget about muscle building, weight loss and fitness. Just swim, walk or row.

8· Play with clay, but don't try to make something with it. Experiment to discover the qualities and limitations of the clay itself. Squeeze it, slice it and poke holes in it with your fingers. Have a conversation with the clay. Write about what you have learned.

9· Open your thesaurus at random, and point to a word on the page. Write a short poem inspired by the word. Repeat this process once a week; if you like, substitute the yellow pages of the phone book, a clothing or novelty catalog, or an encyclopedia volume.

10· Put together a box of creative media: paint, crayons, paper, scissors, glue, etc. Spend an hour a week experimenting with these materials.

Explorations

✤ "Dance" with a pencil or pen. Take out a pad of paper, and write or draw whatever comes to you. Put yourself on automatic pilot. Don't have a predetermined subject or goal; just write or draw. Let your pen play with words and images.

Project

✤ Buy or make a sand tray. Paint the bottom of a shallow cardboard or wooden box to represent water. Fill it with an inch or two of fine dry sand. Make a scene in the sand by scraping away some places to expose the water you painted on the bottom. Build hills and mountains; make roads and paths. Add sprigs from bushes to make trees. Add toy animals and people and houses. Play. Have fun. Write about your experience. Next time, take away all the props, level the sand and start over with a new creation.

Experiment

✤ Cross over to another medium. If you usually write, try painting with brushes, sponges or your fingers. If you usually paint, try playing with clay. Let whatever happens happen. Plunk away on a musical instrument, or thump away on drums you don't know how to play. Write about the experience.

18. Flamingos in the Men's Room

A color photo in a recent *Time* magazine is enough to stop you short, even if all you're doing is flipping pages. The photo shows a flock of spindle-legged pink flamingos gawking into the mirror of a men's room in a Las Vegas casino. What are flamingos doing in a men's room? How did they get to the middle of the Nevada desert? The peculiar image arrests the attention of even the most jaded page flipper.

It turns out, the article reveals, that the flamingos were housed in the men's room overnight to keep them warm and protect them from a hard freeze. Admittedly, as imported residents on the casino grounds, the birds were accustomed to warmer climes. But the sight of them swiveling their necks to peer at the strange duplicate flock reflected in a wide mirror above the sinks was something to remember.

This bit of Useless Information Trivia, what I call U.I.T., is part of a collection I've made over the years with the same fervor as people who collect Beanie Babies. A whole drawer in my bedroom

THE USES

OF USELESS

INFORMATION

dresser is stuffed with U.I.T.s waiting to find their use. (Believe it or not, most of these snipped facts and jotted oddities do find a purpose sooner or later.) At first sight, the clippings and notations and photocopies may seem to be nothing more than just—well—odd. Let me give you some examples and a few of the questions they provoke:

- You can now buy a colorful beetle as large as a New York cockroach in a vending machine in Japan. (They're hot sellers!) Would you keep it on a leash? Confine it in a cage— perhaps creating a market for beetle cages? Let it run free? How much do they cost? Do they come, like some panty hose, in their own plastic egg? What does a beetle eat? Are there beetle-food stores?

- Researchers are trying to find out if clams cavort and, if they do, whether their cavorting predicts earthquakes. How can you tell when a clam cavorts? Do they flop around inside their shells? Giggle? Leap? Should I keep one in the bathtub so I'll know when to run for shelter?

- There's been a legal dispute over ownership of a cave in southern France that has thirty-thousand-year-old paintings on its walls. The dispute goes unresolved because the judge in the case can't squeeze through the cave's narrow opening. Did he try? Did he get stuck? Could he have sent a skinny deputy?

- They say Mount Everest is moving northeast at two and a half inches a year. How many millennia will it take for Mount Everest to walk to the nearest town, Xigaze, Tibet, more than a hundred miles away? (You do the math.)

- Rivers in the sky that are more than 450 miles across and carry as much water as the Amazon have just been discovered by scientists. Wouldn't you think that a 450-mile-wide river would have been noticed, even with the naked eye, if it was flowing over, say, Los Angeles? If you were a sky diver, could you swim in it? Are there any Jet Skis or riverboats floating up there?

You can see how an intriguing U.I.T. can inspire a multitude of questions. These questions are triggers for creativity. Think of them as the engines that drive the tractor that pulls the plow that turns over the soil of your imagination so you can see in a new way. Here is an example of how I used a U.I. T.

Years ago I had collected a few clips about the noise levels in cities and about loud music and its effect on hearing. The clips were stored willy-nilly in a folder with other U.I.T.s. Then one warm fall day I was having lunch on an outdoor deck and heard a sound I'd never heard before: something like "yuk, yuk, yuk." The sound, it turned out, was coming from a squirrel, yukking as it skittered through dry leaves. Why hadn't I ever noticed that squirrels make this sound? In all the years I'd been watching them, why didn't I recognize a squirrel's bark?

I remembered the clippings about city noise. Of course! The squirrel's bark was drowned out by loud noises from lawn mowers and leaf blowers and jackhammers. Combining the noise U.I.T.s with the squirrel sounds inspired the article I wrote called "Listen to the Squirrels Bark." Without the clips, the article idea never would have jelled. Without the squirrel, the clips would have moldered.

You can add items to your collection of U.I.T.s from news broadcasts, PBS programs and magazines. Look through back issues of *National Geographic*, *Smithsonian Magazine* and *The New York Times* Sunday edition, or simply observe what goes on around you. Your own U.I.T. trove might be completely different from the one we just talked about. It could reflect your work, the sports and hobbies you like, the place you live or the things that tickle your funny bone. The bits can be ordinary, or they can be bizarre. To qualify for your own unique U.I.T. list, all the item needs to be is interesting to you—interesting in such a way that you respond in your cells. The thing makes you laugh, guffaw, wonder. Most of all, it makes you ask a lot of questions. Sometimes you won't know 'til long after you've discovered an interesting bit whether it's useful or useless. My claim is that anything that attracts you can be useful.

Collecting Useless Information Is a Form of Play

Collecting U.I.T.s keeps your creative mind alive and fed. It teaches you to value things just for themselves, just because they interest and attract you. Such thinking prevents you from becoming too purposeful. Purposefulness, when it becomes obsessive, can block creativity by allowing logical thinking to dominate. Collecting useless information also helps you find your heart place, the place where creative expression has to start if it's to be satisfying.

The Search for Useless Information Teaches You to Keep Your Eyes Open

You never know where and when some new U.I.T. will turn up. I found one, for example, on the bookshelf of a friend who had traveled the world. May Fetchhiemer (yes, that was really his name) had a carved wooden replica of a narwhal with an ivory tusk in his living room bookcase. The tusk of a male narwhal grows into a spiral sometimes as long as eight or ten feet; it looks like a corkscrew swordfish. I was fascinated. I later read up on narwhals, but until now I had never done anything with this surprising discovery. It was enough just to wonder about these creatures who stab through the ocean waves with their long tusks. The discovery was satisfying all by itself.

Useless Information Cultivates an Appreciation for the Surprising, the Ridiculously Absurd and the Bone-Ticklingly Funny

U.I.T.s keep the fires of creativity stoked. You may see no practical use for your quirky fascinations, but they can generate inspiration just the same—even if all they do is keep the creative spark alive. Many writers, artists and other creatives have told me that if they feed the creative fire, it will burn through to some new realization. A rich supply of useless information may store the exact resource to bring about an "aha!"—a new idea, a new image, a new process. You'll notice how fragments of information begin to come together to make whole ideas, just like bubble bath made islands in the bathtub when you were a kid.

Useless Information Inspires Questions

When we learn about beetle vending machines, our minds immediately fill with questions. Welcoming those questions—even encour-
aging them—exercises our creative, questioning minds. Creativity is
fed by everything that crosses its path, planned or not. Often the un-
planned elicits the most fruitful questions.

I heard a story about a woman from California who traveled
to Japan on vacation. While poking around one of the open-air food
markets, she noticed the interesting white cotton sacks lettered in
Japanese calligraphy that held fifty pounds of rice. Questions popped
into her head: What do merchants do with the empty sacks? Could the
sacks be made into something else: an article of clothing, a kimono?
The merchants, she discovered, discarded the empty sacks, so she
asked if she could have some of them. When she got home, she
stitched them into tops and pants and beach cover-ups. She showed
them to friends who were so enthusiastic about them that she decided
to approach a women's clothing shop to see if the owner would be interested in selling the items. And so a new career resulted from keeping her eyes open and asking questions based on what appeared to be a
useless observation: rice sacks with interesting calligraphy.

What can you do with a piece of useless information? You
don't need to know in advance. Treat it like a piece of puzzle and see
where it leads. It may take you somewhere. It may not. Even if you
never use your U.I.T.s, you'll never be short of conversation starters at
parties. You'll also have a tantalizing source of soul food to keep the un-
canny, whimsical, creative creature inside you fed, alive and growing.

Explorations

❧ For a week or so, collect any odd facts or images that arouse your interest. When you've accumulated at least a dozen, see if they fall into any particular categories. What do they have in common? What attracted you to each one? Write about what intrigued you.

❧ Continue to collect odd information. Periodically, sit down with your trove of useless facts and see if some of them suggest a particular form of creative expression: a poem, a nonfiction article, a novel, a painting, a paper construction. Carry out your exploration based on these insights.

Mental Push-Up

❧ Consult your collection of odd facts. Select one. Write as many questions as you can think of that the odd bit provokes. Be whimsical, brainy, imaginative and profound in your approach. Repeat with one or two others.

❧ Put two pieces of useless information together—for instance, vending machine beetles and decorative rice sacks. Write about the combination. What questions, ideas, images arise? Use your imagination and sense of humor.

ch 19. Visualization

There's a particularly stirring moment in the movie *Mr. Holland's Opus* where the music teacher, Mr. Holland, confronts a red-haired student who has been playing her clarinet out of tune. Desperate to get the student to find a way to feel the music, he asks her what she saw in the mirror that morning that she liked best about herself.

> "My hair," the student says.
> "Why?" Holland asks.
> "Because my father always says my red hair
>   reminds him of a sunset."

Holland's face brightens. He grins. "Then play the sunset!" The girl picks up her clarinet and gradually begins to play the sunset. The reds, oranges and yellows of the sunset enter her music, and she plays as she never has played before.

THE MAGIC

OF THE

MIND'S EYE

When we create, we play the sunset. We play what we see in our mind's eye. This vision is a powerful nudge to creativity because what we imagine inspires what we create. I'd almost go so far as to say that what you create you first have to visualize.

Visualization makes real something in your imagination. It gives substance to feelings and thoughts by actually creating a scene in the mind's eye. In the created experience, it's possible to "visualize" scents, tastes and sounds as well as color, shapes and textures. Sometimes, if you picture something vividly enough it will come to life just like Pinocchio did before the eyes of the wood-carver who made him.

George Ella Lyon, author of several children's books, once told me she visualizes her fictional characters to give them life. After the characters have been created in her imagination, she said, they seem to take on a life of their own. When I spoke to her, Lyon had been on a book tour and away from her work for a time. She said, "I can't wait to get home to see what my characters have been doing while I've been gone!" She had "made real" her characters by bringing them to life in her mind's eye and then just letting them act in their own ways.

Here are a couple of other functions of the mind's eye:

- Visualization provides a *physical* experience in which the whole body participates. Do you believe this? Picture a juicy lemon slice. Imagine that you squeeze a few tart drops into your mouth. Taste the tangy juice on your tongue. Is your mouth beginning to water? Visualization has the same effects as actual physical experience. Recall a time when you remembered a frightening situation. The hairs on your arms and legs stood up. You reacted as if you were right there, right then. The same thing happens when you watch a chilling drama or find yourself being chased by a tiger in a dream.

  If you've ever watched figure skating competitions on TV, you may have noticed your body's response. When the skater braced before going into a triple lutz, you did, too. You found your shoulders tensing and your leg muscles clinching as you helped her through the jump. When she'd completed the rotation and carried the whole thing through

with grace and expert control, you felt your muscles relax.
You had, in your imagination, just done a perfect triple.

• Visualization can be a rehearsal for action or a prelude to it. I
recently wrote an article about artist William Schickel, who
operates out of a studio in a hundred-year-old railway station
in Loveland, Ohio. After the interview, when I was home
with my notes and getting ready to write, I reentered the interview to set the scene for the piece. The way the orange
afternoon sun slanted low through the studio's tall windows
became an image. So did the family's mixed-breed dog,
Chip, who lay like a bear rug near the door. So did the artist
himself, standing on a metal scaffold and wearing his paint-
spattered black carpenter's apron. The images were a prelude
to writing. They whisked me back to the scene where I could
write, mainline, directly from the experience.

When I'm feeling stuck, images remind me why I
wanted to write about a subject in the first place. The sounds
and sights and flavors come back. They energize the writing.

• Visualization balances the two sides of your creative self. A
writer told me he likes to keep images in his mind to help
balance his logical thinking with creative thinking. "When I
keep a picture in my mind, the writing flows better. Visualizing helps me reconnect with the original experience so that
my writing has the feel of solid reality. Airy concepts become
concrete. The reader walks along at my side, looking where I
look, feeling what I feel, seeing what I see."

Some people are better visualizers than others. Swiss artist
Paul Klee could stare at a blank canvas until an image came. What
most people see in their mind's eye, Klee saw on the white page. Once
the image appeared, he began to paint, incorporating what his mind's
eye had seen. His head was aswim with images that easily found their
way onto the canvas.

People who aren't naturally visual thinkers may need a device
to get them started. Leonardo da Vinci found images in wood grain
and used them to inspire his paintings. Renoir played with colored

SEED THOUGHT

"Daydreaming,
as free inner living,
can be taken as a
nuisance by those
who have designs on
our energies."

Eric Klinger, Ph.D.
Daydreaming

spots he turned into landscapes or people. You can practice visualization by looking for images in cloud shapes or bare tree branches or scribbles on a page. When you've mastered these devices, you can try big-time visualization by creating your own mind movies.

You can start anywhere. Let's say you like potbellied pigs. Start there. Visualize a purple pig. Give it pink polka dots, then stripes, then plaid skin. Make it green. Make it blue. Draw a circle around the pig. Let the pig shrink to a tiny dot inside the circle. Now have it grow bigger and bigger until the circle is a collar around its neck. Then see the collar change into a circle of daisies.

Introduce another animal, perhaps a porcupine. What color is it? How big? Let the two animals interact. What do they do? Keep the images changing, moving around, interacting. Put the pig in a dresser drawer. Take it out and let it walk on the ceiling. Give it wings. Let it fly.

You can memorize or record this sequence if you want to, but it's more fun to make up new images as you go along. It doesn't matter what images you use. Try different ones to see which ones create the most vivid pictures—in Technicolor and 3-D.

Visualizing any object expands your thinking from linear to wholistic. You "get it" all at once, like when you see a work of art or a sunset. I like the word Robert Heinlein used in *Stranger in a Strange Land*: *grok*. When you grok something, you see it, you get it all at once. You know, not just in your thought mind, but totally.

Words used alone without a connection to real life have limitations. They're stunted. Images can provide a bridge between words and experience. When we fall in love with words we sometimes forget this missing link. In the early 1930s John Neihardt interviewed Black Elk, the Oglala Sioux warrior and medicine man, for the book *Black Elk Speaks*. Black Elk had attempted to relate the story of his vision and the tribe's many trials to Neihardt, who assured him he understood. But Black Elk, still not completely certain, replied, "You hear it, but do you *see* it?" He felt that a thing had to be seen in the mind's eye—or as he said "with the heart"—before it could be fully grasped. Unless something can be "seen," it remains only words in a concept. It has no life.

Writers, especially, pay attention to such seeing. By putting themselves into the situation, the heart place, and writing from there, they haul the reader by the scruff of the neck to that same place. What the writer says begins to live; no longer is his writing just dry words on a page. Writer and reader cozy up into the same intimate space.

You can find a demonstration of such communication in the writings of Loren Eiseley. Dr. Eiseley, a naturalist and most unlikely source of intimate communication, accomplishes a rare feat. He brings science to life before your eyes. In my favorite essay, *The Star Thrower*, he writes about his encounter with starfish along a deserted shore:

> I picked up the star whose tube feet ventured
> timidly among my fingers while, like a true star, it
> cried soundlessly for life. I saw it with an un-
> accustomed clarity and cast far out. With it I
> flung myself as forfeit, for the first time into some
> unknown dimension of existence.

Dr. Eiseley not only reenters the scene himself in his writing, he pulls us into the experience, too. We respond to his presence with our own. The result is a humanizing of scientific writing—making the subject real through bringing inner images into light.

Most of us would expect that visualization plays a useful role in artists' work because art is a visual medium. But Eiseley shows that mind pictures can have a broader use. Image is the native tongue of the unconscious, where creative ideas live in their prehatched form. It's natural for ideas to emerge as images first. Then they can be translated into words.

Years ago, Elias Howe had an idea for a machine that sews. He couldn't get the idea to work because he kept trying to thread the needle from the dull end, the way a regular sewing needle is threaded. It took a dream image of warriors throwing their spears into a pit to help him visualize a solution: The needle must be threaded at the point.

A mental picture can pull an idea into daylight where it can be acted upon and expressed. That makes visualization a universal donor to creativity in the arts, literature, science, business—even sports. Seeing a situation, visually, in the mind's eye can capture an idea or solve a problem where logic can't. Visual daydreaming can help you play the sunset to bring creativity to life.

❧ Select various kinds of recorded instrumental music: jazz, big band, classical, New Age, marching. Play one of the selections for ten minutes or so. With your eyes closed, picture what the music is saying and visualize a scene the music suggests. Allow images of people, places and interactions to enter your mind's eye. Let them have free rein to do and be what they want. Watch a drama unfold, then open your eyes and write about your experience. Repeat with one or two different kinds of music.

❧ Close your eyes and visualize two people who are opposites, such as a construction worker and librarian or a socialite and a hobo. Imagine them on a small desert island together. What happens? How do they cope? What do they do? How are they changed? Repeat with a different pair in a new setting, such as a rowboat in a stormy sea, up a tree with a tiger pacing below or in a foxhole during a fierce battle.

Visual Push-Up

❧ Concentrate on looking at a simple object, such as a pencil, soft drink can or flower, for five minutes. Now close your eyes, and find out if you can still "see" it in your mind's eye. Repeat at least two or three times. Write about how you did.

❧ Recall an interaction with another person that made you feel uncomfortable or that didn't end the way you hoped. (Let's say someone did something that made you angry but you didn't say anything, or you said or did something you later regretted.) Close your eyes and visually put yourself back in the situation. Reexperience the setting, the other person's presence, your own feelings. See it all in your mind's eye. Restage the interaction so the outcome is more agreeable to both. Write about the encounter.

Site Write

❧ Go to a public place, such as a waiting room, shopping mall or bus station. Bring a pen and a notebook. Find a place where you can write undisturbed. In your mind's eye create a cartoon-type character, such as a ten-foot rabbit with a pink tutu or a green mouse in a top hat or a white mole the size of a large dog. In your imagination, let your fantasy creature interact with people you see: Have it dance among them, talk to them, sing, make faces, beg them to notice. (Once you've tried this, you'll never again be bored in a public place.) Write for twenty minutes on the spot.

ch 20. Can the Cat Kill
Your Curiosity?

Curiosity is a wonderful thing. It lures us from our surefootedness
in the shallows into deeper water. It stimulates imagination and awakens
new ideas. It keeps us on our toes by giving us answers before we've
asked the questions. More important, it creates a storehouse of information that supplies creative expression.

Curiosity always generates a surprise. When your receptors
are turned on, you can learn the most amazing things. For instance, I
learned more than I ever wanted to know about iguanas at, of all
places, a hair salon. I was in for the usual clip when the patron in the
next chair told her stylist that she had a pet iguana. All our ears perked.
Suddenly the air was filled with questions. What's its name? (Magma.)
What does it eat? (Salads, spinach and kale.) What does it look like?
(Green-blue, about so long, with great expressive eyes.) Curiosity took
hold, and the whole salon was off and running.

Our need to know often happens so spontaneously that we

WHAT TO

WATCH FOR,

JUST IN CASE

take it for granted. Sometimes we're even a little afraid of it. After all, who hasn't heard the expression "Curiosity killed the cat"? A friend of mine who owns two black cats claims the old saying is based on reality. "They're very curious, and they get into everything," she says. "I put an empty grocery bag on the floor, and the next thing I know they're in it. I slide out a drawer, and they climb in. Open the linen closet, and they're on the shelf in a flash. After watching these two get into some harrowing circumstances, I know curiosity really could kill a cat!"

Curiosity can also be dangerous for writers and other creative people. It can lead us into new ways of doing things. Trying a different approach can upset those around us who subscribe to the theory "That's the way we've always done it." As it does to my friend's cats, curiosity can lure us into dark closets through its passionate, nosy, questioning, relentlessly questing and sometimes troublesome ways. For these reasons, curiosity itself is always at risk of being killed. Certain conditions contribute. They're the CAT that kills curiosity:

- **C**onformity
- **A**pathy
- **T**abloid mentality

Conformity is the cookie cutter everyone tries to squeeze you into so you'll come out looking and acting like everyone else. Curiosity is a threat to conformity because it inspires you to think outside the mold, to develop fresh ideas and choose your own path.

Conformity teaches you to label everything. It begins in elementary school when the teacher holds up a picture of an elephant and asks, "What is this?" You and your classmates, all together and awkwardly, dutifully say, "Elephant." It may come in handy to know that the gray, big-eared thing in the picture is an elephant, but merely labeling something short-circuits imagination and kills curiosity. Without further questioning, you'll never learn how long an elephant lives, why it has big ears and how it lives in the wild.

When you've labeled something, you tend to file it away so you don't have to think about it again. Before long, such pigeonhole thinking stops questions and keeps imagination on such a short leash

that it can't wander into something new. Curiosity atrophies. We fail to
ask, what if? In Pakistan, where I lived for a time years ago, the sweep-
ers who cleaned our walkways used short-handled brooms, so they had
to squat and duckwalk as they swept. No one thought to make the
handles longer. No one asked, what if? I once asked the gnarled old
sweeper who crept along our drive why he used a short-handled broom.
"Because it has always been done this way, Memsahib," he replied.

"The way it's always been done" is the theme song of conformity. Curiosity prefers to ask, what if? What if I took the bus
cross-country instead of an airplane? Would it offer a new perspective
to write from? What if I spent a year in a log cabin in the wilderness?
Would it generate a novel? "What if" is the vocabulary of curiosity
that keeps creativity speaking to us. Doing things the way they've
always been done leads to hardening of the creative arteries. It freezes
excitement and cuts off questioning, so you'll never know all the
fascinating facts about elephants or iguanas.

Apathy is another wet blanket that can smother curiosity.
Once you've labeled something and filed it away in your mind, curiosity ebbs away. Questions are mothballed. Boredom sets in. We think
we know everything we need to know. Apathy sucks energy.

I hand out Anasazi beans in class to demonstrate that we don't
really know beans about beans or anything we're not curious about.
Anasazi beans, sometimes called Christmas beans, are not only unique
compared to other types of beans; they're different from one another.
Underneath, they're white limas, but the skin of each is splotched in
brown, like the spots on a pinto pony. The ancient Anasazi tribes of
the Southwest are said to have foretold fortunes of the coming year by
seeing images in the beans' irregularly shaped spots. People in the
class who don't care a hill of beans about beans become curious and
interested. Apathy dissolves. I leave them with questions I hope will
continue to nudge their curiosity about how the bean grows and the
shapes that appear on its mottled skin.

Tabloid mentality is still another killer of curiosity. It's difficult
not to fall into its trap. You can't pass through a supermarket checkout
without coming face-to-face with the latest scandalous tabloid head-
lines. And even on the Internet and television you're besieged by

tabloid-style sensationalism. Most of the subtleties of curiosity get buried in the overload.

The need for ever escalating stimulation acts like a drug. It's addictive. Whatever seems shocking in today's news will have to be compounded tomorrow to have the same effect.

"Channel surfing on TV and the hundreds of choices we now have on the Internet have intensified competition for our attention," a teacher told me. "The media have to increase sensational offerings more and more as we develop a tolerance, like we do when we overuse antibiotics. Eventually, everything but the loudest, most shocking, most blatantly violent programming will seem boring."

Pushing the envelope of sensation to its ultimate will eventually dull and finally destroy curiosity. As a result, creativity will wither. Curiosity is like the lure of a chocolate bar. One chocolate bar can be savored; fifty will make you sick. When you're watching a television movie where a ton of explosives detonate on-screen, you won't be too curious about shadow patterns moving across your living room wall or whether your experiences working in a homeless shelter would be worth writing about.

Too much sensation leads to an unquiet mind—a mind that's always confused and busy, like a hamster on a wheel. There's no room for curiosity. The only way to get your mind to slow down and empty itself of mental overload is to take an occasional vacation from sensation. Turn off the TV. Disconnect the PC. Try some of the practices on quieting the mind suggested in chapter thirty-six, or just take time to sit and stare at goldfish.

Curiosity is elusive and fragile. CAT includes just three things that can cripple or eliminate it. But if you're on guard, an attentive goalie at the wicket, and determined to keep your curiosity healthy, the rewards can be enormous.

Curiosity keeps us vital. It is, as writer Elbert Hubbard said, "the peephole in the brain." Through that peephole we see things that lure us off the well-trod path and into new discoveries that fire creative imagination. Curiosity can revitalize us. I even know of a case where it revitalized a whole town.

When my friend Bill ran a nursing home in Edgerton, Ohio, his job was to make sure all the facility's beds were filled. He tried all

the usual marketing methods: advertising, direct mail and tours. But he
found that people in Edgerton didn't really like their town, and without their enthusiasm, the nursing home was doomed to fail.

"I realized if I didn't sell the town, I wasn't going to be able to
sell the nursing home," Bill recalls. He noticed that other towns had
some symbol or special festival that set them apart. Some had pumpkin
or tomato festivals. One even celebrated the buzzards' annual return.
So what about Edgerton? What would make the town stand out and
encourage people to stay? Bill asked the city council for ideas, but
they came up empty.

Every morning as he drove to work, Bill kicked his curiosity into
gear. "I tried to look at the town in a new way. I saw the town hall gazebo,
the railroad tracks, the park. Nothing remarkable here. Then suddenly I
came up with the idea of Edgar—a kind person named after the town."
Bill deputized his wife, two sympathetic council members, the editor of
the town paper and the chief of police for his secret mission.

The group began its clandestine activity by taking out classified ads that read "Edgar is coming." As subsequent ads grew larger
and larger the town started talking. Curiosity began to simmer.

"Our next step was to make a couple of huge banners that said
'Edgar is Coming.' We sneaked into town at 3 A.M. to hang one on the
high school entrance and run the other up the city hall flagpole. Kids
thought Edgar was a rock band. Others thought he was a real person
who would be moving into town. Everybody was curious."

Then Bill began Edgar's random acts of kindness. His group,
in secret, painted the unsightly rusted gate to the city park and left a
sign that said "Compliments of Edgar." The next day the story was
front-page news. Curiosity bubbled. "We planted a tree, dropped
holiday greeting cards at the doors of businesses and hung mechanical
pencils on high school lockers. Each said 'Compliments of Edgar.' At
Easter we made a huge crepe paper egg with candy around the bottom
and a sign 'The Edgar bunny was here.' And when a lady's house
burned down and Edgar sponsored a fund to help her recover, the
whole town was curious to know who Edgar was. To this day, I've
never admitted it was me."

After the Edgar antics, the town's attitude began to change.

People saw their hometown as a fun, interesting place to live. And soon the beds in the nursing home began to fill with people who wanted to stay close to their roots.

Curiosity can energize a whole person or a whole town. It keeps creativity vital. Curiosity can take you to places ambition could never dream of. All you have to do is to keep it from being consumed by the CAT.

Explorations

❧ Play "what if?" with a few other people or by yourself. Have each person write down ordinary or preposterous questions, such as

- What if the world were square instead of round?
- What if no human being had the sense of sight? What if only one or two people did?
- What if someone invented a device that would do all the jobs you hate to do?
- What if people walked on their hands instead of their feet?
- What if dandelions were suddenly considered to be, like gold, the most valuable substance?

Discuss or write about what these "what if" questions suggest.

❧ What were you curious about as a child? If you can't remember, ask some kids what they're curious about. Write about your findings. Are you still curious about any of these things? Why? Why not?

Walkabout

❧ Go for a walk around any place you consider interesting: a car repair shop (if you are allowed), a suburban neighborhood, supermarket aisles, etc. Take a notebook with you and write down things you see that make you curious. Let the questions percolate. If you can, research some of these questions (Where do guavas come from? How do you clean a valve lifter? How long will it take that maple seedling rooted spontaneously in your front yard to grow to full size?). Write about your findings.

Project

❧ Keep a curiosity file. On a small piece of paper, write what arouses your curiosity, and slip it into the file. Try to write one thing each day. If you miss five days, write five things when you get back to it. At the end of a month, review your file. Stack the papers according to category. What are the kinds of things you're most curious about? Why? Write about one of them in a poem, a story or a journal entry, or represent them in paint or clay.

freeing your
creative elves

5

21. Ice Fishing

FOUR STEPS

TO CREATIVE

INSPIRATION

Nimitz was what most of us would call an eccentric. He lived year-round in the north woods where he owned the Lighthouse Resort and where he tended bar every night 'til well past midnight. He was the first person to teach me about ice fishing and, inadvertently, about creativity.

Each spring when school let out, my family and I drove from Illinois to our Wisconsin summer cabin. Nimitz lived nearby and was always ready with new stories about the previous winter's ice fishing. I believed his tales, and not just because he had snapshots of fishermen holding yard-long trophies of walleyed pike and muskie. I swallowed his stories hook, line and sinker because, in my dazzled child mind, Nimitz had magical powers. We'd heard stories to prove it.

One late night in the bar, when smoke hung thick and blue and tall tales and wagers grew like yeast dough in a warm oven, Nimitz settled a bet. He plunged a butcher knife through his pants leg. When we heard, we were amazed. We didn't know then that Nimitz had a wooden leg.

Hoax or not, the spell was cast. His stories about ice fishing stuck with me. But it wasn't until decades later when I was putting together a class on creative thinking that I realized ice fishing follows a path remarkably similar to that of the creative process.

FOUR STEPS IN THE CREATIVE PROCESS

Ice Fishing	**The Creative Process**
1· BAIT. Erect a shelter against the wind, cut a hole in the ice, bait your hook with the juiciest lure you can find and drop it into the water.	1· PREPARE. Form your creative question, define the problem, inventory what you already know, network to get input, research your subject. Now's the time to let your logical left brain do its stuff.
2· WAIT. Sit on your wooden crate and shiver. Pull up your line from time to time to see if you've had a bite. Drink hot buttered rum. Wonder why you came.	2· INCUBATE. Let go. Send your brain on vacation. Relax, take a break, do something mindless, such as taking a walk, washing your car or darning socks. Play. Watch TV. Doze.
3· CATCH. You've got a strike! A big one! Pull it in.	3· ILLUMINATE. Experience a creative "aha!" that can be accomplished only by the inner creator, or the right brain. Relish the moment.
4· WEIGH. Is your catch a keeper? Measure it. Weigh it. If it doesn't make the grade, toss it back and start over.	4· EVALUATE. Your critical self has a function at last! Ask yourself, Will this idea work? Can I change it so it will? If not, return to square one. Do not pass go. Do not collect two hundred dollars.

This four-step process is not the creative act itself, any more than Nimitz's stories are the real experience of ice fishing. The four steps are only the bones—an after-the-fact snapshot of the catch—which can be a helpful guide when you get stuck. Using these steps, you can go back to one of the previous steps or even start over as many times as you need to for as long as your patience and energy last.

When nothing seems to work, it helps to put your original question another way. The restating alone can suggest a solution.

Rephrasing the question proved to be a lifesaver when I was asked to come up with a new name for Ocean Health Products, an East Coast supplement company. Feedback from customers had led the company to change its advertising strategy from mainstream press to religious press. The old name didn't fit this new plan.

I generated fifteen names, but none really clicked. My mistake? I had been trying to force a variation of the old name into the new situation. When I stated the question in another way—What do these customers really want from their supplements?—the answer was easy. Most were cancer patients. They wanted a miracle, or at least a blessing. That's how the new name, Natural Blessings, was born.

Brainstorming is something you can use to ignite your creative process. Set aside an hour to write down every answer you can think of to your problem. Let your responses build upon one another. The important thing is not to judge what you produce. Aim, instead, for a large quantity of ideas directed toward resolving the question. When the time is up or you've run out of ideas, see if anything comes close to what you're seeking. If not, take a break and return to the task later.

One pitfall you can stumble into in the bait/prepare stage is *over*preparation. My tendency is to gather until every resource is exhausted. Another writer I know has the same problem. She's been doing research for a book on the history of the Roman Empire for over ten years. The research alone fills half a dozen shelves covering a whole wall in her bedroom. When last I heard, she hadn't started to write yet. Aside from the fact that her subject is broad enough to produce a whole library of books, she obviously has too much material.

Experience teaches you how much preparation is enough. For a personal profile piece for a magazine, I generally interview for an hour or take about five pages of notes. Sometimes that's not enough, and I have to go back for more. But the idea is to get started. Prepare until your gut tells you you're ready, and then just begin. Don't research the entire history of the Roman Empire.

In the wait/incubate stage, the pitfall is the quick solution. We want to take the soufflé out of the oven before it's completely baked. What happens? It falls flat just like a half-baked idea. If you're the resident creative in the place where you work, socialize or volunteer, then you know what I mean. Someone—usually your boss—says, "You're creative, tell me an idea for _____." You are supposed to answer on the spot. No waiting. No incubating. It's like being a gumball machine: Someone puts in a quarter, turns the lever and expects you to produce an instant colorful handful of ideas.

Sometimes you make the same demand on yourself. You put in a couple of hours. You come up with a bunch of so-so ideas. You want to wrap it up with what you've got. It's hard to believe that doing nothing will get you anywhere, but that may be just what's needed to get the inner innovator to belch up a new idea. Charles Darwin believed so strongly in the value of incubation that he built himself a nature path to walk on while he performed his ponderings.

How do you know when you've waited long enough? You know when you hear the click—the creative "aha!"—in the catch/illuminate stage. The idea fits. It feels right. Of course, sometimes the aha! doesn't happen, or you've got a deadline and you can't wait forever. What then? The only solution is to repeat one of the other steps, probably the first one. Rephrase the question. Get input. Research. Look at the problem or the project in a new way.

Sometimes even after a fiery aha! you realize in the weigh/evaluate stage that you've got a clinker and not a meteor. Something about the idea doesn't work. This is the tedious, disheartening part of the process. It takes courage not to get *dis*couraged.

When you hit a creative snag, get feedback and encouragement from another person. If nothing else, he can help you keep the spark alive until a solution comes. Whether you pursue the four-step creative process alone or in a group, Nimitz would no doubt have a few last words of advice: "Stay warm, and make sure you don't fall through the ice."

SEED THOUGHT

"Let your hook be always cast; in the pool where you least expect it, there will be a fish."

Ovid

Explorations

❦ Keep a list or folder of creative accomplishments. Include those you might be inclined to overlook, such as the time you used an egg carton to start seedlings in your windowsill or you made a greeting card for a friend or you used cold chamomile tea bags to rest your eyes.

❦ Brainstorm a problem. Write three new solutions each day for a week. Don't judge any of them until the end of the week. Build on any promising ones.

❦ What works best for you at the incubation stage? Walking? Running? Household tasks? Watching TV? Reclining on the couch? Other? Write a page about your preferences.

Recollection

❦ Write a case history of a creative accomplishment, dividing it into the four stages described in this chapter. What happened at each stage? What steps did you repeat? In what order? How did you know when you had a workable idea?

ch 22. Bursting Your Shell

The first time I saw a chambered nautilus cut in half so the insides showed, I was astonished. What I had thought was a continuous spiral, like the smoothly curved channel inside a tuba, was actually a series of rooms—"rooms of pearl" as Oliver Wendell Holmes called them in his poem "The Chambered Nautilus." Most remarkable was the fact that each room grew larger the closer it was to the outside. As the creature developed it had made a new, more spacious container for itself. Each room was larger than the last. Each room made way for further growth.

You experience the same process as your creativity develops and you build new mental space to accommodate your growth. Without the new space, growth is restricted and creativity is crippled. Do you remember the tiny tables and chairs you used to occupy in kindergarten? What if you were still sitting there as your body grew and matured? You'd either get stuck, or you'd realize when your seat no

A STRATEGY

TO EXPAND

YOUR CREATIVE

COMFORT ZONE

SEED THOUGHT

" May your
trails be
crooked, winding,
lonesome, dangerous,
leading to the most
amazing view."

Edward Abbey

longer fit in the chair and your legs pressed the underside of the table that it was time to move on.

A writer told me about a time when he had reached this point. The copywriting job at an ad agency that had at first excited him now seemed boring. He didn't feel challenged. Projects he was working on were the same month after month, year after year. Though he'd often dreamed of starting his own business, where he could pursue the kind of clients he'd like to work with, he kept putting off the decision. The ad agency was comfortable. He liked the people he worked with. They liked him and respected his work. The pearly cell was closing in on him, constricting his creative growth. To get out, he had to build a new, larger room—maybe a room that would hold a business. He had to take a leap of faith.

I have on my bulletin board, among fading vacation snapshots, famous quotations and torn newspaper clippings, a greeting card that illustrates just such a leap. It makes my corpuscles laugh every time I see it. A black-and-white photo on the front of the card shows a man in a three-piece suit and a bowler hat caught in the midst of a leap over a puddle on a downtown Manhattan street. It is obvious, even on first glance, that the puddle is too broad and the leap too short. He is not going to make it. But his face wears an arresting look of undeterred faith. Here he is in his polished shoes and his best suit and fancy derby, and he is about to splash into a muddy puddle. Every time I see this photo, I'm intrigued. He must have known he couldn't make it. Why did he try? Was it really a leap of faith? He had seen where he wanted to go, and he gave it his best shot. In the middle of that leap, anything could have happened: The puddle could have drained away, or a strong gust could have carried him across. Either way his gutsiness is impressive.

Gutsiness is a creative requirement. To be creative, you have to have guts enough to expand your comfort zone. This is the zone we usually live in, an invisible fence that hems us in and prevents us from moving into that more spacious pearly room or taking a leap of faith, successful or not. If we're always cozy and comfortable, we're probably not living up to our creative potential. Look at it this way: Unless you're making someone, including yourself, uncomfortable, you're probably not being very creative. I'm not talking about anything illegal or immoral or even anything deliberately bizarre. What I mean is the act of pushing your comfort limits—gently, to stretch your creative experience to begin to build that more spacious, pearly room.

When is the last time you planned an adventure? Learned something new? Did something perfectly normal that scared you silly? The more you dare to expand your experience, the more creative you can be. You don't need to think about whether or not the new thing will be useful. There is usefulness in the attempt alone, as our puddle leaper demonstrated.

A guy I know borrowed my friend Harriet's sewing machine so he could learn how to sew. "In the process, I created new curtains for the bedroom," he said, "but that wasn't the point. The point was to learn something new—to learn something I'd never normally even *think* of learning." The learning itself is the lesson, but you never know when such learning will be just what you need.

The creator of a TV commercial for a national toilet tissue brand apparently hasn't taken this message to heart. In the commercial, three cartoon women are busy quilting the toilet tissue—with *knitting* needles! Within a few weeks, the commercial disappeared and was replaced by one showing the women using sewing needles for their quilting. (Oops!)

I have tried to imagine the commercial creator. Was it a woman who lived in New York City and jogged in Central Park and kept a potted plant in the window—a woman who had never made a quilt or seen someone else make one? Or was it a man who might not have tried the craft even if he had the chance because—unlike my friend who made curtains—he thought quilting was a "woman thing"? Obviously, in the commercial creator's defense, we can't know everything. But whatever we do know firsthand will help prevent us from making the knitting needle goof.

One reason we don't try new things is that we think we have to be experts before we start. Sometimes that's true. I wouldn't recommend attempting brain surgery before you've had the right training. You may also want some thorough instruction in such things as high-wire acrobatics and bridge building and rocket launching before you try your hand. Beyond these exceptions, a whole universe of discovery can be made through the creative leap called trial and error.

Though the opportunity probably wouldn't come to a novice these days, I once wrote a musical commercial for a carpet store sponsor at the radio station where I worked. I'm about as musically talented as a stone. By way of proof, a dulcimer that has only been strummed to play an off-key "My Dog Has Fleas" and other compositions of similar difficulty now sits in the corner of my living room. So the sponsor was not exactly getting a pro.

Nonetheless, I began to write words extolling the company's broadloom as musical notes tinked away in my head. Later, I hummed the imagined melody to an assorted crew of station staff who just happened to be able to sing or play an instrument and were willing to get together to give it a try. We sounded, starting out, like a kindergarten band tuning up. Surprisingly, the sponsor liked the finished commercial and ran it long enough to drive the control room announcer slightly over the edge. No one had told us, as no one had told the puddle leaper, that what we had set out to do couldn't be done. If we'd thought that, we couldn't have done it.

Creativity is the ability to meet a seemingly impossible situation and stretch yourself to fit; and just like the stretches you do before a long run or an exercise session, you can do practice stretches to warm up and keep in shape creatively. "I always repot myself whenever I get too root bound and comfortable," a poet told me. "The repotting can take many forms. Sometimes I pack up and move to a new place. Sometimes I take a class in glassblowing or kickboxing or flower arranging or Greek history. Sometimes I just take a walk around the block. I try to keep myself on my toes. It's dangerous to my creative ability to get too comfy."

Breaking out of your shell, nautilus or otherwise, is an effort aimed at expanding your comfort zone so you won't get "too comfy." The effort to expand necessarily involves discomfort. Like Homer Simpson in the TV cartoon *The Simpsons*, you prefer your old corner of the sofa because you've sat there so long it has come to take on the shape of your body. It's easier just to stay put.

I once heard a story of a man who was searching for a lost key under a streetlight. A friend happened by and asked the man what he was looking for. "My key," the man said. "Where did you lose it?" the friend asked. "Over there, in the bushes," the man said, pointing to a place in the shadows several yards away. "Why are you looking here, under the streetlamp?" the friend asked, perplexed. "The light is much better here," the man said.

We look for creative inspiration, too, where the light is better, where we feel more comfortable. To step out of the old pearly room, the one that has become too small and constricts our growth, is to step into unknown space, dark and uncomfortable. Breaking into that larger space requires no less than a leap of faith—a leap much like vaulting a broad mud puddle.

YOUR COMFORT INDEX

Directions: Circle "ℭ" for comfortable or "𝒰" for uncomfortable for each item in the list below. Where does most of your discomfort lie? Are these areas you'd like to work on? Write about ways you could do this (take a class, discuss with a friend, join a group, design your own program). Write a page outlining your plans and how you'll put them to use.

ℭ 𝒰 being alone with myself and liking it

ℭ 𝒰 setting my own goals

ℭ 𝒰 speaking before a group

ℭ 𝒰 asking a favor of a friend, stranger or family member

ℭ 𝒰 refusing an unwanted invitation

ℭ 𝒰 refusing a request from a friend or associate

ℭ 𝒰 terminating an overly long phone call

ℭ 𝒰 standing up to an aggressive, steamroller-type person

ℭ 𝒰 revealing my feelings to family, friends and others

ℭ 𝒰 stating an opinion contrary to others'

ℭ 𝒰 expressing affection in words and actions

ℭ 𝒰 accepting myself "warts and all"

ℭ 𝒰 using and expanding my abilities and talents

ℭ 𝒰 taking a constructive risk

ℭ 𝒰 experiencing failure

C U relying on myself, not always on others, for affirmation

C U meeting new people; talking with people I've just met

C U moving to a new city; going to a strange place

C U allowing others to be their true selves

C U fulfilling my own needs (not expecting others to)

C U accepting a compliment

C U accepting criticism

C U telling a friend or family member when I am hurt

C U being in charge of a group

C U terminating an unrewarding relationship

C U saying no without feeling guilty

C U going somewhere alone

C U complimenting or giving strokes to others

C U taking responsibility for my actions (not blaming others, circumstances, etc.)

C U feeling free to change my mind

C U completing started projects (or writing them off once and for all)

C U taking time *regularly* for myself and my interests

C U pursuing an interest no one else shares

C U complaining about inferior service

C U saying something good about myself

C U disciplining children, employees

C U criticizing another person and pointing out offensive behavior

C U making the first move to introduce myself at a party

C U coping with new situations (job interview, travel, moving, etc.)

C U feeling good about how I look

C U resisting comparing myself to others

C U saying no to myself (with regard to overeating, over-spending, etc.)

C U standing up to someone who puts me down

C U thinking positively in crisis situations

C U dealing with someone who doesn't consider my rights

C U making a decision

Explorations

❧ What kind of people make you feel uncomfortable? Why? Write a dialogue between yourself and one of these people. Express your feelings, and let the other person respond. Did this interchange give you any new insights into the source of your discomfort? Does it have roots in the past? Write about what you discovered.

❧ When the weather is warm enough so you won't freeze and cool enough so you won't melt, try going without electricity for a day. (You can keep your refrigerator plugged in and use candles, a flashlight and a battery-operated radio, but no fair eating out or going to someone's house to watch TV.) Write about how you coped. What was the hardest part? Were there any pleasant surprises? Unpleasant ones? How did it feel to go back to electricity again? What did this experiment tell you about your ability to stretch your comfort zone?

Field Trip

❧ Visit a place that stretches your comfort zone—someplace you've never been before, such as a tattoo parlor, a soap factory, a nursing home, a landfill or an unemployment office. You can get ideas by thumbing through the yellow pages. Take a notebook when you set out on this field trip, and jot down what you see and hear and feel. Later, write about your experience and how it affected your comfort zone.

23. Deliberate Ridiculousness

Absurdity is creativity's next-door neighbor. You can't be creative unless what you do is unique enough to tempt at least one person to say, "That's ridiculous!" Giving yourself the freedom to be ridiculous creates wide-open spaces where your ideas have room to roam and develop and feed each other.

Geralyn Curtis, founder of Chesapeake Group, Inc., tells how her prospering six-year-old Cincinnati-based package design company had its origins in absurdity. "I was working for another design company and was stuck on the tarmac waiting for a flight to take off for Boston, where I was going to make a pitch to Dunkin' Donuts for a design contract," Curtis tells. "While I was sitting there, I was thinking about what a design company really ought to be. Businesses often are run in ways that inhibit creativity. I saw a company with no titles, no time sheets—a company that nurtures creative people."

BUMP UP AN

ORDINARY IDEA

AND TAME AN

OUTRAGEOUS ONE

But the idea seemed like wishful thinking. Absurd. Too airy for real life. "I knew if I could come up with a name for the company, that would make it more real and get me going," Curtis says. She thought about rivers, lakes and bodies of water that are life-giving symbols of creativity in its ever-changing process. "For some reason I thought the Chesapeake Bay was near Boston, and I liked the name. It was easy to say. Once I named the company the idea took hold. A whole philosophy began to emerge from this."

From seemingly ridiculous ruminations in a plane on an air-port tarmac she created the idea of a new company. "You have to take something to the ridiculous level to begin with so you can see its full potential," Curtis says. "Otherwise you just grab an old idea and try to dust it off rather than think of a new approach. Actually, to call an idea ridiculous is a judgment—a prejudgment—and you can't create and judge at the same time."

Instead of creating a new company from the confines of her seat on a grounded plane, Curtis could have told herself, This idea is absurd. I have a good job. What proof do I have that this idea would work? Could I really run a business like this? Like many of us do with creative ideas, she could have killed her innovation before it lived long enough to deliver its message and inspire action.

Creativity is, by definition, a departure. Usually, it's a huge departure from what we've come to accept. Walt Whitman, for exam-ple, had to publish *Leaves of Grass* at his own expense because it was rejected by publishers as too controversial for Victorian tastes. Even though Whitman was hailed later as "the most original and passionate American poet," and poets and revolutionaries saw him as a hero, his work was seen at first as too bizarre for the appetites of regular readers. If Whitman hadn't believed in himself and allowed his unusual ideas to live, the world would have been denied a considerable gift.

To allow an idea to live, you must treat it with as much re-spect as you would an unconventional stranger who could, if you got to know her, become a friend. New ideas face the greatest danger of becoming casualties of rejection. This idea is too blah. That idea is too bizarre. Slam! The door gets closed in its face, and it never gets a chance to become a valued friend capable of the most wondrous feats.

Instead of rejecting an idea out of hand, pause. Give it a minute to sink in, to change its clothes, to perform its song and dance. Think about why some ideas don't click. They belong to two clans. In the first clan are boring old ideas that couldn't raise an eyebrow even with a facelift. These ideas need rethinking to give them some jazz. The second clan, at least at first look, appears to be too ridiculous to be workable. They need to be unbuttoned to expose each one's heart and learn what makes it tick.

Bump Up an Ordinary Idea

Boring ordinary ideas don't go far enough. They end up being a hackneyed replay of an old way of doing something. They don't command attention. Let's say you want to sell your car. You park it in the front yard, if the neighborhood allows such things, and plop a sign on the windshield: "For Sale." You're finished. This is the old, accepted, uncreative way everybody follows. But last week I saw a car for sale whose seller had gone a step further. There was a huge red bow tied to the top of the car. What's the unspoken message now? It says, Here's a wonderful car in such good condition you could give it as a gift. The red bow carried the idea a step beyond the ordinary.

There are lots of ways to bump up an idea. Here are a few:

1 **MAKE IT BIGGER OR SMALLER.** A writer I once knew had always wanted to be a book publisher but feared she couldn't compete with the biggies. She put her dream in mothballs. One Christmas, as a special gift for her sister's children, she wrote a story about a mouse and made it into a miniature book, about the size of a gift enclosure card. The children loved the book so much, she hit on an idea: Why not publish miniature books? Here she could have the field almost completely to herself. With little competition, her company flourished, and she went on to publish many titles, some as small as a postage stamp but still readable for those with good eyesight. She had taken an ordinary idea and made it smaller. Conversely she could have made the book bigger than usual—with large type for people whose eyesight needs assistance.

2 ADD TO IT; REMOVE FROM IT. Some years ago, the Art Academy of Cincinnati staged a promotion at a shopping mall featuring a quickie class in making greeting cards. Passersby could sit at a table surrounded by colored papers, ribbon, string, feathers and bits of lace and use them to put together, with an instructor's help, a card.

One man worked for a minute or two and then said, "I give up. I guess this just isn't my thing." The instructor told him he hadn't gone far enough. "Keep adding a few more things. Try different textures and color harmonies. Make a center of interest. Keep going until the piece feels finished." The man looked doubtful, but he kept working on the card. Finally he turned to his son and blurted, "Hey, look at this! It turned out after all, and not too bad, if I do say so!" The man had continued to add to what he was ready to dismiss as an unsuccessful project, just as the car owner had added a red bow to what might have become an unsuccessful sales effort.

Does your project need a finishing touch? Could something be added? Is something there that's unnecessary or that doesn't belong? Ask yourself these questions to keep from quitting too soon.

3 DO THE OPPOSITE OF WHAT'S EXPECTED. There's a retaining wall on a busy street in our town that was continually defaced by graffiti. It always looked a mess. Maintenance crews tried whitewash, paint remover—everything they could think of. Police stepped up their patrols to no avail. The minute everyone's backs were turned, the vandals spray-painted a new layer of graffiti. Then someone came up with a novel idea: If we can't stop them, why not encourage them to do more of what they're already doing? A few of the perpetrators were invited to produce a mural based upon their ethnic heritage: athletic heroes, musicians, people they respected. The mural has been in place for at least a decade. It has been repainted a few times, but since the mural went up there's never been the slightest blip of graffiti to deface the wall. Doing the opposite of what's ordinarily expected succeeded where other efforts had failed.

4 GO THE EXTRA STEP. I once told a friend that I liked to make microwave tea with fresh ginger cut into half-inch cubes but the

SEED THOUGHT

"*The act of being* deliberately ridiculous is the whole heart of creative excitement. It creates freedom. It's a way of energizing something that can later be tamed."

Geralyn Curtis
Chesapeake Group, Inc.

gingeryness wasn't flavoring the water enough. The friend suggested I "stick a toothpick through the ginger cube." That would work, to a degree, but it would be tedious to punch enough holes to do any good.

We could have discarded the idea. Instead, we built on it. What was it about the toothpick idea that had merit? Holes. Breaking down the cube to release more of its flavor. Why not use a garlic press or whomp it with a meat-tenderizing mallet? We came up with two good ideas in a few minutes by going one step further, building on an ordinary idea to put the extra touch of creative frosting on the cake—or the ginger cube.

These are a few ways to jazz up a ho-hum idea. They work in any media, whether you're struggling with a novel, a poem, a painting or just a better way to make ginger tea. If you learn to see the ordinary as just an idea in need of completion, as a work in progress, you're halfway home.

Tame an Outrageous Idea

But what about ideas that are, already, as the English say, "over the top"? These are ideas that immediately get tossed aside because they seem too far-fetched to be useful. Before you add your own original ideas to the scrap heap, give them another chance.

Creative ideas always have at least a thimbleful of ridiculous impracticality in them. If they didn't, they wouldn't be creative. In nearly every ridiculous, outrageous, bizarre, impractical idea there's at least one N.O.B. (Nugget of Brilliance). If you search for and find this nugget at the heart of your most preposterous idea, you'll know how to put the idea to use. Let's consider the classic story of the slow elevators to see how this works. (I've heard the story so many times that I'm not sure where it originated.) The elevators in a high-rise office building ran slowly. People complained. Engineers couldn't find a way to speed up the elevators, and there was no room to add more, so management called in a group of creative people to brainstorm ideas. One idea proposed was to have a circus in the lobby so people would be entertained and not notice the slow elevators.

There were a dozen reasons, of course, why this idea wasn't practical. The lobby was already overcrowded with people waiting for elevators. Circus animals were messy. Lions and tigers in close quarters might eat the clientele. Building managers could have rejected the idea as bizarre and unworkable, but they didn't. Instead they looked for the N.O.B. in the idea.

The N.O.B. was that a circus could distract and entertain people until they could be whisked away by the elevator. A circus was just one way. Management and the creative people finally chose a distraction that was practical *and* creative: install mirrors in the lobby. Mirrors, the story goes, did the trick. Office workers were entertained by watching themselves and each other in the mirrors and didn't seem to notice how slow the elevator system was. There were no more complaints.

Usually, bizarre ideas need taming, but sometimes they work just the way they are. As a case in point, Joe Webb tells in his Cincinnati *HomeTown* TV series about red-lensed goggles for chickens. When chickens get to feeling feisty, they peck each other. The sight of blood can send them into an aggressive frenzy that ends in a pecking to death, causing substantial losses for the poultry raiser. The solution, a bright idea of National Band & Tag Company's founder, Joseph Haas, was to manufacture red-lensed goggles for chickens.

The goggles looked funny, but they worked. The chickens saw everything as red, so the sight of blood didn't result in chicken mayhem. The bizarre idea worked. Later, a new solution was developed—simply clipping the chickens' beaks as one might clip a fingernail—and the red-lensed goggles were discontinued, but not before they sparked more creative thinking.

Bizarre ideas, like boring ones, can be made to work if they're not immediately rejected. The trick is to see value in every creative brainchild, no matter how outrageous or mundane. When you're stuck on an airport runway or waiting for an elevator or driving to work, let the crazy innovations and the ordinary ideas come. Welcome them. Sit on them like a chicken sits on an egg. Know that when they hatch and grow, they can make elevators seem to run faster, produce new companies that take off and thrive, and help chickens behave more politely.

Explorations

❧ Practice hatching absurd ideas. Write down five problems in your work or personal life, and spend ten minutes on each one listing ideas for solving them. Pull out all the stops. Let your bizarre, crazy, funny ideas flow. Write at length about how one of the ideas could be tamed and put to use.

❧ With a group of five or six or on your own, review the problem list above or list five challenges facing your community, workplace or organization. What unsuccessful attempts have been made to solve these problems? Why didn't the methods work? How could they be bumped up to give them a greater chance of success? Write your ideas. If you're working with a group, share and discuss.

Project

❧ Make two separate files. Label one file "Ridiculous Ideas." Put all your bizarre ideas in it as they come up. Jot them in as much detail as possible on small slips of paper. On the back of the paper, write why the idea is ridiculous or ought to be dismissed as undoable (like a circus in a building lobby), then write the N.O.B. (Nugget of Brilliance) contained in each idea. Title the second file "Ordinary Ideas." In this file keep lists of ideas that didn't work or weren't very innovative. Use these two files to work on taming ridiculous ideas and bumping up ordinary ones.

ch. 24. Learning to Wiggle

The problem is, we don't trust ourselves. We have little faith in that creative part of ourselves that asks us to dance and gently suggests taking the lead. To enter the dance, to flow along with the creative process, you have to let go, move to the music and improvise as you go along. You have to wiggle around a little. We're often uncomfortable with wiggling.

American author and spiritual teacher Alan Watts said, "It seems that rigid people feel some basic disgust with wiggles; they cannot dance without seeing a diagram of the steps and feel that swinging the hips is obscene." We've been taught, at least to some degree, that rigid is good. Nice people don't swing their hips. It's important to stay in control and plan everything in advance—every step, beginning to end. In our compulsive need to preplan a goal, step by tedious step, we don't allow the creative work to have its say along the way or, heaven forbid, allow it to lend a hand in our efforts. Like lemmings in a

TO BE
MORE CREATIVE,
LOOSEN UP!

SEED THOUGHT

"The process has an intelligence that can be trusted, and the gift of creation is the ability to work with it."

Shaun McNiff
Trust the Process

relentless march to sea, we're so obsessed with getting there that we forget about the trip. We keep all the wiggle out of our lives.

How did we get this way? Our whole cultural network is in cahoots to teach us the "right" way: First you learn how, then you do. Plan ahead. Focus on the goal. Almost no one tells us that doing can also be a way of learning. The process itself can teach if we loosen our stranglehold enough to let it. Many writers and other creative people get bogged down because they cling so tightly to control that they can't dance in rhythm with the creative process.

The creative process is like a stream. It flows. If you let your boat be carried along, you never know where the stream will take you. One writer told me he starts off writing about one thing and often ends up on an entirely different subject. "I like to go to different places to write, and when I get there something I see gives me an idea. I once sat out on my porch writing about the tall maples in the backyard and ended up writing about my father—his strength and the way he kept the family together in difficult times." Anything can be the inspiration; once you start, just let the inspiration take you where *it* wants to go. Giving up control and allowing the process to have its own way removes a lot of stress. You can always edit later.

A piece of writing or a painting has a life of its own. What you had envisioned and what results in the end are almost never the same. Sometimes words come out of a pen or keyboard or images come out of a brush as if they'd been imprisoned there, waiting for release. They surprise even their maker.

"The inner dream and the objective fact can never permanently coincide. They can only interact," Joanna Field says in *On Not Being Able to Paint*. The two have to dance together. There's a certain arrogance in assuming we write or paint or create all by ourselves. A helper stands at our elbow ready to assist; we just have to step aside to let it. Give in and let the process lead. When this happens, we're in unmapped territory following a fragile path of bread crumbs.

People tend to get anxious on such a path. They want more direction. They want a preprinted map of all the twists and turns. In writing and art classes, I deliberately hide the map and withhold direction on the theory that doing alone can give guidance and can lead to places unimaginable beforehand. One project I propose is building a three-dimensional object from cardboard using just scissors, no glue. Someone always asks how to do it. I reply that the object is to find out how to do it as you go along. Some students discover that their creations collapse, and they have to find a way to keep the structures from toppling over. Others find that some of the pieces are boring and cut holes in them to make them more visually arresting. In twenty minutes, after much trial and error, they create the most amazing objects! They've learned to take part in the process, to wiggle their way out.

There were a couple of writers in one class. They said it was helpful to experience visually and manually how the creative process works. "When I can actually see and feel what it's like to get deeply into something and work out the kinks as I go along, I can apply those same principles to my writing and other creative work. I can even apply it to my life. I don't always have to know ahead of time how everything will turn out. I don't have to control everything," one of the writers said.

Keeping the ultimate goal in the back of your mind while you let go and enter the creative process is a lot like trying to pat your head while rubbing your stomach. It's hard to do both at the same time. Because the creative process is subtle and hard to define, it requires concentration to maintain momentum. Without concentration, the process gets lost. The stream goes on without you. "I can usually tell when I'm really immersed in the work," one writer says. "But when I wander away, it's hard to find my way back again."

One force that can jerk you right out of the process like a wiggly trout at the end of a fishhook is placing too much importance on the results of your work: focusing on the goal and paying little attention to the experience as it unfolds and changes.

A few summers ago, I was hooked by just such a dilemma. No matter how many times I recite the litany in class that process will carry you if you relax and enjoy the trip, I have to keep learning the lesson over and over. It never sinks in once and for all. In this case, I had the go-ahead to write an article for a humanities journal I'd long admired. The brainchild of two M.D.s who also happened to be extremely accomplished writers, the journal had national circulation. I was intimidated down to my socks.

That summer I spent months writing and rewriting an article that should have taken a few days at most. The goal loomed large. This piece had to be really good. Finally, in desperation, after more drafts and rewrites than I could count, I asked a friend for feedback. "It's OK," she said. "It's even good, but there's an awful lot of blood on it." The process, my revered dancing partner, had deserted me. I had tried too hard again. Because I hadn't lost myself in the writing, let go, given up control, I'd lost my ability to dance. I'd become too rigid to wiggle, and it showed.

There are only two things to remember about staying in the process: Maintain contact and lose control.

Maintaining contact with your creative expression at every point in the process is like white heat that dispels mental fog. Your entire self is invested in what you're doing. You can tell by the fact that you lose track of time. Hours go by like minutes. Does this sound familiar? If not, maybe you should ask yourself whether you really want to do this project.

A newsletter editor I once worked with told me she was having trouble writing an article about a board meeting at one of the facilities. No matter how hard she tried, nothing would come. "Are you interested in the subject?" I asked. "No, it's boring," she said. "Well then, ask yourself if there's anything about the subject that's interesting. If not, write about something else." A few minutes later the editor returned and spouted, "I finished the article! Once I forgot about just getting it done and started to think about what was interesting, I could get into the writing."

There are lots of ways to create contact. My poet friend Lynn says she needs to write by hand. "I can't create on a computer because it's too distancing. I need the intimate contact and the slowed pace of writing on a yellow legal pad in my lap." Other writers and creative people have developed rituals to warm up and lose themselves in the process. Some lay out their equipment in a special way or work in a particular place that triggers the creative response. One writer plays a tape of Sousa marches to summon his muse.

Losing control seems like the opposite of maintaining contact. Is it possible to do both at the same time? To demonstrate, I sometimes have classes try out a practice called "push hands" that I learned years ago from a tai chi instructor. Two people stand facing each other, arms bent with palms forward and nearly touching. Then each person moves her palms while at the same time following the other's moves—all without speaking and all the while keeping their hands palm to palm, nearly touching. The object is to give up control and follow the other person's motion while maintaining contact with one's own. Like patting your head and rubbing your stomach, it's difficult to do both at the same time.

When you apply the ritual of push hands to your other creative work, you can take your foot off the brakes and surrender to whatever comes. The process carries you. It allows you to welcome mistakes, and even failures, because they are part of the creative process. You feel free enough to start in the middle, write nonsense, improvise, wiggle with playfulness.

When you loosen your hold on the creative process, you also reduce the importance of the ultimate goal. You're free to explore the back roads and enjoy the trip as well as the arrival. You don't need to preplan quite so much.

"It's like the time I spent the Fourth of July weekend at a bed-and-breakfast north of Columbus," a workshop participant once told me. "To get there, I took the four-lane interstate. I was in a hurry. All I could think about was getting there. But after I'd spent a couple of days relaxing, I didn't feel like facing that seventy-mile-an-hour traffic, so I took a road that was just a faint squiggle on the map. It wound through a tiny town where the citizens were having ice cream socials and picnics on the green. In a gazebo in one town's square, a brass band played patriotic marches. It took me four hours longer to get home, including the stop for ice cream; but I enjoyed the trip, and I learned a lot."

The creative process is the trip, not just the destination. It's the ability to go with the stream, make changes as you go along and be in intimate contact with the unfolding of your work without losing sight of your destination. When you're in the process you don't have to preplan too much. You don't need to know exactly where you're going. You can trust yourself to read the instructions, then set them aside and go your own way—with a little wiggle in your step.

Explorations

❧ Set aside at least an hour where you can be alone without interruption. Get ready to write by performing any rituals that help you get into the mood: moving to music, taking a walk, reading a few favorite passages. Gather pad, pens, etc. Sit down and write spontaneously for an hour about the first thing you see—your desk, a picture on the wall, the zipper on your sweatshirt. Let the process carry you wherever it wants to go. (Don't worry if beginning to describe the zipper on your sweatshirt leads you to write about a walk along the beach. Just welcome whatever comes.) When you're finished, write for ten more minutes about the process itself. How was this experience different from your usual writing? Where did you hesitate or stop altogether? What was going on in your mind? Did you feel a perceptual shift?

❧ Find someone who is willing to do the push hands exercise with you. Stand and face each other, fingers pointing up, palms out and about an inch apart. *Slowly* move your hands to match each other's motions. Continue for five minutes without speaking, then write about your experience. Share what you wrote. What did you learn about process?

Recollection

❧ Remember a project that you were so immersed in that time seemed to stand still. Write about your feelings, thoughts, fears and pleasures. What were you doing? Did the project turn out as you expected? Were you disappointed? Elated? Frustrated?

Project

❧ Mold in clay or draw on paper an image of a person, animal or thing that represents your creative muse. Write a dialogue with it. Place it in your work space to remind you of the dance between your muse and you.

Site Write

❧ To remove the paralyzing effects of self-judgment and intense pursuit of a goal, set aside an hour to write just for yourself. Find a setting you really enjoy: a rented rowboat on a lake, a tent in the mountains, a bench in the park, a folding chair on a hillside overlooking the river. Write with enjoyment about whatever comes to mind. Immerse yourself in the process. Don't worry about grammar, spelling or organization. Just write. Let your writing take whatever form it wants: poetry, fiction, prose, haiku or some new form you invent on the spot. Repeat this process once a week or whenever you can spare the time and spur enough energy.

25. How a Man Jumped Off a Building

A Hollywood stuntman once described how he learned to jump off tall buildings. "First you jump off the curbing," he said. "Then you practice jumping from a chair, then from the roof of your garage. You practice each step. You increase your challenge, little by little, until you get to where you want to be." The point is that the stuntman didn't start out jumping from a five-story building. He divided his goal into doable steps, and he practiced.

When we see him spring in a gutsy leap from the roof of the Last Chance Saloon to the back of a saddled palomino, we forget about the steps and the practice. We say, "Whoa! I could never do that!" It's a phrase I often hear in classes. People compare the place where they're standing—on a six-inch curb, contemplating their first leap—to that of the accomplished stunt person sailing through the air from five stories high. They forget that the stunt jumper once stood at the very same height and practiced elementary risk.

RISK PRACTICE,

STEP-BY-STEP

You have to start from where you are. It's as simple as that. You can't skip a few steps before you try a high leap or you'll break your neck. Philosopher Friedrich Nietzsche once said, "When I ascend I often jump over steps, and no step forgives me that." Trying to leap over steps keeps us creatively stuck.

A woman in a writing class was about to read what she'd written, but the man who had read before her had left us all dumb with admiration over his moving description of a childhood memory. "I could never write like that," the woman said. The man had been writing for years and understood how she felt. He turned to her and said, "I should hope you wouldn't write like that. Rather, I should hope you would write like *you*."

You have to take your own creative risks; start from where you are and move from the curbing to the chair. I'm told that novice mountain climbers are instructed not to look down. That way they have to focus on where they're going, to build on their strengths and to inch upward little by little. I often cite this example in classes when someone says, "I wish I could write like Arthur Rimbaud." Look up at Rimbaud. Climb toward Rimbaud. But inch up slowly so you don't fall off the mountain.

Why take risks at all? Why not just curl up in your sleeping bag by the toasty fire at base camp? No one says you have to climb Mount Everest, and if you tell anyone you want to, they'll try to talk you out of it anyway. Each of us has an Everest, a creative mountain we're itching to climb. It could be the chapbook of poems you've dreamed of having published. It could be the life experiences you're longing to write about or the two-week painting class in Maine you're aching to take. You feel if you don't try to climb your mountain you'll miss something important. You will.

Jeff Bezos, head of Amazon.com and said to be worth ten billion dollars or so, operates within what he calls a "regret minimalization framework." He says he doesn't want to look back with regret someday over what he hasn't done. Viewing every creative challenge from the point of view "Will I be sorry if I pass up this chance?" keeps him inching up the mountain. When you're motivated by regret minimalization you don't want to look back on missed opportunities, even if they don't turn out the way you'd hoped.

To check out Bezos's theory, I've been conducting an unscientific survey to see what people regret most about their pasts. So far, the polls are running overwhelmingly toward regret for something not done as opposed to feeling sorry for a mistake. Here are some of the more interesting responses: I regret

- turning down a chance to dye my hair brunette and be a model for a weeklong fashion photography shoot on a cruise ship
- declining a request to fill in for a TV talk show host
- not pursuing my goal of becoming a playwright like I'd always wanted to be
- missing an opportunity to fly to Paris for a few days on a friend's special low-fare airline ticket
- entering a well-paid career I didn't like and giving up my dream of being a sculptor

People's regrets fall into two groups: missed adventures and derailed creative opportunities.

The *missed adventures* could have fueled creativity by supplying a rich source of experiences to draw from. A writer could have created an article or a novel about a white-water rafting trip. A painter could have used a weekend campout as a springboard to new work. Adventures involve taking risks: risks that jeopardize old habits, reconfigure long-held attitudes and, plain and simple, just make you feel uncomfortable in unfamiliar territory. Risks push your envelope.

The risks don't have to be supersize. Rearranging your creative work space can be a small risk to your conventional way of dong things. You can up the ante by going a step further. Maybe you decide to paint the walls red even though you've heard a red room can drive you crazy. Or maybe you decide to cut off the back half of a small evergreen tree, as a friend of mine once did, and nail it to the ceiling so you have something to look at if you happen to look up. Some may think that's stupid, but as *The Simpsons* character Bart Simpson says, "Stupid risks are what make life worth living."

This is not to say you should take up high-wire walking or

SEED THOUGHT

"So be sure
when you step
Step with care
and great tact
And remember
that Life's
A Great
Balancing Act."

Dr. Seuss
Oh, the Places You'll Go!

skydiving or bungee jumping from bridges where at least forty-six people have been killed. There's a big difference between taking risks and thrill seeking. Thrill seeking aims for a death-defying high. Creative risks aim toward helping you define who you are as a creative person. Positive risk helps you discover your strengths and limits.

The other kind of regrets people mentioned in my survey were their *derailed creative opportunities*. Being a creative person is risky. Lack of nerve can be a greater barrier to innovation than lack of talent.

A magazine writer once told me that it took her nearly twenty years to make her way to the career she loved. "My parents tried to talk me out of becoming a writer," she said. "They thought I should be a secretary or a teacher so I'd have a dependable income. I ended up getting a teaching degree and spending half my working life instructing high school English classes. One day I woke up to the fact that if I was going to be a writer, I'd better hop to it. So, despite my trepidation, I did it. I took the leap." She started small, writing as a part-time reporter for the local paper. Then, with published clips, she approached a few regional magazines and, finally, the biggies.

Marsha Sinetar, author of the popular career guidebook *Do What You Love, the Money Will Follow*, says, "All of us can take steps—no matter how small and insignificant at the start—in the direction we want to go." It's comforting to know that you don't have to get there all at once. All you have to do is to take the next step. In fact, if you look too long at the whole mountain you aim to climb without thinking about the next step, you might not be able to climb it at all. You'll be frozen into inaction. The task will seem too great.

I love the story my mother used to tell about how her uncle Anton taught her to cut a formidable project down to size. Newly arrived from Sweden, untutored in English and already getting on in years, Uncle Anton took a job at a gravel pit to pay his room and board. One day my mother and Aunt Vi stopped by the work site to see what he was doing.

"There he stood beside a mountain of sand," my mother remembered, "shoveling it bit by bit into a wheelbarrow and hauling it to another place." My mother looked up to take in the enormous pile of sand that stood waiting. She was awestruck by the size of the task.

"Uncle, how are you ever going to move all that sand?" she asked. "My dear, I plan to do it one shovelful at a time," he said.

The bigger the goal, the more ferocious the dragon. Start with a small dragon. It's easier to tame.

A woman told me she'd always wanted to write a novel using as the background a two-year stay in Africa. But she just couldn't get started. The thought of writing several hundred pages stopped her cold in her tracks. "Then I realized that if I wrote only one page a day, I'd have over three hundred pages by the end of a year. Instead of thinking of the whole book, I just pictured the project page by page. That got me started." Without realizing it, she had determined what she needed to be comfortable with the risk she wanted to take.

Not that you can completely remove the anxiety of risk. A few stomach butterflies come with the territory. As David Viscott writes in *Risking*, "If you have no anxiety, the risk you take is probably not worthy of you." You just need to ask, as our writer did, "What do I need to help make my anxiety manageable?" Here are some ideas from writers and other creative people:

1 **DIVIDE THE TASK.** What's the first, curb-level step? If that's still too threatening, divide it again. Let's say you'd like to write a column for a local paper. First step: Write a sample column, and contact the paper. Still too scary? New first step: Subscribe to the paper, review several issues to find the editor's name and study the publication's style.

2 **GET HELPERS AND COLLABORATORS.** Is the project too formidable to tackle alone? Find a coauthor to help write or a business manager to organize your finances or a marketer to sell your crafts. Organize a think tank to share ideas and critique. Find cheerleaders and nags to keep you going. Read your writing aloud to others. Have an open house to show your artwork.

3 **SCHEDULE YOUR PROGRESS.** All the planning in the world won't move you one step closer to climbing your mountain. What day, hour, minute will you actually gear up and go? Write it down.

Tape it to your refrigerator door. Rewrite steps as you go along, if you need to.

4 **HOLD A TRIAL RUN.** Practice. Even NASA does this. So do Olympic figure skaters, who wear harnesses to learn their jumps and flips so they don't crack their heads on the ice. Write a rough draft, do a thumbnail, play with colors and shapes, cut a model sculpture from a bar of soap. Try out your creative ideas to see what works and what doesn't. An attitude of investigation rather than mountainous expectation reduces performance paralysis— what some call stage fright.

5 **REWARD YOURSELF.** "If I finish this chapter (or draft or painting or poem), I'll thank myself with an hour-long bubble bath, a walk in the woods, dinner out—no cooking." Write down your reward: "I owe you _____." Fill in the requirements and the promise. Sign it. Date it. Then get to work.

This is not a foolproof system. Risk takers have been known to take pratfalls even from curb level. Applaud yourself wholeheartedly for trying, whether you succeed or not. Dr. Seuss sent out his first book more than fifty times before he found a publisher. I know a number of creative people who have failed grandly time and again, but they continued to take risks. Mistakes and misfires are just as important to creative expression as right-on-target hits.

Before you jump from the roof of the Last Chance Saloon, you have to practice in ever increasing steps. But you can start right here, right now with a flying leap from the curb.

Explorations

✤ Make a list of five things you've dreamed of accomplishing but have never begun because the risk seemed too great (e.g., write a book on sea turtles, learn sumi-e painting, teach a workshop on exotic travel). Break each of your dreams into smaller, less scary steps. Circle step one in each of the five. Does the first step still seem formidable? Break it down further. Write about your thoughts, feelings, plans, fears, enthusiasms related to step one of one of the dreams. Schedule a time to actually do it.

✤ Talk to creative people you consider successful: writers, poets, artists, dancers, architects. Ask them what risks they've taken to get where they are. What have they learned? How did they cope with setbacks and failures? Write your findings.

Project

✤ Keep a risk record on scraps of paper or small notepads. Each day note at least one risk, large or small, that you've taken. File the note in a shoe box or pocket folder. Keep a companion risk list posted on your refrigerator door that details risks you'd like to take to broaden your horizons: learn to scuba dive, write a sonnet, paint in gouache, build a writing desk, redecorate your bathroom, file article ideas, find time for solitude, read up on novel writing. After two weeks, consult your risk record and write about what you've accomplished.

befriending

your beasts

6

26. Spinning Straw Into Gold

IDENTIFYING

AND COPING

WITH FEARS

The creative act generates fear and anxiety just as surely as hot asphalt summons heat ghosts. No matter how broad and deep your experience, there's always a gremlin of fear lurking under the next briar bush, waiting to pounce and paralyze. Whether you're intent on producing a science fiction story, a haiku or a silk screen print, when the gremlin confronts you, it can turn your creativity to stone.

No story better demonstrates what creativity consultant and author Doug Hall calls "The Fear Factor" than the classic Grimm brothers' fairy tale *Rumpelstiltskin*. The tale begins when a poor miller brags to the king that his daughter can turn straw into gold. Impressed, the king has the girl whisked away to a cell in the castle where, upon threat of death, she's commanded to perform her magic by morning. The girl, who hasn't a clue, sinks into fearful despair. Suddenly an ugly gnome appears and claims he can fulfill the king's wishes. The grateful girl bribes him with a necklace, and he gets to work.

The next day, when the delighted king spies the gold, he commands the girl to repeat the process. The girl bribes the little man with a ring, and he sets to work. The king, amazed and ecstatic upon seeing the gold, proclaims he'll marry the girl if she can perform the feat a third time. Trouble is, the girl has nothing left to offer the little man. What should she do? Desperate, she promises him her first child, and the man once again spins straw into gold.

True to his word, the king weds the miller's daughter, and she becomes his queen. A year later the queen's first child is born, and the ugly little man shows up to claim the infant. The queen's sobs soften his heart, and he says if she can discover his name in three days' time, she can keep the child.

A kingdomwide search fails to turn up the right name. On the third day, with time running out, a messenger reports hearing a little man dancing round a fire, singing his name: Rumpelstiltskin. Aha! The queen confronts the little man and blurts his name. Livid with rage, the gnome stomps his foot so hard he disappears and is never seen again.

In the tale, the ugly gnome and the gold-spinning genie embody the positive and negative sides of creativity. They're Siamese twins. They occur together. In the beginning, the girl experiences only the dark side—her fears—but when she is able to name the gnome, to face her fears, the curse is broken. Fears disappear or at least diminish. How does she do this? She makes the magic of the positive genie her own by giving birth to creative expression despite her fear. She spins cells into human life much like other creative people spin paper, paint, clay, ideas into something beautiful and valuable.

When you see other people's creative treasures, you want a little gold spinner all your own. Like the miller's daughter, you'd like someone else to do the work. But there's a catch. The genie doesn't work for free. He keeps asking for more and more. Because it's easier to let someone else do the creative thinking for you, you pay. You ask someone else to design the poster, write the flyer, create the solution. You never dream you can do the spinning yourself, that you have your own creative genius.

As long as the little man who is the essence of undeveloped creative capacities stays in the dark, he will inspire fear and loathing.

Once you learn his name, once you recognize your fears and your own unique potential, he loses his fearsome ugliness. He disappears. You don't need him anymore, because you now know your own genie.

That doesn't mean fear disappears forever. You still have to continue naming and overcoming your fears. A blank computer screen, an empty canvas or an unformed lump of clay can call them all up again.

New York–based poet, writer and editor Peter Stillman believes that fear is part of the creative package. "Any sensitive being has experienced a bit of that. As for those who haven't, I'd hate to spend an evening with them. But I think you have to work around or through or past fear. If you're honest (and reasonably articulate), fear can be perceived as no more than a by-product [of creativity] or at worst a handicap one can compensate for—sort of like being the shortest guy on the basketball team."

In my experience, virtually all creative fears spring from anticipation of a particular result, either positive or negative. Fear of rejection, fear of failure, fear of looking silly, fear of the blank page and fear of not achieving a desired goal all originate in this place. We're driven to meet someone else's requirements or our own. In the fairy tale, the miller's daughter lands in a predicament of impossible expectation: spinning straw into gold. It all begins, familiarly, with her father's boast to the king. Who hasn't been in such a situation? Your parents and your friends brag about you, and you get stuck with trying to fulfill their expectations. Sometimes you set your own impossible expectations, like when you tell yourself you should be able to write an article in just one draft, no editing.

The miller's daughter's fear was compounded by an impossible deadline and a death threat. Does this sound familiar? You have six weeks to produce an annual report for your company. Your whole career is riding on this project. It's a life-or-death situation that has you tied in such knots that you can't get started. You huddle, like the miller's daughter, in the corner of your cell, drowned in despair. In your heart you know Clarissa Pinkola Estés was right when she wrote in *Women Who Run With the Wolves*: "Fear is a poor excuse for not doing the work." If you're alive, you are fearful. You're alive. You're certainly fearful. What now?

Undress Your Fears

Look your fears in the eye. Name them. Question them: Are these fears the result of impossible expectations—mine or someone else's? On a scale of one to ten, how pervasive is my fear? What will happen if my worst fears are realized? Can I deal with it? What will happen and how will I feel if I give up on this project (or path or idea)? Is this goal beyond my present abilities? What do I need to meet it? Have I had this same fear before? Under what circumstances? Can I think about this in another way to reduce my fear?

If your fears are wrinkled and ugly like the little man in the story, can you still muster some loving acceptance of them? Can you see them in all their unappealing reality and admit to them as part of yourself? We are, after all, not supposed to feel afraid. When we do feel that way, we're not supposed to let on. As a result we never get to know that the little man is supremely gifted and that his ugliness lies only in our ignorance of his potential.

Know When to Say When

Fear and anxiety can be like "no trespassing" signs. They can keep us out of places we shouldn't go. They can help us speak up about our limits. In the story, the miller's daughter voiced not a single objection to the impossible demands from her father and the king. Her father put her life at risk with his bragging, but she didn't say, "Hey, Dad, I don't have a clue how to spin straw into gold. Tell the king you fabricated just a teensy bit." Nor did she object when, having made straw into gold once, the king demanded she do it again and still again.

Enough is enough. Creative integrity has to be defended.

Stay Connected

Fear causes you to step outside yourself and lose contact with your creative genie. That's how we've come to say, "I was beside myself." Erich Fromm in the respected classic *The Art of Loving* says, "The experience of separateness arouses anxiety; it is, indeed, the source of all anxiety." Close contact with your work edges out fear and anxiety and leaves no holes where gremlins can enter.

Fear is a sign of separation. It usually comes before the creative act. After you've become deeply involved in a project, you unmask fear, and it stomps its foot and disappears. Peter Stillman tells about the panic that precedes performance. "I was sitting on the starting grid in my race car, waiting for the flag to drop. My clutch foot trembled so much I was always afraid I'd slip and stall the car. The moment the flag dropped I was solid as a rock. No tremor at all, even at ferociously high speeds. Maybe fear is part of getting started. I'll be nervous as hell for the first thirty seconds of a talk. After that, I'm totally relaxed, no matter who and how large the audience is."

A woman writer in a recent class said it helps her if she's motivated. "If the article or piece of writing I'm working on is something I'm really interested in, I don't have too hard a time staying connected. If I'm not interested, it's difficult to focus enough energy to concentrate. But sometimes I can do a little mental refocusing and find something about the idea that really hooks me. When that happens I get into the work and I don't worry so much how it turns out."

The miller's daughter was motivated, too. She operated under a three-day deadline and threat of death. Deadlines and death threats are motivators of a sort, but without self-motivation to move you beyond fear, they aren't very effective. Like the little man, you just have to sit down and get busy. Physician and author Hans Selye said, "Action alleviates anxiety." Any action.

Sometimes a little mental judo helps. Often, on days when I've finished researching an article and sit down to write, I can't get going. I sit and stare at the page, hoping a little gnome will show up to pen in a lead. After a couple of false starts, I try mental judo. Here are some strategies I use:

- Write an imaginary letter to a friend describing what I'm going to write.
- Write the beginning of the piece on a small notepad so it doesn't seem like I'm really writing.
- Tell myself I'll start in earnest tomorrow, but today I'll write whatever comes.

- Just begin. Write fast. Edit later.
- Jot a painful and awkward lead and just keep going until the momentum carries the pen. Go back and rewrite the lead.
- Try to turn the project into a game. Make it fun. (Creativity guru Doug Hall says, "If fun is done right, it can be a tool to reduce fear.")

Bribe the Muse

The most intriguing part of the Rumpelstiltskin tale is that the miller's daughter bribes the little man with a necklace, a ring and finally with the promise of her first child. Since the man would likely have no use for women's jewelry, these baubles must represent something else—trappings of the outer world such as we've come to cherish. Material goods. Status. A burgeoning bank account. Everything that relates to self-interest in our everyday world.

But the little man is not a part of the everyday world. He works nights. He doesn't go out. What does he really want? He wants you! To know the creative little man and get him to do his work for you at night while you sleep, you have to sacrifice your usual way of thinking. This sacrifice, this bribe, overcomes fear and keeps the genie on the job. "To become aware of the subtle, creative mind—the mind that is in touch with visions, imagination and memories—the conscious mind that normally dominates and masks must be silenced," says Peter London in *No More Secondhand Art*. So you give up your jewelry—the trappings of the outer world—to lose your conscious mind, your ego self that can stand in your creative way.

The miller's daughter gives up these things. She has to because her creative muse is still outside and she hasn't learned to spin straw into gold all by herself. She's afraid to try. But then she gets married; she becomes a queen and has a baby. She's performed the ultimate creative act: spinning cells into flesh. Does she realize what she's done? No, not yet.

She has to face her fears and fight to keep her only creation—her child. The fire of feminine feeling and the water of tears are her only defenses, but they're enough to buy time for her to learn the name of her fears and face them down and make them vanish (or at least shrink).

How many times have you heard a creative man or woman say, "That's my baby!" about a project the person is working on? How many times have you said it yourself? When you begin to write the book, paint the picture, dance the dance, sing your own song, you begin to develop a passionate attachment to your work. It does become your baby. Like the miller's daughter, you can sacrifice all your worldly goods and even some of your logical intelligence, but not the golden offspring of your inner creative self. There, you draw the line and hold firm.

EARLY WARNING SIGNS OF FEAR AND ANXIETY

- [ ] Inability to concentrate
- [ ] Trouble getting started
- [ ] Feelings of panic and resistance
- [ ] Physical symptoms: butterfly stomach, overbreathing, sleeplessness
- [ ] Diminished enthusiasm and enjoyment
- [ ] Seeing the project constantly unraveling into obsessive rewrites or repaints
- [ ] Lack of spontaneity
- [ ] Procrastination ("I'll start tomorrow.")
- [ ] The sense of being forced to march rather than leading your own parade

❧ Review the section in this chapter, "Undressing Your Fears." Make a list of fears that have arisen in past creative projects or about a project you're planning. Expose and interrogate each of your fears by writing answers to the questions in that section.

❧ Keep the Early Warning Signs of Fear and Anxiety (see the sidebar on page 182) posted on your computer or bulletin board—someplace you'll see them from time to time. What signs have you recognized before beginning new work? Were any of these signs of fear a valid deterrent? Write about your experiences.

Recollection

❧ Think about how your creative process has grown and developed in your particular area of work. Visualize individual projects, successful or not. What were your fears at the outset, as you got into the project and after you were finished? Did you face these fears? Overcome them? How? Were there times when you gave up on a project because fear and anxiety overwhelmed you? Would you see things differently today? Write for a half hour about your insights.

27. Uncle Wiggly and the Giant Squid

My brother and I used to play a board game called Uncle Wiggly when we were kids. The object of the game is to move a playing piece along a meandering rabbit-hole path booby-trapped with hazards and snares. You throw the dice. You move that number of spaces. Sometimes you land in one of the snares or come perilously close. The most fearsome snare is the giant squid. Its tentacles can squeeze the life out of anyone who wanders too close, and if the dice throw turns out wrong, you can step right into its dark maw.

To this day, when I'm stuck for an idea and lost in a black hole of confusion I blame the giant squid. Some wrong throw of the dice has landed me in this dark place. Nothing comes. Grasped in the squid's choking tentacles, it's impossible to move, to see the light, to think straight. This is hell. This is chaos.

"Chaos . . . is the state in which everything is, but so undifferentiated that nothing can be manifest in particular," says David

Maclagan in *Creation Myths*. In simple terms, chaos is the storm before the calm, an uncomfortable layer every creative act goes through to reach the aha! of a new idea, a new piece of writing or work of art. If you didn't enter the chaos layer, the strange disquieting place you've never been before, your creation would be condemned to repeat the same old boring, trite, repetitious stuff. Chaos is the space between you and the creative thing. To come out on the other side, you have to go through it.

Creativity is the ability to sustain immersion in chaos. Sure, sometimes an answer comes right away when you're in an early stage, just fooling around, preparing, researching or brainstorming ideas. This is how most people see the creative act. You prepare and presto! The creative aha! comes. But generally it doesn't happen that way. What usually does happen—and you can't detect the struggle in the finished result—is you complete the preparation step and then get bogged down in chaotic primal ooze. Something happens against your will. You can't seem to get a handle on what you're doing, or you get off track and can't figure out how to get back on. The thing you're creating doesn't quite work. You despair. You begin to lose faith in yourself. When this unwelcome chaos closes in, you know you're in the grip of the giant squid.

Being in what R.W. Gerard in *The Creative Process* (Brewster Ghiselin, editor) calls "that all important no man's land between the end of the receptive process and the start of the expressive one" feels mighty uncomfortable. Your feet are itchy. You want to move on and be done with this. Like being stuck in traffic, it's agonizing to sit there, but that may be just what's needed. My artist friend Jack says that when he used to get impatient for a resolution in his work, his brother Harry would advise, "Don't just do something. Sit there!"

Give yourself an "incubation interim." Sit with chaos for a while until you can decode its message. "The biggest mistake I make is the recurring need to push through and get the job done," a graphic artist told me. "On those rare occasions when I can hold off, the idea continues to develop; and when I let it, I'm much happier with the way the project turns out."

It helps to cultivate what John Keats calls "negative capability"—when a person is "capable of being in uncertainties, mysteries, doubts, without any irritable reaching after facts and reason." Someone with negative capability resists the temptation to forge ahead, control, force, be done with it. Instead of cracking the egg and reaching in to grab the chick before it's ready to come out, you wait until the egg is ready to hatch. You give the idea time to enrich and develop so what you end up with is more than a sloppy raw egg yolk.

Charles Eames, the internationally respected furniture designer, artist, filmmaker and teacher, had a nifty way of prolonging immersion in a developing creative project. He'd ask his students to take the problem apart, dismantle it piece by piece into a hundred parts, and then research and brainstorm each of the parts. The lengthy preparation effectively and intentionally extended the chaos state. By preventing premature conclusions, the approach opened the way to breakthroughs into new ways of thinking.

Eames's solution isn't the same as getting stuck in the preparation stage, researching and sifting forever. By chopping the problem into a hundred parts and researching and brainstorming each of these, he creates a kind of "idea soup." The mix gets richer and richer. There's a deliberate immersion in chaos that nonetheless preserves the students' sense of where they're going and how they plan to get there. The first step is to chop, break up and destroy the old configuration.

"You have to destroy before you can create," an artist friend says. "The way I work is to get something down and then take a lot of risks, which effectively destroys any preconceived notions. Before I began to work this way, my painting lacked freshness. I was in a rut and in danger of stagnating."

Deliberately entering the maw of the giant squid can help reduce feelings of irritation, unease, frustration and discouragement when an immediate answer doesn't come. But it can't do away with the feelings entirely. There will always be at least some frustration and discomfort in this state of disorder, which poet Paul Valéry called "the condition of mind's fertility." Accessing creative fertility is like slipping a note under the door and waiting for an answer from the other side. The agonizing wait for a creative solution engulfs us in the chaos of confusion. It's frustrating. Why doesn't the other side respond?

Gradually, the uncomfortable waiting begins to erode self-confidence. We feel we ought to be able to come up with an easy solution if we're any good at what we do. One writer told me, "I thought because I was having so much trouble coming up with a lead for an article that I must not be much of a writer. If I was really any good, I ought to be able to sail along in my work and not get stuck at every turn in the road. I look at other people's work, and they make it all seem easy. Why can't I do the same?"

When I told this story in class, everybody grinned. They recognized their own doubts and struggles with chaos. One of the students said that the trouble with the chaos layer is that it comes right after the preparation phase, when you feel in control of the project and its outcome. "It's really a shock, then, when chaos hits," she said. "It throws you into a state of confusion. But if you can hold the tension, the wait is almost always rewarded. I've developed a practice where I *invite* it. Before I begin a project, I just sit with my ideas awhile. Sometimes a whole new approach comes out of this; sometimes it doesn't. At least I've let my muse have its say."

Letting your muse have its say is part of the creative process. It can't be forced or rushed. That still, small voice speaks so softly you have to listen carefully to hear it. You also have to know its language and meet it on its own home territory: in the dark. Once you begin to see the chaos layer as an essential part of creativity—the door to new ideas—you can start to make friends with it. Four tips can help you begin:

1. **POSTPONE CONCLUSION.** Resist the urge to force an immediate resolution. Have patience. Slip your note under the door and wait. As Maureen Murdock advises in *The Heroine's Journey*, try not to "move into the light prematurely, holding the tension and letting things unfold in the appropriate time." Instead of rushing to find answers, rush to ask more questions:

   - Have I gotten off the track? Where? What's missing?
   - Do I need help on this? From whom? How can I broaden my outlook?
   - Have I prepared enough? Too much? Are there questions I haven't asked?

SEED THOUGHT

"One must still have chaos in oneself to give birth to a dancing star."

Friedrich Nietzsche

- Should I give the project (and myself) a breather? Or should I forge ahead?
- Do I trust my experience and skill level enough to wait for a resolution?
- What other approaches can I use? What if I looked at the project from someone else's point of view?

2 **WELCOME CHAOS AS A PRELUDE TO A CREATIVE BREAK-THROUGH.** Think of the chaos layer as medicine you have to take to cure an ill. It won't taste good going down, but the results are worth it. You won't know this until the creative lightbulb goes on in your head. Until then, all you can do is trust the dark. As Gertrude Stein once said, "Naturally, one does not know how it happened until it is well over beginning happening." When the spark ignites, you'll say, "I don't know where it came from. It just came to me out of the blue."

3 **THINK OF CHAOS AS EVERY CREATIVE PERSON'S HOMETOWN.** Goethe, German poet and novelist, said that the roots of consciousness are in the unconscious—that is, in the dark. So are the roots of the creative process. If you're a creative person, you spend a lot of time going down into the dark, into chaos. Sometimes you come up with an empty pail. That's no reflection on you or on your abilities as a writer, an artist, a dancer, a composer, a scientist or a cake decorator. The whole subject matter of creation is chaos, abstract expressionist painter Barnett Newman once claimed. Don't be ashamed to be in it. It comes with the creative territory. You may not have to live there, but it's a good idea to visit often.

4 **LET THE GIANT SQUID OF CREATIVE CONFUSION BE A WAKE-UP CALL.** Nagging doubts and stubbornly resistant questions can be clues to a better solution or a need for change. You may be stuck for good reason. Invariably, when I point out a portion of a student's writing that needs untangling, the person will say, "I really knew that all along. It had me stuck, too, but I didn't know how to fix it." Vague feelings of not-quite-rightness can signal

the need to look deeper, to consider a change, to find a new way. The message may first be experienced as an intuition or feeling you can't quite define. This is the still, small voice from the creative underground that requires an attentive ear if you want it to make itself known. The voice can advise you to forge ahead or to pause. Only experience can tell you how to read it. And maybe not even then.

The dark layer of chaos contains everything in potential readiness. It's the soil from which the creative seed grows. As modern human beings, we want instant answers, the way we get fast food at the drive-up window. We can't wait until chaos resolves itself in its own way, in its own time.

As my way of dabbling in chaos and exploring other ways of thinking, I like to read English gardening books. Gardeners have first-hand experience with nature's primordial chaos and are able to muster an acceptance, even a puckish enjoyment, of such uncertainty. Their struggle with weedy overgrowth and the unpredictability of seasons lends grounded reality to what they say. Despite my own handicap of congenital black thumb, I feel an immediate kinship with gardeners such as Mirabel Osler of Shropshire, England, whom I have never met. Her delight in nature's surprises and unexpected blossomings, as expressed in her book *A Gentle Plea for Chaos*, delights me, too. She states the need for chaos—for spending time in the realm of what I've come to call the giant squid—so charmingly that we share her enthusiasm. Her garden is our garden. Her words sum up the positive role of the unpredictable and unknowable:

> So when I make a plea for havoc, what would be lost? Merely the pristine appearance of a garden kept tightly manicured, which could be squandered for amiable disorder. Just in some places. Just to give a pull at our primeval senses, a mild desire for amorphous confusion which will gently infiltrate, and, given time will one day set the garden singing.

Explorations

❦ When have you had an encounter with the chaos layer between preparation and the creative aha!—your own giant squid? How did it influence your sense of confidence? Your ability to complete the project? Your satisfaction with the result? Write about your experiences.

❦ What ways have you discovered to work through the chaos layer? Write and share your breakthroughs with others who do the same kind of creative work you do. What did you do? Was it constructive? Did it work? If the same experience occurred again, what other ways would you use to hold the tension? Write for twenty minutes about your ideas.

Project

❦ Draw or visualize what a chaos experience feels like for you (A black hole? An earthquake crater where the ground opens up beneath your feet? A dark cave where you're lost in one of the tunnels? A monster?). Write a description of your chaos place.

Creative Retreat

❦ The next time you encounter the chaos layer, take time to let it work in you. Set aside a day or at least a few hours to sit with it, and give it your attention without trying to force it or change it or determine its shape too soon. Try not to think too analytically while you're immersed in this. Make it a practice to set aside time for contemplation before you begin a creative project (but after you've researched and prepared). At the end of your retreat, write about how you felt, your resistances, discomforts and breakthroughs. Reread these notes before you begin the next project.

28. Aiming for Join-Up

John Nell is a no-nonsense, Gary Cooper kind of guy. In every-day life he sells real estate in his hometown, Glendale, Arizona. But his passion, his hobby as he calls it, is training his own and other people's horses in the natural, nonviolent way popularized by Monty Roberts, author of *The Man Who Listens to Horses* and subject of the PBS documentary "A Real Horse Whisperer."

Nell says, "I used the system long before anyone heard of Monty Roberts. It's just a commonsense thing to work in a gentle way with a powerful twelve-hundred-pound wild animal, especially a breeding stallion. They could kill you! You need to get them to want to cooperate. The object is to reach a stage of join-up, a word Monty uses for the moment when the horse trusts you enough to willingly follow you."

I was amazed how closely Nell's method for training wild horses resembles the way creative people tame their inner critics. The same techniques that work for taming a wild stallion also work for

HOW TO

TAME YOUR

INNER CRITIC

taming a nagging inner critic. If you've never begun to tame your critic or if it's been grazing open fields all summer, chances are it's running as wild and headstrong as the most undisciplined range pony and ripping your work to shreds. Nell has a couple of tips to help when you first step into the corral:

1 **OBSERVE.** "You start by observing and getting a feel for the animal. To get him to cooperate, you need to know how he thinks and functions. I show displeasure if he doesn't do what I want. Horses mouth a lot, loll their tongue, work their ears. I pay attention to what they say."

You can get to know your inner critic the same way, through observation. But how can you observe something you can't see? How can you lasso this invisible, intangible, amorphous thing that runs loose and can trample your petunias if you let it? You can't know your critic directly, of course, but you can learn to recognize its effects. Are you blocked in your creative work? Has your idea font dried up? Suspect the critic run wild. Is there a voice that prattles in your ear, "You aren't any good at this. What makes you think you can write (or paint, play an instrument, compose, act, dance)?" Suspect the untamed critic. Learn to recognize that itchy trigger finger that can't wait to interrupt, to edit, to take control, to tear apart your work.

- Know that its comments may be valid or they may not.
- Talk to your critic. Ask it to wait. Say, "Let me do this. I'll call you later."
- Let your critic have a voice. Listen. Weigh what it says. Let it write you a letter stating its case. What does it need? What does it like? What is it afraid of? How does it see your creative work? What can it contribute?

2 **HONOR EACH OTHER'S SPACE.** "The horse respects your position, and you need to respect his and not get into his space," Nell says.

In creative work, too, critic and creator have their own spaces where each performs in its own way. Allotting the critic its own space and opportunity to function can transform it from a rigid, obsessive control freak who finds flaws in everything you do into a cooperative helpmate who has your best interests at heart. To bring about such a transformation, the critic must be treated with gentle authority to prevent it from breaking out of its corral and overpowering the shy, quiet creative process.

The problem arises in knowing when to let the critic out of the corral. Have you had this experience? You're working on a project and the critic gets out too early. It begins to edit and criticize prematurely, as you go along, until the piece begins to unravel. If any life remains in it, you think it to death. Your work ends in shambles. You're stuck.

"Until I learned to refrain from premature judgment of my work, I always felt like I was driving with my brakes on," a writer once told me. The critic has a positive function. It can organize, edit, shape, revise, evaluate. But it can't create. To have anything to judge, your critic has to stay in its corral long enough to let your creator self do its work.

3 **PROCEED CAUTIOUSLY, IN SMALL STEPS.** "You have to gradually accustom the horse to accept the weight of a saddle," Nell says. Trainers start with just the light touch of a rope flung on the horse's back as he circles the corral. Later, when the horse is ready, he's fitted with a small light saddle and finally with a full-size, heavier one. Gradualness decreases the animal's anxiety and builds trust. It can do this for your inner critic, too.

A man in a writing class tells how he learned to approach his critic one small step at time. "When I first decided to write the novel I'd been thinking about for years, the idea was terrifying. How was I going to produce several hundred pages? The very thought brought out my critic in full force and launched me immediately into anticipation of failure and rejection. I decided the only way to beat the anxiety was just to sit down and write a few pages. The next day I'd do the same, until I had a chapter. In other words, I would just plod on through one page at a time."

SEED THOUGHT

"Some people are born with a more focused and flexible neurological endowment or are fortunate to have parents who promoted unselfconscious individuality. But it is an ability open to cultivation, a skill one can perfect through training and discipline."

Mihaly Csikszentmihalyi
Flow

Just beginning to think about a creative project can awaken the censor. As you continue to work and anxiety builds, the censor has to be temporarily bound and gagged. "As the creative process progresses, censorship is increasingly reversed and the creative person experiences increased anxiety," says Albert Rothenberg in *The Emerging Goddess*. Gradualness can reduce anxiety by increasing comfort. A shift occurs when you decide to plod on, not in a heroic leap, but feeling your way inch by inch. Writing a few pages isn't nearly as forbidding as authoring a whole book. Doing a thumbnail sketch isn't as scary as anticipating a life-size oil painting. The trick is to start with a small saddle so the horse won't bolt.

4 **DEVELOP RESPECT.** "You can't treat a horse like a slave. You need to treat them as if they're worthy—get them to want to cooperate, not break their will. That's true for getting along with any living thing," Nell says.

It's especially true for getting along with your inner critic. Treating your inner critic with respect builds trust, and trust is necessary for *join-up*—that state where your critic becomes helper, not saboteur. You achieve join-up when both sides work together, each performing its own function—the thing it does best—without trying to take over the other's territory.

You could force your critic to behave by treating it as trainers used to when they tried to break a horse by tying it down and brutally slamming the side of its head with a two-by-four. But if you break your critic's spirit, you'll lose a valuable ally. Your creativity will fly like a kite with its string cut into a never-never land of indecision and undisciplined, directionless meandering.

A dispirited critic is a liability. So is its opposite: the overzealous critic who tries to saddle you with shoulds.

- You should know more, be more proficient and get more done.
- You should be as talented, quick, resourceful, convincing, creative and energetic as _____.

- You should never run into snags, get tired, make mistakes or be less than perfect.
- You should never have doubts about anything.

With such an overactive critic cracking the whip as you run around your pony ring, you're apt to begin to doubt your own ability. Sometimes creative people feel that if they have doubts, they must not be very competent. Not so. Researchers say that incompetent people usually don't know they are incompetent, while competent people think they're doing a poor job. What does this say about the inner critic? It says that people with an active—sometimes even a smidgen overactive—critic tend to be more competent. The critic has to do its work to keep you on track, and you have to do yours by treating it with respect. That means listening to its nagging with at least half an ear and accepting a certain amount of self-doubt and anxiety as a necessary prelude to creation.

5 **DON'T CONFRONT IT DIRECTLY.** "You must avert your eyes if you want a horse to follow you. Looking them in the eye, challenging them eyeball to eyeball, makes them flee. You should not take an offensive position, but instead keep your body moving away from wherever the horse is. I learned this the hard way, by being beat up too many times," Nell says.

This is Nell's most important piece of advice. It works just as well, if not better, for training the inner critic. *Don't confront.* Try to work without arousing the critic's fear and compulsion to control. This requires—how can I put it delicately—a sacrifice of the head, of thinking. In his book *The Holy Grail,* Malcolm Godwin says there's an ancient belief that if a severed head is thrown into a well, it will enhance the well's power. Likewise, temporary sacrifice, or at least a reduction, of the critic's rational thinking capability will enhance creative power. Willem de Kooning, founder of abstract expressionist painting, once said that his secret of creating art and beating the critic was "to work so fast you couldn't think." This method for sacrificing his head enriched his creative well.

So how do you sacrifice your own critic's head? How can you avert your eyes and approach the critic indirectly so you don't arouse its fear and compulsion to take over? It's helpful if you reduce the baggage your creative animal carries. Here are a few ways to unload:

- **DEVELOP AN ATTITUDE OF EXPERIMENTATION.** The surest way to arouse the critic's compulsion to control is to place huge importance on the task by wanting to do it perfectly, or by trying to compete or excel.

  Last summer, I fell into the importance trap. I was doing a painting for a faculty show, and all I could think about were all the B.F.A.s and how accomplished their work was likely to be. As a once-in-a-while painter, my ability was less than polished. What's more, I've never functioned well under threat of a deadline. After three weeks of frustration and more paintovers than the Grand Canyon has strata, I finally finished a half hour before the deadline. The result was passable but not very free. I had forgotten to sacrifice my head to the well and had saddled the creative genie with too much baggage.

  By contrast, my artist friend Carol isn't particularly interested in art shows. She's too deeply involved with experimentation and exploration. "I keep boxes of images, in different categories, clipped from magazines, greeting cards, junk mail. When a box is nearly full, I sort through the images until an idea comes. Then I play with the idea in paint."

  An attitude of experimentation can be a sneaky way to edge into creative work without awakening the critic so it rears up to throw you off.

- **HAVE A WORK ROUTINE.** Sharpen pencils, clean brushes, turn on the computer, and then plunk yourself down and begin to work. Have a routine you follow and just plod along. In my case, I write for four hours or so every morning, at east five or six days a week. Afternoons I file, edit, research, interview; sometimes I walk in the woods or swim or take a nap. A science fiction writer I used to know had a different routine. He drove a bread truck by day and wrote from after dinner until midnight. Each person is unique. Do whatever works for you.

Know that the critic tends to ignore routine. It gets bored. It hungers for the sound of bugles and the battle cry, "This is a really big deal." By plodding along, day after day, your critic loses interest and may let you work, undisturbed, for long stretches.

• **BORE IT TO SLEEP.** Do a lot of experimenting. Practice as if you were learning to play the violin. Write, draw or dance the same thing fifty times. The critic will be lulled into inattention. Tell yourself (and your critic) that this is a trial run, a thumbnail sketch, a rough draft, a shot in the dark. Your critic will snooze loudly.

• **AVERT YOUR EYES AND WALK AWAY.** Like any good horse trainer, act like there's no need to force the issue. Change direction. Do something physical. Chop wood. Make the bed. Walk around the block. Let the ripples in your mind go smooth and the water in your well come clear. (See chapter thirty-six for other ways to calm a chattering brain.) Take a break, but promise your critic that when your ideas have had time to jell, you'll be back to ask for advice.

Join-up happens when creativity and critic learn to dance together, to work as a team, each performing its own function, each respectful of the other. When you reach join-up, you can throw away the two-by-four. This doesn't guarantee your critic will never again get cranky or nag or try to take over. It will continue to test your limits. That's its nature. But now at least you know what those limits are and you can hold the reins in both hands.

Explorations

❦ Write a letter to your critic. Ask for its cooperation. Tell why your creative self needs to be able to express its ideas first, in whatever media you use, without being interrupted by premature criticism. Thank your critic for past input and suggest ways that it could be helpful in the future. Write a letter in response, as if it came from your critic. Mail the letter to yourself.

❦ In a journal, keep a record of occasions when your critic has been annoying or has actually stopped your work in its tracks. What did you do to alleviate the situation? What worked? What didn't? What could you try next time that you haven't tried before? Revisit your notes from time to time or whenever the critic begins to get out of line.

Project

❦ Visualize your critic. Is it a screech owl that nags and objects? A skinny Ichabod Crane type who keeps whacking you on the shoulder with its cane? A person who criticized you excessively as a child or someone whose approval you sought? Or is your critic a helpful wizard who performs magic on command? A lovable, bumbling munchkin? A zany English teacher you remember from high school? Do you see your critic as menacing? Humorous? Helpful? Crushing? Mold your vision in self-hardening clay. When it's dry, paint the figure with bright-colored tempera or acrylic. Give it a name. As your critic transforms over time, create a new figure that embodies your current vision. Ultimately, you can collect a whole lineup of figures representing the progressive development of your critical abilities. As you complete each figure, write your thoughts about what it represents. Save your entries in a loose-leaf notebook to review from time to time.

29. Sailing Through Seaweed

On one of Columbus's voyages, the story goes, the ship that carried the explorer and his crew sailed into a broad expanse of seaweed floating on the ocean's surface. It looked like the ship was heading into a vast green island. The superstitious crew panicked. "We will mutiny if you don't turn back," they threatened Columbus. The ship had slowed and now stood eerily still in the midst of the tangled weeds. Pandemonium broke loose. The crew feared they were stuck in the middle of the ocean. They had failed to notice that the wind had ebbed, and this lack was the real cause of their difficulty. They were engulfed in the doldrums.

That the bones of Columbus and his crew were not found moldering on the ship's deck proves that the doldrums can be sailed through. All aboard survived the dangerous ebb of wind energy and the tangled tentacles of seaweed. They sailed on, no doubt, with a fresh appreciation for tedium, ennui, torpor, malaise, listlessness, slump, funk. They met the doldrums and prevailed.

WHAT TO DO

WHEN THE WIND

WON'T BLOW

(AND YOU'RE

STUCK)

What creative person hasn't experienced days, months, sometimes even years of stagnation? You're a writer who sits down to work, and all you can turn out are reams of crumpled paper. You're a painter who looks at the past year's work and turns all the canvases to the wall. You're a creative person who's consumed by an energy drought. All your ideas have ebbed. The wind refuses to blow.

"I knew I was in the doldrums when things I once did easily suddenly seemed insurmountably difficult," a student offered when we were discussing the situation in class. I had told them the story of Columbus and the doldrums. "When I'm in it, my body feels as if it's tangled in seaweed. I can't move. Everything seems to take longer than usual. I can't seem to muster enthusiasm for anything. To try to do any work feels like I'm rolling a ten-ton boulder uphill."

You know you're in the doldrums when

- your life and work cease to be exciting or even interesting
- you're spent, dried up, worn out
- you seek distraction to feel better
- you're tired but can't cut back or slow down
- you need to be constantly busy to feel alive
- every creative project seems beyond your ability

If you've had these symptoms from time to time, you're not alone. Well-known writer Anaïs Nin, when she was going through a difficult time, had recurring dreams of pushing a heavy wooden ship across a desert. Artist Jackson Pollock became so overcome with stagnation he gave up hope and took his own life. Many other writers and artists have tried to fend off the doldrums by using alcohol and drugs, only to see their creativity further diminish.

When you are sunk deep in the doldrums and experiencing an extreme energy ebb, it's natural to think you're the only one this happens to. Yet even experienced writers and other creative people frequently find themselves caught in the seaweed tangle, unable to move ahead. I got a call just a few days ago from a friend who was in a seaweed situation, even though she has written several books and is working on another. "I'm in despair!" she said. "I just can't seem to get this chapter to come together." Her despair came on the heels of a grueling trip and a host of holiday distractions that sapped her energy. But true to her courageous style, she tried to forge ahead, and she found the wind had gone out of her sails.

The first step in getting the wind to blow again is to look closely at what might be causing your energy deficit. Ask yourself questions. Mull the answers.

- Is my muse well fed? What nourishes it?
- Am I getting enough rest?
- Is my creativity appreciated and rewarded by others (and by me)? Am I working in a hospitable setting?
- Is there enough variety in my work? Too much? Are the demands of deadlines and workload daunting?
- Am I working on at least one thing that energizes me? Am I bored?
- Is the rest of my life sapping my energy? Have I taken on too many commitments?
- Do frequent distractions derail my creative thought?
- Do I plan for and insist upon time for myself?

Asking yourself questions about the state of your inner weather is like sticking up a damp finger to see which way the wind is blowing, if it's blowing at all. Questions assess. The answers tell you what areas bear watching and what areas may need to change. Questions can help you determine if your creative life is in balance or seriously skewed. Usually, we're too busy putting out fires to worry about the water supply.

"I used to think I could do everything and have energy left over," a newsletter editor and parent of two preteens once told me. "I'd just take on more and more, and before I knew it there was no time left for any creative work outside my job and family and the organizations I belong to. What's more, a lot of the responsibilities I took on were things that weren't necessary and that I really didn't want to do. The whole mess sent me into a funk. I couldn't do anything."

If you find yourself in the same seaweed situation—a situation most of us fall into at one time or another—don't give up hope. The wind will fill your sails again. Meanwhile, it might help to develop an energy plan.

Three ways to get your creative wind to blow are to

- conserve energy
- create energy
- focus energy

We all own lots of devices designed to help us conserve our energy. Cars take us places. Cell phones and faxes and the Internet make communication almost effortless. Microwave ovens and dishwashers and other household appliances ease our chores. So why are we always so drained?

I think it's because these so-called energy-saving devices lead us to believe we have more energy to spare than we actually do. We develop a casual attitude toward taking on commitments, and with every commitment, our energy supply springs another leak. Too many leaks and our boat sinks.

Conserving energy means plugging the leaks. Sometimes leaks slip in right under our noses, and we don't even bat an eyelash. They're sneaky leaks. They sneak up on you, and before you know it, you've taken on another responsibility you may not want. Before long, your creative energy is riding so low in the water from so much excess baggage that even a hefty wind can't move you.

One way to get a handle on where your energy is going is to record how you spend your time. I call this clarifying your basic values. Write down what you did, how long it took, the energy it used (on a scale of one to ten) and the satisfaction value of the activity (rated one through ten). Make four columns on a sheet of paper to keep track of each of these. Try keeping this energy inventory for at least a week. Meanwhile, list your priorities, creative and otherwise, placing the most important things at the top and descending to the least important. At the end of the week, look at both lists to see if your priorities are reflected in the way you spend your time. Can you see any places where leaks need to be plugged? What kinds of things rated highest on the satisfaction scale? How much time did you devote to these things?

How much rewind time—time for rest, relaxation and soul restoration—did you allow in your week? It's important to know when your energy is apt to be low so you can schedule time for restoration. If I'm involved in a demanding creative project, I schedule a few hours at the end to refuel. If it's a longer job, I try to leave time in the late afternoon or early evening a couple times a week to walk in the woods or dabble in paint. I try not to schedule meetings or creative projects on the day before or after a trip. To make sure I don't, I cross out these days in pencil, so nothing sneaks in.

Once in a while, I also schedule a "soul day" for just drifting, putzing or doing whatever comes. The idea came from a student who visited Zurich on a trip to Europe. Walking down one of the city's narrow streets, he noticed a sign in a shop window that read: "Closed. We are taking a soul day." He liked the idea so much, he adopted it himself and passed it on to me.

Sometimes the doldrums can be a healthy thing. We are so supercharged in our modern attitudes that it seems inconceivable that unfilled time can be a positive respite. Sometimes just riding out the duration of the doldrums can be like waiting for snow to melt. Eventually it does, and the melting nourishes the ground. The doldrums can be the sign of an idea getting ready to happen. If you try to push though, the idea may emerge half-formed or it may not come out at all. So should you push through or wait? It depends. It never hurts to give unfledged ideas a chance to develop naturally, in their own time, conserving energy until the time is right.

Creating energy requires a different strategy than conserving energy does. It's a lot like stealing fire. Where can you find energy when you have none? You strike stones together until you ignite passion. Like Jonah in the whale, you're in a dark, doldrum place. What do you do? You light a fire! You find your passion.

"For truly creative work to be done, the drive of passion must be produced," Harold Rugg wrote in *Imagination*. You can't write or create from your idea place without the fire of passion. Lacking this excitement, the will—the whipcrack—of the logical mind takes over and produces a lifeless wooden facsimile.

There ought to be a loudspeaker at every work site that

SEED THOUGHT

"If we wane, as all energies must, it can only be to wax more ardently, more wonderfully."

Wendy Beckett
The Mystical Now: Art and the Sacred

blares, "It's 9 A.M. Do you know where your passion is?" Unless you know what drives you, you'll be forever imprisoned in the whale. You can determine your drivers by writing down five or six things you like to do. Ask why you like to do each thing. Write your answer. Ask why again. Here's how the dialogue might go:

> "I like to bake giant decorated chocolate chip cookies."
>
> "Why?"
>
> "So I'll have some to give friends and neighbors."
>
> "Why is this important to you?"
>
> "Because they enjoy the cookies."
>
> "Why is that important?"
>
> "Because I enjoy doing things to make people happy."

When you can't say why anymore, you've likely hit a driver, a motivating force, a passion. Maybe it will turn out that you bake cookies to try something new or to exercise an artistic bent by decorating them with raisins, sprinkles and frosting. You could be doing the same things as someone else, but your drivers might be different.

Another way to track your passion is to keep a running list of things you love to do. What turns you on? When do you lose your sense of time? Noted ballerina Maria Tallchief, when interviewed late in her career, said her work was her passion. The interviewer asked how, at her age, she was able to muster enough energy for long hours of dance. "When you do something you love, you never get tired," she said. Keep an energy diary. Discover where your passion lies by recording times of high energy, times when you don't get tired.

And then focus that energy. Undo the seaweed tangles of distraction, busyness, aimlessness, indecision. As Al Pacino said in the movie *Scent of a Woman*, "When you get tangled, tango on." Passion will carry you if you undo the tangles. When you were a kid, did you ever try to untie a knotted yo-yo string? The temptation is to yank the string, which only makes tighter knots. As your big brother or sister showed you, first you have to loosen the knots. Let yourself be in the doldrums. Wait until things settle and clear. Then, ask a lot of questions to get your bearings, and make sure that when you set sail, it's in the right direction. Ask, What do I *really* like to do? Where is my passion? Focus like a laser on that.

I once asked a class to tell where their passion bubbles up. One woman said, "What I really love to do is sew, but I can never find time to do it." Someone piped, "Do you *really* love to sew?" The woman cocked her head and thought a minute. "As a matter of fact, no," she said. "I actually hate it. What I really love is to coordinate fabric and design new ways to use patterns. But I never realized it until you asked." Questions help concentrate the heat of passion and focus the sunlight of common sense 'til it ignites creativity.

So there you are. If you want the force to be with you, conserve the energy you've got. Generate more by connecting with your passion, and focus the whole energy rush so it doesn't leak away. Simple, but not easy.

A friend says that a jolly romp with the muse can leave us inflated, like an overblown balloon, and in danger of going bam! and losing all the energy. An energy drought, the interior or exterior doldrums, helps us come face-to-face regularly with our vulnerability. It keeps us humble. It rivets our feet firmly to the ground. Most of all, the doldrums keep us in shape and practiced by giving us seaweed to row through.

✿ Fold a piece of notebook paper in half lengthwise. At the top of the left column write "Spark Plugs." At the top of the right column write "Wet Blankets." Under "Spark Plugs" list everything you can think of that nourishes your muse. What energizes you? What do you really love to do? What kind of environments, people, work, routines (or lack of) boost your creative energy? Under "Wet Blankets" list all the things that dampen your creative spirit. What saps your energy? What makes you feel drained at the end of your workday? Where, when and why do you get tangled in seaweed? Do your answers show need for a change, whether in attitude or circumstances? Write about your findings.

✿ Describe in detail your ideal work situation, using your lists above as guidelines. Do you like a predictable schedule or a flexible one? Rather work alone? With a small group? In a large company? High- or low-tech? At home or in an office or studio?

Project

✿ Write down half a dozen things you've always wanted to try: ice skating, collage making, bookbinding, carpentry, rock climbing, line dancing, boxing, oriental ink painting, poetry writing, acting, choral singing, building a snowman, playing chess, learning to juggle or whatever strikes your fancy. By the end of next week, take at least the first step toward fulfilling your fantasy (sign up for a class, collect materials, etc.). Write what it felt like to make your ideas come to life.

Research

✿ Reread the description on clarifying basic values in this chapter. On the left side of a page turned horizontally, write five or six things you like to do. Write from left to right why you like to do this thing, until you distill your ideas into basic values. Write about your findings. Did you discover anything unexpected? Do the values seem to fit? In what ways are these values expressed in your life? Which ones are most important to you?

30. Leafing Out in Impossible Places

There's a particular mulberry tree I've known for years. We've had conversations. It has, in fact, become a kind of creative mentor. The tree grows in an impossible place—some four stories above the street, where it has taken root in the marquee tower of what used to be the 20th Century theater a few miles from my home. Apparently it sprouted from a seed excreted by one of the pigeons that roost in the marquee's crannies. But how did it grow ten feet tall with no soil to plant its roots in and only an occasional storm to bring water? It's a mystery that can only be attributed to sheer stubborn, resourceful tenaciousness.

      The tree flourished abundantly while the theater stood vacant for nearly a decade. It was during that flourishing time that I first saw it, standing tall like the torch at the top of the Statue of Liberty. After that, I continued to look for it when I drove by, seeking the inspiration of its resourcefulness. One day it was gone. I despaired. But a year later, I was surprised to see a small green tuft emerging once again from that lofty place.

THE THREE D'S:

DIFFICULTIES,

DETOURS AND

DISTRACTIONS

"We had taken the tree out in the early nineties when the building was rehabbed," a new tenant says. "But the top of that tower is a precarious place to get to, and we had to leave the root. That tree just keeps coming back! Something about it must appeal to people because we've had all kinds of publications do stories about it."

What I think appeals to people is the fact that the tree grew, even flourished, in an impossible place. Who can't relate to that? The creative place in each one of us reaches out to embrace such a symbol. It reminds us of our own trials and triumphant breakthroughs, our own persistent tenaciousness as we bump along on rocky roads.

Difficulties

That creative people succeed at all is due more to perseverance despite difficulty than to any sort of wished-for boon. The painter El Greco had serious eye problems. Beethoven composed beautiful music even thought he was nearly deaf. Author William Styron wrote his way through debilitating depression. None of them let difficulties stifle creative work.

Misfortune and difficulty are our teachers. They tune our creative instrument. As Frank Herbert says in *Dune*, "People need hard times and oppression to develop psychic muscles." Difficulties as fodder for creativity give depth to expression. Nothing resonates with a reader, an art observer or music listener so much as a shared experience of struggle, difficulty, detour and eventual victory.

Sometimes the difficulty itself can be motivating. Earl Shaffer, who at age twenty-nine, in 1948, was the first person to hike the Appalachian Trail, beginning to end, was no stranger to hardship. He saw those hardships not as deterrents but as motivation. "I often ponder whether the difficulties provided me with the impetus to carry me along," he says.

Just a few years ago, writer Linda Ellerbee told in an article for *New Choices* magazine that she had run into Shaffer near the end of the same trail, three-quarters of the way to Maine. Shaffer was seventy-nine.

Adversity is as much a part of creative life as an arm is a part of your body. We all, no matter what our medium of expression, swim like salmon—upstream, against the current. As Wendell Berry once said, creative people go in at exits and out at entrances. Only such swimming against the current makes further progress possible.

In Olympic competition, for instance, there can be no new record until a competitor realizes that the old record can be broken. Triple-jumps in figure skating championships had become standard, but no one thought a quadruple-jump was possible—until someone actually did it. What holds true for creative athletes also applies to creative writers, artists, composers, dancers and others. Overcoming adversity and the status quo helps you think beyond accepted possibility.

Creativity can be generated even at times when life hands you its severest blow or confines you in extreme conditions. Ernie Pyle wrote and drew on the battlefield during World War II. Viktor Frankl recorded psychological ideas while he was in a concentration camp. Creative people have managed to function during illness, war and hard times. You can, as J.D. Salinger advises, "Write your way out"—or paint or doodle or dance or scheme. You can create your way through, and your work can be a candle in the dark for others close on your heels.

Detours

Besides difficulties, false starts, confusion and blind alleys are also parts of the creative process. We often think of the creative act as an orderly progression from where we are to where we want to go. It isn't. It's messy and vague with lots of places where we get off track and don't know how to get back.

A student once asked eminent Swiss psychiatrist Carl Jung what the quickest way was to individuation, or the realization of one's whole creative person. Jung replied, "The detour." We usually consider detours a nuisance, but sometimes a jog in the road can take us to just the place we want to go.

A detour can present us with a whole new view. An artist tells that when she was a student she was too poor to afford many of the supplies for her oil painting class. At the end of the semester, with still one more painting required, she had run out of paint except for a conglomeration of color that remained on her palette from a previous work. In desperation, she picked up a palette knife and troweled the leftover paint onto a canvas someone had discarded. As she worked, an image of a ghost ship began to emerge and the knife motion created the texture and feeling of waves. She liked the result, but wondered if her instructor would see through her desperate act. Apparently not. Her painting received a high grade. A detour had led to an even better place.

A detour is an invitation to meander. And meandering, said Lao-tzu in the *Tao Te Ching*, "leads to perfection; the crooked becomes straight, the empty full and the worn out new." Meandering keeps us from becoming too purposeful. It keeps us artistically open and growing so we don't box ourselves in. It's possible to plan deliberate meandering detours.

- When you look up a word in the dictionary or thesaurus, examine the words that precede or follow the one you're seeking.
- Do something backward. Eat dessert first. Write the end of a story before you write the beginning.
- When you're on a car trip, get off the highway from time to time to see what surprises you might find. Snoop around. Notice.

Detours happen when you're trying to get somewhere and you end up somewhere else. Sometimes "somewhere else" can be more interesting than "somewhere." If you're open to change, a detour can lead you to a place you never dreamed.

A few months ago, I drove a half hour into the countryside to Rouster's Apple House where I regularly go to get my "apple a day." On this trip, Evelyn the apple lady told me about a one-hundred-year-old covered bridge a few miles off the main highway. Intrigued, I set off down the narrow, winding road until I came to an old, red, wooden, tin-roofed bridge that stretched across a shallow creek. The car skuttered along rickety planks into the near dark of the bridge's vaulted interior and came out into sunshine on the other side. There, in a clearing where the road ended, reposed a quaint red brick church surrounded on all sides by a tall forest of ancient trees. What a discovery! I sat in the car with the door open and wrote to the creek's music for an hour in this peaceful place. An unexpected detour had led me to someplace I never could have found by design.

Not all detours are productive. Sometimes all you learn by taking a detour is where *not* to go. And yet, if you look back on your creative life, you're likely to see that even these nonproductive forays eventually led somewhere. Have you ever watched an ant? It wanders in every direction but eventually winds up at the front door of the anthill. Your own wanderings will get you someplace, too. Just remember that mulberry tree growing stubbornly out of a theater marquee.

Distractions

Downright stubbornness can keep you coming back to the main road after an intentional or unintentional detour, but can it help combat the third D: distractions. This morning, as I'm trying to write, I get a call. I can't find the phone, which is under a pile of papers beside me, so I have to get up to answer the other one (two minutes lost). The Dow Jones people are trying to sell me *The Wall Street Journal*. I tell them I'll keep them in mind, but I can't afford the time to read right now (five minutes lost). As long as I'm up, I look for a book I haven't been able to locate. It turns up where I last left it (three minutes lost). I sit down once again to write. The doorbell rings. It's a tyke from Saint Something or Other selling grapefruit for a school fund-raiser (five minutes lost). Finally, I get back to work, and jackhammers start up outside, noisily digging up electric lines that our historic village demands be planted underground (my morning is lost). Do you recognize this scene? Have you ever gotten deep into a creative project without being interrupted by someone calling to sell you aluminum siding or a time-share? Is there ever a stretch of more than five minutes without the doorbell's ring, an ambulance scream or a lawn mower's drone?

The best advice I've found on how to overcome distractions came many years ago from author Phyllis Martin. She happened to call on a snow day when all three of my kids were home from school and half the neighborhood had gathered in our basement. I prattled on about the noise, the interruptions, the constant inquiries about the way to the bathroom. "I'm trying to write an article," I wailed to Phyllis, "and all I'm getting are distractions." There was a pause at the other end of the line and then she said, "Can't you do it anyway?"

The message comes back every time I'm besieged with distractions. Over time, I've learned to write anyway. In the front seat of a car, in the bathroom, on a barge on the Ohio River, in a rowboat, in a nylon tent, and even on a balcony outside my bedroom in Pakistan during the war with India, while jets pursued each other across the sky and artillery fire resounded all around.

You can, of course, attempt to reduce distractions. Thomas Carlyle built a soundproof room. Marcel Proust lined his walls with cork. Another writer I know nailed egg cartons inside a whole room. We often feel that if we had a garret somewhere, private and removed, we could be more creative, have more energy, get more done in less time. But I believe that some distraction helps sharpen the intensity of your concentration. Like the mulberry tree in the theater marquee, creativity can grow anywhere. It doesn't need ideal conditions, only an open mind and tenacious roots.

The three Ds—difficulties, detours and distractions—don't have to destroy innovation. When they threaten, you can ask yourself like I often do the question posed by Phyllis Martin and that mulberry tree: "Can't you do it anyway?"

✤ Make a list of the roads not taken in your creative life:

> **buds:** ideas or projects that were mothballed before they could bloom
> **duds:** ideas and projects that, once launched, didn't fly
> **detours:** false starts and forays off the main path

Write about one or more of these experiences. What did you learn? Do any of these untraveled paths still hold promise for your creative life?

✤ What was the most demanding, most difficult, most frustrating creative project you've ever tackled? What trials did you experience? How did the project turn out in the end? Write your thoughts and feelings.

Research

✤ Find a symbol, like the tree growing out of the top of the theater marquee, to serve as your beacon when you're slogging through the muck of a difficult project. Write about why you chose the symbol you did and what special meaning it has for you.

Recollection

✤ Have you ever gotten sidetracked and found that the other track was a better one? Have you made a mistake that turned into a fortuitous move? Have you unexpectedly wandered into a wonderful discovery when you didn't expect it? Take twenty minutes to write your thoughts.

creating from
the inside out

31. Setting Out on a Steed, Riding Backward

THE COURAGE

TO BEGIN

Beginnings are uncomfortable. They stir feelings of stepping off a cliff into empty air. Our ideas aren't quite clear just yet. We think we ought to do more research, get some training, wait a while. The truth is we're just not ready to set out. Maybe next week or next month would be better.

There's a story about beginnings that someone told me years ago that I like to tell to classes at the first meeting. I call it "Setting Out on a Steed, Riding Backward." As we go around the room and say our names and what we do, we inevitably find that there are several experienced pros in the class. You can see the beginners start to shrink into their shirt collars. So I tell the class that beginners will have an advantage. They will have less to unlearn. Nobody believes me. Then I tell them the story.

There once was a king whose kingdom had fallen on hard times. He hears of a fabulous treasure and a beautiful princess being guarded by a fierce dragon and sends the eldest, most experienced and best trained of his three sons to slay the dragon and bring the treasure home. When the eldest son fails, he sends his middle son, the next most experienced. He, too, fails to win the treasure.

So what's a king to do? Reluctantly, he sends his youngest son, the fool. There's not much hope that this untutored simpleton will succeed when the others, older and wiser and stronger, have failed. But the foolish boy sets out in all his impetuous awkwardness—riding backward on his horse. Everyone gathered to see him off laughs. The boy, undaunted, goes trustingly on his way. He doesn't even know enough to be scared.

Then miracles begin. The boy's inept innocence stirs the hearts of birds and beasts in the forest. The helpful animals guide him through difficulties and lead him to find the magic sword to kill the dragon and free the captive princess. He slays the dragon, marries the princess and returns to the castle with a bountiful treasure to save the kingdom.

If you've ever begun a creative project, you know what it feels like to start out in bumbling backwardness. You're besieged by false starts and blind alleys and feelings of confusion that are woven into every innovative act no matter what medium you use. Are you tempted to give up? Turn back? Wait? Or will you forge ahead? The youth's story, like many other fables, can show the way. It can be your magic animal to guide you on your path. In class, I offer four questions to start the wheels turning:

1 **WHY DID THE OLDER BROTHERS FAIL?** The older we get, the more stuff we file away in our brain computers. This stuff tells us the right way to do something. It saves us time because we don't have to figure everything out from scratch. The light turns green, we walk. Our noses run, we grab some tissues. We don't have to think before we do something.

We run into difficulty when the rules we've learned don't apply. In our boxes of coping supplies, we've stashed only a few tools. When those tools don't work, we're stymied.

The older brothers didn't realize they had to unlearn the old ways before they could kill the dragon and capture the treasure.

They relied on experience, on what they'd learned from their elders and on what had worked before. In short, they trusted what the world valued as the right way. They lacked the innocence to be creative and to let that creativity carry them through the confusion of the unknown.

"The birth of every new venture begins in some confusion because we are entering the realm of the unknown . . . [and there is] a profusion of elements struggling to take form," says R.L. Wing in *The I Ching Workbook*. We can't possibly know what these elements are. They've never existed before, and they don't exist quite yet. We have to empty our minds like that naturally blank slate of the innocent youth in our story. When we do that, miracles will happen. But first, we have to start out, however awkwardly.

2 **WHY IS IT A GOOD IDEA TO BEGIN EVEN IF YOU'RE NOT COMPLETELY READY?** When I asked that question in class, half a dozen people piped, "Because we're *never* completely ready. We go on preparing and preparing, and we just can't decide when and how to start." One woman added that she couldn't decide about anything, even something insignificant. "When I'm in a drugstore, I can't even decide whether to buy the red pencil or the blue one. So I buy both." A man added, "I've been trying for five years to decide whether or not to leave my present job. One day it's go; the next it's stay." They said what they really needed was a decision-making machine.

So before the next class, half as a joke and half as a way to see what would happen, I drew up a Rube Goldberg-style handout with a diagram of a decision-making machine complete with gears and levers. The idea was to list all the deciding factors, assign them a value and then rate each factor for choice A and choice B. The totals were at the bottom, in the "out" slot. All you had to do was see which total was higher. Everyone set about enthusiastically to fill in the blanks.

Before long, their pencils stilled, and they began to look perplexed. I asked what the trouble was. "Well, I got an answer," one man volunteered, "but it's not the right one." Several others echoed, "Yeah. It's not the answer we wanted." When I asked how they knew it wasn't the right answer, one woman spoke up. "Because it doesn't come from *here*," she said, patting her heart place. "I guess we don't need a decision-making machine," she added. "We've got one right here."

This other kind of decision-making machine, this uncorrupted intuition of the heart, had inspired our awkward young hero to set out—even though he didn't know which way to sit in the saddle.

IS THERE SOMETHING TO BE SAID FOR BACKWARDNESS?

Riding backward on a horse is a wonderful image of life, creative and otherwise. We know only two things: where we are and where we've been. No matter how eagerly we try to look ahead and see what's over the next hill, we can't know what we'll find when we get there. In his bumbling way, our hero knows that. He sits in the saddle so he can see where he's been and where he is. And he trusts his instinct, represented by the horse, to take him where he needs to go.

Like the people in the class, he relies on instinct, on his inexplicable, amorphous heart place, to be his guide. Can you imagine how much less worried we'd be if we focused on where we've been and where we are and let the heart place, the trusty steed, trot on to its natural destination? In creative work, especially, we can't always know the goal before we set out. Maybe we don't have to.

"The artist is uniquely placed to embrace the enigma of commencing a journey to an unknown destination. He can search without knowing what he is looking for, yet recognize his quarry the moment it appears," Edward Adamson says in *Art As Healing*. Many fairy tales are just such journeys into the unknown. They're meant to teach us at an early age that it's not always possible to figure things out in advance. At an early age, we already know that, of course, but the tales help us remember to remember as we grow older.

We think we learn deliberately, by our own aim or someone else's. Just open the lids on top of our heads and pour stuff in. Maria Montessori, the Italian educator who created a new learning system bearing her name, saw it differently. She says, "All knowledge comes to us or is possessed by us gradually, in stages. At first, we are simply aware of something new, then there is a long period of rumination, or almost-knowing, finally, at a certain point we do know."

Was she saying that we are all, in a sense, backward riders? I think so. I think she was also describing the creative process and how it begins in unknowing—the unknowing of an untutored youth who knows no better than to set out riding backward.

4 **WHO ARE THE HELPFUL ANIMALS?** The mere act of setting out can provoke magic. If, in trusting your heart place, you take one step into the unknown, as awkward as that step may be, something awakens in the universe. All manner of birds and beasts and fortuitous happenings come to your aid. The old saying "Take one step and the cosmos moves with you" says that when you begin the way that is uniquely your own, helpful beings arrive to assist.

When I first decided to pursue writing full-time I was scared witless. I kept asking myself if this was the right decision. Voices in my head kept saying, "Are you crazy? Do you want to end up a bag lady?" Then I had a dream where I set out in a rowboat without oars in a stream so shallow I feared the boat wouldn't float. Not only did the boat float, it carried me to a magical place of deep quiet water and tall flowering trees, exotic singing birds and sunshine. The universe had begun to move.

Not that there wasn't a lot of frustration and hard work and discouragement after that. I was plagued by all of these. There were also many happenings of amazing synchronicity that came just in the nick of time, when visions of becoming a bag lady looked like they might actually materialize.

Along with the synchronicities and helpful animals, there came a sense of the bumbling fool inside me who nonetheless knew the way to the treasure. He made me chuckle. In his awkward way, my inner fool was taking me to places mental cautiousness never could have discovered. As Sallie Nichols says in *Jung and Tarot*, "The joker connects two worlds—the everyday, contemporary world where most of us live most of the time, and the nonverbal land of imagination. . . . [T]his energy is undirected, but seems to find its own way, connecting end with beginning."

Gordon, a photographer I once coached and told the steed story to, recently told me, "I started out riding backward, not knowing where I'm going, but now I'm sitting on the horse, facing front." Gordon is one of the most accomplished photographers I know. But even experienced people are beginners when they first venture into new territory. Some fiction writers have never written poetry or perhaps never tackled a novel. A graphic designer in one of my classes had never worked in clay.

Everything begins in awkwardness and uncertainty. If you try to begin in complete assurance, to iron out all the kinks beforehand, you will also flatten the life out of what you do. Not knowing where you're going at first doesn't mean you can't begin anyway. You may start out riding backward, as our hero did, but the road will unfold as you ramble. The knowing, in truth, may be found in the going.

SEED THOUGHT

"Being empty is a beginning."

Sue Bender
Everyday Sacred

❧ Write a dialogue between your creative fool and your sensible thinking self. What part did each play in your most recent creative project? What does each side have to say about the other's contributions, resistances, and positive and negative qualities?

❧ Knowing where you've been is one way to know where you're going. Think back over your past creative life and background. What mistakes have you made? What opportunities do you regret not pursuing? What traumas have you suffered through? What goals have you accomplished? Write how these elements have shaped the creative person you are. Based on past experience, in what direction do you see your future path leading?

❧ What fairy tale or myth does your past creative history recall? Write your history as if it were such a tale, using second-person point of view and naming your characters imaginatively.

Assessment

❧ Divide your past creative life into at least four or five stages. What precipitated the end of one stage and the beginning of another? How long did each stage continue? What similar elements can you discover in each? Are you now in the beginning, middle or end of a particular period? Write your thoughts.

32. A Knight to Remember

"What I need is one of those tin suits that knights wore back in medieval times," a writer once told me after she'd received a rejection letter from a publisher. Anyone who has ever put a creative offspring on the judgment block knows the feeling. Rejection hurts. Your tender insides are vulnerable.

Not all creative people jump at the chance to act like Don Quixote and go where the brave dare not go. Most of us hang back and look for shelter. We wonder how we can be tough and tender at the same time. Tough enough to do battle with a world that's hostile to new ideas. Tender enough to connect with the moment-to-moment experiences that form our creative ground.

If we become fierce and arm ourselves too well, the armor that keeps out slings and arrows also keeps out feelings and sensations. Can you imagine yourself in one of those knight suits? You wouldn't be able to feel the breeze through your hair. The metal would cut you

MENTAL ARMOR

FOR YOUR

SOFT SPOTS

off from sensitive contact with your creative home country—the source of ideas and images, the place where your creative muse lives.

But if you face the world in your own vulnerable skin, you also open yourself to criticism and rejection. What writer hasn't felt the sting of a rejection letter? What artist hasn't experienced the walking-on-hot-coals sensation during a class critique? Without our knight suits, we're as defenseless as shelled oysters.

Every creative act begins in vulnerability. Filled with uncertainty, you pen the lead for your article about how to organize a home library. Your hand shakes. Your head is filled with cobwebs. No tender snail extending a soft foot out of its shell ever felt so vulnerable! This is a time to be gentle with yourself, to allow mistakes and false starts and getting lost in sidetracks. The key word here is *allow*. "You cannot begin to recollect yourselves by force, but only by gentleness," advised Saint Teresa of Avila. A creative act is a re-collection, a gathering of all you are and know. In the beginning, you're not yet ready for exposure.

The main thing is to know when you're vulnerable so you can dust off your tin suit or take other precautions. Assume you are in a tender state when

- you're beginning a large creative project
- you're completing a project you've worked on for eons
- your creative energy is compromised by a heavy load of demands from other parts of your life
- you're going through an important life transition: divorce, beginning or ending a job, ill health, death of a loved one, a move to a new place

A couple of decades ago, I learned a large lesson in vulnerability when someone gave me a tropical air plant. Well, they didn't actually give me a whole plant, just a starter—one large leaf about the size of a pair of pouty lips. The leaf edges were scalloped, like a piecrust, and I was told that the leaf, kept anywhere—even pinned to living room drapes or stuck in a drawer—would sprout baby plants along its scalloped edges in about three weeks. It sounded like the perfect plant for someone like me who subscribed to the notion of benign neglect.

I watched eagerly every hour for about a week. Then I checked every few days. Finally I forgot to look at all. When I came across the leaf again, it had sprouted around its edges ten tiny new plants about a half inch tall. Each plant had two or three microscopic leaves and a thready bunch of roots. I plucked off the fragile sprouts one by one, pressed them into the soil in ten tiny pots, watered them and set them in a warm, sunny window. The next day I was surprised to find them wilted and prostrate in their pots, nearly dead. Frantically, I called the garden center, and after a lot of asking around I heard, "The new plants are too tender for direct sun. Put them in a sheltered place with just a little light until they're strong enough to be in the window." I did as I was told. The plants flourished. They managed to live in captivity for another twenty years. I learned an important lesson about vulnerability: Before you can protect something, you have to recognize that it needs protection.

There's an unborn "something" inside you that needs your care and protection to survive. Sometimes, like the air plant leaf, that something is in such an early stage of development it can't be detected. Sometimes when all you've got is the seed of an idea, you have to wait until you can find good ground to plant it in and let it grow.

When women in Suriname were being enslaved by the Dutch, they would steal rice, corn, wheat, bean and squash seeds and hide them in their voluminous hairdos. When they escaped to a jungle refuge, they'd shake their heads to propagate the new fields. They saved their seeds until the time was ripe.

Others, too, have "saved their seeds." Viktor Frankl carried notes for his idea for a new therapy on a tiny scrap of paper in his pocket while he was in a World War II concentration camp. Two executives I know met regularly for years to develop and preserve a new concept for a retirement community until they could find friendly soil to plant the idea. My artist friend Bev worked out a revolutionary idea for creating the effect of three dimensions in an art poster. Ten years passed before she found a use for it. "The poster showed a face and hands that looked as through they were pushing out of the canvas," she said. "When you look at it, it's as if a barrier has been broken. The poster was published in several magazines and won many awards, including being selected for the exhibition of fifty best posters of the decade."

Ideas can be like the thousand-year-old east Indian lotus seeds that were discovered in southern Manchuria. They had been stored in a protected place, and when conditions were favorable and they were planted, they sprouted!

Even when ideas have sprouted, like our fragile air plants they need care and protection at first. One thing we commonly do with a new inspiration is to tell everybody we know. The talk alone leaches energy from the idea. Hermann Hesse wrote in *Demian*: "We talk too much. Clever talk is absolutely worthless. All you do in the process is lose yourself."

To protect an embryonic idea, it's necessary to "crawl completely inside oneself, like a tortoise," Hesse says. This means setting boundaries, both inside and outside. It means creating mental armor. It means becoming the dragon that guards your own treasure.

When you crawl into your imaginal space, you enter a place of aloneness. Here you can make your mind tender, receptive, virgin. Here you can be free to imagine preposterous things.

The danger comes when you present your newborn ideas to the world. As remarkable as these ideas may be, when they emerge fragile from the creative soil they can be flattened as quickly as a newly sprouted air plant in a hot, sunny window.

A writer friend tells about such an event. She was part of a four-person, online writing group and decided to share with the group a story she had just finished. "They started tearing my story apart until it was in shreds. After that I lost all inspiration," she says.

Like it or not, criticism is part of the creative process. At some point, your work will be judged. You can protect yourself by making sure that judgment happens in the right way and at the right time.

In grade school, my teachers always marked the report card box that read, "Does not accept criticism kindly." I was told I was too sensitive, too bullheaded, too reclusive (they didn't actually use the word *reclusive*, but something like it). As a result of my vulnerability to criticism, I've collected every tip I could find over the years that would help me out. Here are some of them:

1 **ASK FOR THE KIND OF CRITICISM YOU WANT.** I don't know about you, but this thought never occurred to me. If you're feeling fragile or your work isn't quite ready for bright sunlight, say, "I'm just starting this and I want to know what's *good* about it. Maybe later, when I'm feeling more confident, you can pull out all the stops and tell me the whole truth, but right now let's stick to positives."

2 **REMEMBER THAT YOU HAVE TO TAME YOUR INNER CRITIC FIRST.** (See chapter twenty-eight.) If you don't, you'll likely take outer criticism personally. This can lead to paralyzing self-doubt that can cripple your creative process and intensify your inner critic's faultfinding.

3 **KNOW THAT SOMETIMES THE FEEDBACK YOU GET FROM OTHER PEOPLE IS FLAT-OUT WRONG.** Be your own knight defender. Listen carefully to input, consider what's useful and then go your own way.

4 **REMEMBER THAT YOU MAY HAVE A FEELING OF OWNERSHIP TOWARD YOUR WORK BUT YOUR WORK IS NOT YOU.** Learn to stay centered and not be put off balance by either positive or negative comments. "Thou art not the better for being praised, nor art thou the worse for being blamed," Thomas à Kempis once said.

5 **ASK FOR SPECIFIC CRITICISM THAT'S RELEVANT TO THE STAGE THE WORK IS IN.** Specific criticism says, "You could add more active verbs to pep up this short story," instead of, "This story lacks something; it seems a little fuzzy to me." Relevant criticism does not include nit-picking of spelling and punctuation in the first draft.

In classes, I use positive feedback almost exclusively. I feel immense enthusiasm for the place in someone's written or visual work that contains the creative spark. Nita Leland advises us in *The Creative Artist*, "Learn from the things you do right." This is the method I try to follow in class, sometimes adding a suggestion on how to continue in a fruitful direction.

The creative act gathers strength as it develops. Weak at the start, like a newly sprouted air plant, it thrives when it's given care and protection. In the end, despite all the support you're able to muster, the creative act is a lone enterprise requiring vulnerable resilience, immense courage and limitless perseverance. As someone once advised me, "You've got to have guts to go in naked, stripped of all defenses." And it goes without saying, armored only on the inside.

SEVEN STEPS TO REJECTION PROTECTION

Or

How to Build a "Bomb" Shelter

1·Expect failure sometimes. Creative people fail more often than uncreative people.

2·Keep several pots cooking. Have an alternative fallback plan. Don't invest your whole self in just one project. (Remember the saying about putting all your eggs in one basket.)

3·Hold a failure rehearsal. Imagine how you'll feel if your idea doesn't fly. Can you cope? Plan some ready therapy if you need a morale boost (be with friends, take a walk, tinker with a hobby). If failure is too scary to consider, postpone your idea's debut.

4·Remember that every rejection or failure you survive lessens future fear.

5·Don't quit when you're behind. Submit the article to one more publisher. Try your idea in one more place. Work through kinks to finish your project no matter how it turns out. Start over. Keep plugging.

6·Approach every project with a "let's see what happens" attitude, not an "everything is riding on this" frame of mind.

7·Learn to laugh at yourself. It gives perspective.

Explorations

❧ Think about a time when you felt creatively vulnerable. Maybe you had an idea for a new poetry form or decided to do an old project in a new way. You were not quite clear about how to proceed. Write out the idea with as much detail as you can. Then write what kind of input you'd like if you were to proceed at this stage in your work. Consider what kind, who, etc.

❧ Let's say you're sending a short story to a magazine publisher. Or you're designing a logo for a contest. Or you're taking a class in sumi-e for the first time. Write about the worst thing that could happen as a result of putting your creativity on the block. Devise a worst-case safety net. How will you cope?

Creative Retreat

❧ Plan a few hours, a day or a weekend to yourself when you're at a vulnerable stage in your creative life or the life of a creative project you're working on. Let your creative life and/or your project speak to you. Write as if each is talking in its own voice and telling you what it needs. What does it need to feel safe? To fulfill its potential? How can you cooperate?

33. The Mother of Invention

HOW LIMITS

PROMOTE

CREATIVITY

Creativity craves challenge. The two are locked in an inseparable embrace. Without the gritty problem of an irritating obstruction, the creative oyster lacks incentive to form a pearl. These obstructions, these limitations, can come from outside or inside. Outer ones include deadlines, budget constraints or market demands. Inner limits are ones you set yourself, such as when you decide on a focus before you write an article or create a painting.

Whether limits are imposed from outside or deliberately set by your own inner promptings, they urge you over, under and around the wall of conventional thinking. They inspire breakthroughs. Sometimes limits themselves can lead to new ways of seeing and doing, as they did years ago for a bunch of us who worked at a small radio station in Illinois. Out of admitted self-interest and desperation, we devised a unique way to market airtime. Our predicament became the mother of invention.

The radio station where I worked as a copywriter occupied the rear of the ground floor of a dingy downtown hotel. The hotel had become, over the years, a home to released mental patients and practicing alcoholics. It had atmosphere. Anyone who entered the lobby on the way to the radio station was assailed by the smell of cheap wine and stale tobacco smoke. Sprawled on the overstuffed maroon mohair couches and chairs at least one nearly lifeless body inevitably snoozed.

None of our station staff looked forward to summer. The hotel's ancient wiring and high ceilings prohibited air-conditioning, and the grimy windows looking out over a walled alley let in little air. That hot July the very bricks breathed heat. With no other alternative, we prepared to sweat it out in our business suits as we had done in other summers.

When temperatures were predicted to soar to the nineties we asked the boss if we could wear shorts to work. He refused, saying it wouldn't look professional. So we proposed a deal: Would he change his mind if we could boost ad revenues by 50 percent? Intrigued, and no doubt influenced by slow summer ad sales, he consented.

Our small staff rolled into high gear. Motivated by the heat and lack of air-conditioning, we came up with the idea of Keep Cool Week. We did remote broadcasts from the city's swimming pool, an ice cream parlor and the shaded picnic tables at Wing Park. We wore shorts to work. And we sold ad time like crazy! In the end, the irritating limitation of no air-conditioning turned into a pearl of a cool idea. Each of us enjoyed a week of breezy knees. And, as a bonus, we earned an extra day's pay for turning a negative limitation into a positive innovation. Without the limiting situation we might never have produced the bright idea.

"There is no creation unless the urge to life has been impeded in some way," says Andrew Brink in *Loss and Symbolic Repair*. We write or paint or think around those impediments just like water flows around a rock. It's the rocks that keep us on our creative toes. They provide the limits that spur creative imagination.

In our abundant world, we hate the thought of limits. All our scientific and technological innovations have been aimed at erasing limits and widening options. We feel good about having 150 program choices on cable TV. We wax ecstatic over limitless information on the

Internet. Who needs limits? It turns out, creativity needs limits just like sweet peas need poles to lean on. "Having limitless choices and possibilities (or thinking one does) really means having very few," Robert Woolfolk and Frank Richardson point out in *Stress, Sanity, and Survival*. In our time of excess, unlimited choices can lead to creative paralysis. There are no stones in our streams to direct our creative juices and exercise our capacities.

You can see how this happens when a writer sets out to string words together without a guiding, and necessarily limiting, idea of where those words are going. A middle-aged corporate executive who was trying to write about his ideas for running a business once told me, "After I'd finished some five thousand words, I read over what I'd written, and the writing didn't seem to go anywhere. To get a fix on what was wrong, I had a friend look over the story. He said, 'What's your point? What are you trying to say?' I hadn't set enough limits. The writing was all over the place."

The same thing happens to artists who fall in love with the view of the Ohio River from the top of Mount Adams, a neighborhood in Cincinnati. They paint the whole scene, all 180 degrees of the landscape: the river's twists and turns, and the quaint buildings on the Kentucky side, and the skyscrapers on the Ohio side, and interstates 275, 71 and 75 as they interweave through the misty hills and off into the horizon. Maybe it can be done. Maybe somebody could actually paint that whole scene successfully. I haven't seen it happen yet.

What a lot of creative people do is impose limits on their own work. These very limits seem to bring out untapped creative genius. Hiro Clark quotes Pablo Picasso in his biography, *In His Words*, as saying, "Forcing yourself to use restricted means is the sort of restraint that liberates invention. It obliges you to make the kind of progress that you can't even imagine in advance."

There may be no better example of the triumph of such liberation than Robert Pinsky's poem "ABC." Each word of the poem begins with a letter of the alphabet in proper sequence, beginning with *A* and ending with *Z*. I tried it once. It took days. And I could never capture the grace of Pinsky's brilliant choice of words. "Sweet *time* *u*nafflicted." Can you beat that?

Writing poetry isn't easy, even when you don't have to keep your words in alphabetical order. Why make it harder? Why impose an extra limiting factor when you don't have to? You do it to make a framework to hang your thoughts on. You can't think without a framework any more than you can walk without bones to support the soft sag of your body. When you make an outline, that's a framework. When you sketch an image before you paint, that's a framework. When you get an idea and figure out a way to make it happen, that's a framework. A framework is a limitation. It gives you structure.

"Limitation is what differentiates a flood from a lake. In the making of things, limitations allow you to choose from something rather than everything," Corita Kent and Jan Steward explain in *Learning by Heart*. As creative people, most of us want the whole ocean, not just some puny puddle. That's how a manageable two-thousand-word essay can turn into an unwieldy two-thousand-page book. We think that limitation destroys the whole. We're right. We're also wrong.

No matter what you create, it will never be as glorious and shining as the vision that inspired it. The moment you write the first word on paper or dab the first brushstroke on canvas you impose limitations. You destroy the whole. Every creative act is a translation from an amorphous idea into a particular expression of that idea. You never capture the whole thing. It's like the time a man showed Picasso a wallet-size picture and said, "This is my wife," and Picasso responded, "She looks a bit small and flat." Photographs, words, paints—whatever you use to express creativity—never do the whole job. Going in we are limited by our mediums.

Add to that the multitude of budget constraints and deadlines and other limitations imposed from the outside and it's a wonder creative people can function at all. How do they do it? Most of the people I've talked to say they see limitations as a challenge, not as an insurmountable barrier. My photographer friend Connie was recently preparing for a show and working on an extremely tight deadline. Exacerbating the time crunch was the fact that the photographs were being made into lightboxes in Hong Kong and she had to fly there just weeks before the show to check on her work. "The project was highly

SEED THOUGHT

" *. . . you must break through* old structures, develop broader structures, break through those and develop still broader structures."

Ram Dass
Journey of Awakening

condensed timewise, but this limitation made me more aware of how the creative process grows and changes and develops as it goes along," Connie said. "I understand better what I'm trying to do because of the time limit. I'm forced to concentrate in a certain way, and that gives my work greater intensity. Time pushes you to do more."

Recognizing a limitation as an opportunity can open vistas of possibility. If you're not intimidated by limitations, you can often break through to an even better idea. I once had to develop a brochure promoting gifts to a fund that supplies care to nursing home residents who run out of money. The budget for the job was severely restricted. I joked to someone that for so little money all we could afford was to run the brochures on the copier. "That's a plan," that someone said. It got me thinking. I found clip art of a rainbow and put that on the front, then I added copy on the inside. The whole thing—you guessed it—could be run on the copier. And there was a bonus I had not anticipated: Residents of the nursing home could color in the rainbows with markers before the brochures were mailed. The residents gained a useful, sociable, fun project to occupy their time. I experienced the satisfaction—you might even say the triumphant ecstasy—of staying within a severely limited budget.

Every potentially creative situation imposes limits. You don't necessarily have to be limited by those limits. Whether it's a constricted deadline, a tight budget or the lack of air-conditioning that motivates you, the obstacle itself inspires a new creative solution just as the irritation of the grit inside an oyster creates the pearl. Love the obstacle just as much as you value the pearl.

Explorations

❧ Write about a recent creative project and what limits were set from outside (deadlines, length, budget, format, etc.). Were these limits challenging and inspiring or frustrating and insurmountable? What did you learn from wrestling with them?

❧ To get a firsthand feeling of working within limits, write your own poem where each word begins with a letter of the alphabet, in sequence. Arrange the lines of your twenty-six-word poem as you like. Give your poem a name.

❧ Deliberately set limitations in a medium in which you regularly work. For example, write a short story in two hundred words. Paint using a stick instead of a brush. Make a clay sculpture with your eyes closed. Write about your experience. How did the limitation affect your final result? How did the experiment compare with your usual way of working?

Assessment

❧ Review a recent creative project. What limits, conscious or unconscious, did you set for yourself? At what point in the process did you impose these limits? Write for twenty minutes about all of your insights.

Research

❧ Talk to people who are considered to be successful in their work. Ask what limitations they've overcome, what limitations have spurred creative solutions and what limitations they've learned to live with in a creative way. Write about your findings.

34. The Value of Being Weird

Each of us begins life desperately desiring to be a one-of-a-kind, uniquely shaped, raspberry-jelly-filled croissant. But as time goes on, the world turns us into pretzels. We become, in fact, pretzels on an assembly line, molded by upbringing and education into the same shape as everyone else. We sacrifice our weirdness.

Parents, teachers, neighbors, churches and communities want to shape our weird, wild, exotic dough into an acceptable pattern. They can't tell from our unformed potential what we'll turn into eventually. They do know what it takes to get by in the world, so they fit us into that mold. No one says we have to stay there. We don't have to be pretzels for life. Trouble is, however, the longer we stay that way, the more people expect us to be pretzels forever.

So we rebel. We become antipretzels. We dye our hair purple and spike it with hair gel. We drill holes to hold nose rings. What we fail to see is that different isn't the same as authentic. By the time the truth dawns, we're well past puberty. One day we blurt, "Who am I?"

"I spent the first part of my life learning the ropes and the rest of my life trying to untie them," says one middle-aged writer. He says he had a fantasy of being tightly bound and unable to move. The product of a strict upbringing, he spent the first part of his life doing things by the book—his parents' book, his school's book, his religion's book. He didn't begin to learn what his own book had to say until much later.

You can create from only one place. That place is your real, honest-to-goodness, warts-and-all self. This is the self that the world begins to pretzelize and judge even before you outgrow the training wheels on your first two-wheeler. Jeanne Carbonetti, artist and author of *The Tao of Watercolor*, sums up the situation: "When I was a child I was whole. I simply painted, and I was glad. Later, as life grew more complex, I split into many selves, and I learned to judge them all. Some parts were good, others bad. Some were to be loved, others rejected."

Creativity is being all we are. It's living everything flat out. Expressing a creative idea becomes more important than money or status; working from the heart, more important than approval and fitting in.

Someone once told me an old Hassidic tale about Yasha and Moses. Yasha complained to the rabbi that he felt terrible that he couldn't be more like Moses, his idol. The rabbi said, "God won't ask you why you weren't like Moses, but why you weren't Yasha." Likewise, your creativity won't be enhanced by being like Shakespeare or Rembrandt, but by being like you—in all your weird uniqueness.

Trying to be like Moses, live up to other people's expectations or conform to the rules, valid or not, takes all the bubble out of life. It begins to taste like flat champagne. But flat can be a good thing. It can be an early warning that you're sacrificing your own weird, quirky creative self. Waking up to the loss is the first step toward recovery.

I've been in just such a flat state of mind more than once. The bubble and sparkle disappeared from my creative work, and I didn't know why. As Charlotte Joko Beck writes in *Nothing Special*, "at any given moment we are the way we are, and we see what we are able to see." I wasn't able to see what was corroding my creative work. After all, hadn't I tried to do just what the editors wanted? Wasn't I trying to live up to everyone's expectations? Obviously, whatever I was doing

SEED THOUGHT

"*The ordeal of being* true to your own inner way must stand high on the list of ordeals. It is like being in the power of someone you cannot reach, know or move, but who never lets you go; who both insists that you accept yourself and who seems to know who you are."

Florida Scott-Maxwell
The Measure of My Days

wasn't working. I saw what I was able to see: very little.

Then, while driving through a small village one afternoon, I saw something that made flashbulbs go off in my head. The rear license plate holder on the yellow Volkswagen ahead of me bore the message: "I'm a S.W.P.—Super Weird Person." The driver, from what I could see of her through the car's rear window, certainly didn't look weird—long blonde hair, young, probably pretty. Here was a perfectly normal-looking person who claimed to be weird and proud of it. The experience was an eye-opener. Weirdness could be celebrated!

You can't reclaim the missing parts of your creative self until you realize they're missing. And you can't begin to own your wild, weird creative self until you realize you've disowned it in the past. When you wake up, you can start to recover what you've lost. Your creative peculiarities can come out of the closet.

I once knew an African-American aide who worked in a nursing home. In his off time he made magnificent sculptures out of tar. The black asphalt nudes were shiny and thick and immensely powerful. The sculptor himself was intent on keeping his talent secret. Amazingly, he kept the black tar nudes in a closet, fearing that if they saw the light of day they'd be criticized as being weird. They were indeed weird, but in the best sense: unique, unusual, inspired.

Like this sculptor, we tend to hide our most startling innovations, our most personal creative expressions. Why do we do it? Because we're afraid people will think we're weird. Yet it's that weird, original, quirky, authentic way of being that gives us a creative standpoint where we can take a stand, declare inner truth and plant a flag on the mountaintop.

If you've lost your weird, creative self, it's not too late to get it back. With a little effort, you can reclaim the disowned and unrecognized parts of yourself that can hold enormous potential. Here are some ways that have worked for other creative people.

Accept Imperfection Without Shame

I like the Japanese concept of Zen, or "human heartedness." It implies a state of down-to-earth humanness, not just high-flying pursuit of

perfection. It means loving and accepting your lacks as much as your
lovableness. It means allowing foibles and shortcomings and anxieties.

Charles Shulz, creator of the "Peanuts" comic strip, once told
an interviewer about his lifelong struggle with lack of confidence and
persistent anxiety. Yet he accepted these as parts of himself and went on
to forge one of the most successful cartoon enterprises since Disney.

"Liberation comes when we lose anxiety about imperfection,"
says Jack Kornfield in *A Path With Heart*. One way to accept imperfection is to filter it through a sense of humor. Laugh at mistakes. Make a
joke out of what my neighbor Anne calls a "Charlie Chaplin moment."

Another way to accept imperfection is to listen to what you
tell yourself in one of those Charlie Chaplin moments. "Every time I
made a mistake or goofed in some way or let some shortcoming show,
I'd always call myself Dumbo," a woman once told me. "It wasn't until
I had a dream of this pitiful little elephant, this Dumbo, traipsing after
me looking for affection that I realized how I'd been treating myself."

Learning to accept your Dumbos and your Charlie Chaplin
moments is an ongoing process. No one will tell you to do it. The
world doesn't place much value on a free, authentic self. You can try
carrying around this mantra by Lucia Cappacchione from her book *The
Creative Journal*: "To be free is to value all that I am proud of and all
that I am ashamed of in myself and to accept the whole as being me."

Resist Coercion

Don't play dead for others' benefit. "Only dead fish swim with the
tide," Malcolm Muggeridge once said. If you feel your creativity going
dead, look around to see whom you're trying to please, what mold
you're attempting to fit, what threat you're crouching to avoid.

A woman I once knew told me about a time she had an executive position with a company where all her co-workers were men. She
was afraid to express ideas that sounded typically feminine, so she tried
to act like the men. Then one night she dreamed she was on a men's
football team and couldn't seem to get the hang of the game. After
that, she realized she'd been trying to play by other people's rules.
She'd allowed her natural creativity to be coerced into a masculine

mold. It was an awakening. The realization prodded her to step outside a self-imposed cage and use her authentic creativity in her work.

Remember a Time When You Were Your True, Authentic Self

Who were you before the world tried to make you a pretzel? You may have to go back to the time when you were twelve and built a tree house all by yourself. Or the time when you were eight and, despite your terror of the deep water, learned to do a back flip off the diving board. Or the time in college when you took a creative writing course and, on a whim, sent your short story to a magazine that accepted it! It could be a time way back when or just yesterday. The idea is to remember your freewheeling weirdness, your creative bravado, your spunk and your spirit. Call it up. Let it inspire you.

Know Your Creative Needs

Even if your needs are weird, honor them. Do you have to write on blue legal pads that you can order only from a specialty stationer? Order them. Can you paint only to the strains of Mozart? Plunk in your CD and get cooking! Other people do it. Violinist Itzhak Perlman watches baseball or cricket on TV while he practices his instrument. It's a personal quirk that meets a creative need. He does it even though the voice of a long-ago instructor may be resounding in his ear: "You can't do that. You must give your music full attention."

When Brian Wilson, one of the Beach Boys, ran into a dry spell in his composing, he put his piano in an enormous sandbox so he could sit on the bench and feel the sand of a simulated beach under his bare feet as he composed. The sand met a creative need. You can find your own sand, your own creative ground to sink your toes into. Know your creative needs, and do what you can to meet them.

Every choice you make is for or against your authentic creative self. You can be a lopsided raspberry-jelly-filled croissant in all its quirky weirdness. Or you can get stuck on the assembly line and let the world pretzelize you. You choose.

Explorations

🌼 What's unique about you (talents, preferences, hobbies, way of looking at things)? What's good about that? Make a list of ten ways you're different, and keep adding to it as you become aware of new areas. Choose one thing on the list, and write about how your particular uniqueness makes you valuable.

🌼 What's unique about other people you know? How can you support their constructive uniqueness? How can you stand up for them in the face of other people's ridicule? Write your ideas.

🌼 What has happened in your life (positive or negative) that hasn't happened to other people? How have these events shaped you as a unique person? Use these experiences as a starting place for creative expression. Write, draw, sculpt, dance, act your own drama.

🌼 Write for twenty minutes about your personal response to this statement: You are fine just as you are. Pick up your pen, and write as fast as you can.

🌼 List ten things you've done in the past few weeks. Were you *drawn* to do them, or were you **driven** to do them (out of feelings of duty, fear, compliance)? Write your thoughts.

Project

🌼 Make a scrapbook of what's unique about you. Divide it into various periods in your life. Use snapshots, clippings, drawings, etc. Write about each segment.

dancing with your
creative spirit

35. The Big Awe

The creative source is a room hidden inside you. Wonder is a door that—for an instant—opens to give you a glimpse inside. Wonder entertains mystery, builds a nest for the unknown and unknowable, and lures you down the path less traveled.

My poet friend Karen told me about such an experience: her first encounter with the raw fearsomeness of Big Sur, California. "I was in the redwood forest among towering trees, looking down from a cliff at the wide, endless ocean. It gave me a primordial feeling," Karen says. "Outside the structure of the man-made world, untamed and awesome, this place made me feel what I've come to call 'the big awe.'"

A sense of awe doesn't have to be big. It doesn't have to come from being in the presence of mountains or redwoods or the sea's broad horizon. Creative people ooze awe at the drop of a hat. They look at the network of finely etched lines in the palms of their hands and are amazed. They're enchanted by a broken robin's egg, fragile and blue. They're fascinated by the ordinary as well as the extra-ordinary, by the miniscule as well as the magnificent.

Even animals can be hypnotized by an awesome sight. Some-one once told me about a gorilla that scientists had come upon in the jungles of Africa. When the scientists met up with the gorilla standing in a clearing beside a stream, the animal was staring, transfixed, at a waterfall tumbling from a high ridge. The gorilla was no doubt experiencing "the big awe."

Human awe is often buried under layers of familiarity. People, creatures, plants and things we see every day tend to fall out of our awareness, and they no longer arrest our attention. A few Saturdays ago I asked a group of students the usual question, "What did you see on the way to class?" It was one of those rare, breezy, sunlit spring days when in the space of a few hours everything had burst into bloom—yellow daffodils, deep purple magnolias and pink cherry blossoms. Runners clad in their Nikes and shorts, babies riding in their strollers, dogs surging at the end of their leashes, fountains burbling, bees scuzzing—"the big awe" was present in full force.

So what did the students see on their way to class? "Cars," they said, "and people." What else? What else? Silence. Suddenly they remembered other things. They were enthusiastic, now, filled again with what they had seen, blurting impressions, summoning mind pictures. They had experienced awe but they hadn't been aware of it at the time.

That's how our ability to wonder gets obscured. We operate on automatic pilot. We drive along and don't notice that trees and flowers are blooming all over town. We're half asleep. It usually takes something dramatic to startle us into wakefulness.

One sunny day last fall when I was walking in the woods—yellow and red branches arching over the path, quiet resounding everywhere—I was startled awake. I heard a loud *pop!* Then another. Then another. *Pop! Pop! Pop!* What was making the noise? It sounded like exploding popcorn in a metal pot. Soon other people began to gather along the path. Our mouths were agape in awe. We watched and waited. Then we saw them: wisteria pods detonated all around us. *Pop!* A pod blew open and flung its seeds into the air. We were astonished.

SEED THOUGHT

"*Penetrating so many secrets, we cease to believe in the unknowable. But there it sits, nevertheless, calmly licking its chops.*"

H.L. Mencken
American author, editor and critic

We had been in the presence of an awesome happening, and lucky for us, we were alerted by a loud noise. The students on the way to class had no such wake-up call. Few of us do. So if we're going to open ourselves to experience, to all the wonders we want to capture in word, paint, stone, motion or sound in our creative lives, we have to find a way to intercept awe. Wisteria pods can't be depended upon to pop us out of somnambulism. We have to keep dusting off our sense of wonder so it doesn't become encrusted with apathy and inattention. And we can't depend on the presence of redwood trees to draw our attention or the magnificence of mountains to sustain our wonder.

If you want to be an artist in any sense of the word, you have to learn to experience self-generated awe in even the simplest things: shadows, a mud puddle, grass.

Annie Dillard, a master of capturing the wonder of simple things, gives us this passage in *Holy the Firm*: "The land's progress of colors leads the eye up a distant hill, a sweeping big farm of a hill whose yellow pastures bounce light all day from a billion stems and blades; and down the hill's rim drops a dark slope of fir forest, a slant your eye rides down to the point, the dark sliver of land that holds the bay." Can you feel the awe Dillard felt over "a billion stems and blades"? Have you ever looked closely at grass?

Look at everything as if for the first time and you will be awed. You will never run out of fuel for your creative work. When you were a toddler you never lacked for wonder. The world was new. You had a million things to explore, touch, taste, see. Then as you grew, your rational mind began to get in the way; you forgot to notice the blossoming things. As Jonathan Swift wrote in *Gulliver's Travels*, "what use is a flower to intellect? He would tear them up to measure their breadth and circumference." The rational mind can't tolerate mystery and wonder. It has to have answers. To be awed is to allow mystery to live, to sit beside you, to make you wonder.

The wondering mind doesn't have to figure things out. It doesn't have to have answers like some scientists I read about in *Smithsonian Magazine* do. Author Robert Evans wrote that a group of scientists was fascinated by the dozens of what he calls "dancing rocks" discovered at the Racetrack playa, a dried lake bed in Death Valley

National Park, reachable only by twenty-five miles of bumpy, unpaved road. The rocks, some weighing hundreds of pounds, moved across the clay of the desert floor. No one ever saw them move, but they left curious tracks to prove it. The tracks circled and crisscrossed, turned, doubled back, veered sideways.

Scientists were baffled. They had pitched their tents to launch serious studies. Determined to find answers, they mapped and tracked by computer and satellite. They painted identifying numbers on the rocks. They built small corrals around some. They proposed wind theories, ice theories, wet mud theories, but in the end mystery prevailed. The site remains, as far as I know, a source of wonder to those with the fortitude to get there. Something inside me cheered when I read that the scientists were eventually asked to leave. The mystery remains intact, with wonder still smiling its secret smile.

In our compulsive drive for answers, we miss the creative importance of mystery, wonder and awe. We want answers fast, like turning on a light switch.

Mystery, wonder and awe slow you down, take you deep, generate more questions than answers. For creative work to have depth, the creative person has to go below, to where the wonder is. In the underground are few answers to satisfy rational purpose. But anthropologist Gregory Bateson reminds us, "Mere purposive rationality, unaided by art, religion, dream and the like, is necessarily pathogenic and destructive of life." Especially creative life. By limiting our awareness to what we can understand, we erect barriers to our creative homeland. Awe keeps the creative mind open and flexible. If you let it, awe can be inspired by almost anything.

Dom Perignon, the French monk who invented champagne, became exultant over the tiny bubbles in his glass. "Brothers, come quickly," he shouted to his fellow monks, "I'm drinking stars!" To be awestruck calls for an openness to experience, a generosity of spirit that's capable of being agog over the simplest things. Even bubbles.

Awe is, in a sense, spiritual. It's a deep, moment-to-moment appreciation of and respect for all you experience. Such gratitude shows up in creative expression as it did in the work of the classic composer Beethoven. "Beethoven was grateful, and his music said thanks," recalled Italian conductor Riccardo Muti. Your work, too, can be an expression of gratitude and awe.

Abstract expressionist artist Mark Rothko showed his own feelings of awe and respect for unknowable mystery in massive paintings eight or nine feet across. A woman told me, "I never cared much for abstract painting, especially Rothko. But a few months ago I was in a whole room full of Rothkos in a gallery in Washington, DC. People sat for hours there, just looking and absorbing. What I'd always thought were simplistic renderings of rectangles smeared at the edges began to speak to me when I was surrounded by them in a darkened room with light focused only on the paintings' subtle tones. I was awestruck."

To be in awe is to entertain something that's beyond understanding without trying to explain it or to unveil its mystery. As Albert Einstein said, "The most beautiful thing we can experience is the mysterious. It is the source of all true art and science." The experience of mystery can inspire creative expression. When you can't explain something, you're compelled to express it in paint, word, sound or movement. The mystery itself, the state of awe—whether it's inspired by dancing rocks, the raging seas of Big Sur or an ordinary dandelion—can, if you follow it, lead you to new realms of insight and creative expression.

Explorations

❧ What tickles your awe bone? What inspires your sense of wonder? The changing colors of the sea as clouds move by overhead? The tiny fingers of a newborn wrapped around your thumb? The majestic presence of mountains? A new snowfall at dawn? Make a list of ten experiences. Write, in depth, about one of them without trying to explain or analyze.

❧ Practice the wonder of small things. Write about the higher value of something ordinary or even repulsive (an old shoe at the city dump; your grandfather's wooden toolbox; a soggy telephone book left out in the rain; the stump of a dead, rotting tree).

❧ What mystified you as a child? How did you feel when you found out what was behind the mystery? (For example, you found out who Santa Claus really was, or you learned how a magic trick was done.) Fill a page with your thoughts.

Walkabout

❧ Walk around your neighborhood, a park or your city's downtown. Carry a notepad, and write down anything that inspires wonder (how a tall building got built, what makes a seed sprout, how robins know when to sing before the first light dawns). Later, choose one thing on your list, and write for twenty minutes. Explore your wonder without being tempted to try to find answers.

36. Being There

PRACTICES TO

CALM YOUR

SKITTERY MIND

AND TAP YOUR

CREATIVE SOURCE

I once knew a woman named Aldyth who kept a wild squirrel in her family room. What the circumstances of the squirrel's confinement were, I don't remember. Maybe it had been injured and Aldyth nursed it back to health and decided to keep it, as she did a growing number of stray cats and dogs. Or maybe she captured it on purpose. I don't know. But there the squirrel was, confined in a cage that took up most of the room. The squirrel cage contained, in addition to a food dish and water basin, a leafless tree and a revolving wheel where the creature cavorted in constant fits of nervous energy.

One day while we watched the squirrel skitter up and down its tree and scamper around its revolving exercise wheel, Aldyth mused, "It's like the inside of a human brain with all the squirrely thoughts running around in there."

Exactly! It was as if we could see our own minds. How well we know those improbable leaps from branch to branch, the incessant

chatter, the pointless circling round and round as our mind clings to
worries, teasing them over and over. The squirrely mind is like a wild
thing out of control. It babbles and blurts. It runs around in our heads
like an untamed animal caught in a cage. It blocks creativity.

Stimulation from the everyday world only makes it worse.
Have you ever surprised yourself by humming the latest dish detergent
commercial? Do the scenes from a violent movie replay themselves in
your head? You're not alone, say Mike and Nancy Samuels in *Seeing
With the Mind's Eye*. "In modern society, stimulation from the outside
world has become so intense that people are daily, hourly, bombarded
with a flood of visual and auditory stimuli—bombarded so continuously that they have to make a conscious effort to shut out the
outer world in order to become more aware of inner experience."

Outer and inner mental junk obscures our mind's connection
with its creative home ground. It's like the Ohio River when it floods
every spring. All kinds of things wash downriver to impede the water's
flow. I've seen car tires, whole trees, a kitchen chair, even a refrigerator, entire and intact. The mind, too, is full of junk. The junk clogs
and muddies creative thinking.

Like our squirrel on its wheel, we probably don't even notice.
We're too busy fending off thoughts, batting them aside like someone on
the receiving end of a barrage of Pete Sampras serves. Our place of
awareness becomes cluttered and enshrouded. To restore our minds' clarity, we have to slow down and let the junk settle out. "Once we slow the
constant creation of new veils by minimizing our thoughts, we begin to
notice how much they shroud and constrict our inner perception," says
David A. Cooper in *Silence, Simplicity, and Solitude*. Therein lies the problem. Until your mind slows, you don't know you're missing anything.

You may have to find out by accident. During a frantically
hectic time in your life, with thought moths swirling in your head,
your mind may suddenly clear when you come face-to-face with unexpected quiet. A man told me he once had such an experience. He'd
ordered a cord of wood to use in the family fireplace that winter, and
the delivery truck had dumped the whole thing in his driveway right in
front of the garage door. By the time he discovered the pile, the truck
had left. He had to be at work in an hour, but he couldn't get his car

out of the garage. There was nothing else to do but carry the wood, log by log, to the backyard.

The man began in disgruntlement to move the pile. "Thoughts buzzed around in my head like angry bees," he said. "As I worked I rehearsed that morning's upcoming workload and my busy day a dozen times in my head. But as I carried each log to the growing pile in my backyard and placed it neatly in a stack, my mind started to calm down. After about a half hour I was physically exhausted, but my mind was as unclouded as crystal."

Japanese poet Bashō calls this clarity of mind "slenderness." A slender mind can slip through junk and clutter to penetrate creative solutions. This may be why creative inspiration often occurs during downtime—when you're doing something else, when your mind is slender. You can be driving, washing the car, stirring beef stew in a pot, chopping wood, scrubbing the kitchen floor or carrying logs. By being present in what you're doing, you pull the cork on the bottle, and the genie breaks out ready to do your bidding. A mental shift from cluttered consciousness to imaginative insight occurs. This mental shift, the slenderness of mind, can be learned.

Descending to a place that's free of mental clutter is like sending your mind through a car wash. It comes out clean and sparkly. All you have to do is give control to that part of yourself that knows more than the squirrel mind that's usually in charge. But trying to give up control stirs the ego's defenses. It hangs on with clenched teeth and won't budge. It's afraid to explore the dark rooms in the rest of its mansion, so it confines itself to a tiny cell.

Going into those unknown, dark rooms can be scary. But, as Old Woodie says in Anna Fynn's *Mister God, This Is Anna*, "My reason for preferring darkness is that in the dark, you have to describe yourself. In the daylight, other people describe you." You don't know who you are as a creative person until you let go of the clutter in the daylight world and walk bravely into the dark.

Going into the dark, into your unknown rooms in quiet solitude ultimately leads you to find the font at which your creative life drinks and is refreshed. This watering keeps your creativity from drying up. When you look at your time apart in this way, you're more apt

to see the necessity of taking time to let your mind settle and clear.
When you do, you can

- expand your ability to concentrate, even under less-than-ideal circumstances
- free yourself from blocks by descending to the depths where they occur
- cultivate a condition of receptiveness and detachment every creative person needs in order to till the ground of innovation and release the mind from the control of habit and the censor
- overcome mental rigidity and loosen capacities for learning to *allow* things to happen rather than to *make* them happen
- erase mental static that can block creative thinking
- penetrate the membrane that separates conscious and unconscious and learn to come and go with ease between these two worlds—the daylight world and the creative dark

There's nothing mysterious about quieting the mind. It just takes practice. You don't need a mantra to chant repeatedly. You don't need fancy cushions. All you have to have is a few minutes in a quiet place to let your mind sort itself out. The quiet place becomes a chrysalis for creative insights. As author and Jungian analyst Marion Woodman says, "The chrysalis is essential if we are to find ourselves. Yet very little in our extroverted society supports introverted withdrawal."

You have to build your own chrysalis, working with whatever you have at hand. Try everything. If something works, make it part of your practice. Saint Francis of Assisi, for example, drew up the collar of his monk's robe when he wanted to enter his inner chamber. When my own mind feels squirrely, I put on a stocking cap or a hooded sweatshirt to literally hold in my thoughts and keep them from running wild and uncontrolled. It's a lot like covering a parrot's cage so the bird will stop chattering and leave you alone.

Going into your chrysalis means simply being with yourself in silent companionship without letting your squirrel mind run away with you. To reach that place, just sit. Sit anywhere there's quiet and freedom from interruption. On a bench in the park. In a lounge chair at the beach. On a stool in the corner of your living room. Or, if there are people there to distract you, try the corner of a large closet, bathroom, garage or basement. Sit on the floor if you're able, back straight, hands in your lap. A cushion for your tush is nice. So is a pad for your knees. I began sitting on an overturned bucket with a couch pillow on top. Unlike other sports, sitting doesn't require a lot of equipment.

What it does require is fifteen minutes to an hour and a place to sit. You can lower your eyes or close them if it helps keep you in your chrysalis, but try not to fall asleep. If you feel a need to time your practice, keep a clock in view. Then just sit. At first you may be plagued by extraneous thoughts babbling in your head:

> Did I remember to turn off the stove? What was the name of the plumber I wanted to call to fix the pipe in the basement? My knee itches. I should be making out my grocery list. What did Sarah say about having surgery next week? I should call her. There's a fly on my forehead. Now it's gone. My legs ache. Why am I doing this? There are so many other things I should be doing. . . .

Your squirrel mind runs around in its cage at the speed of light. What should you do? Just let thoughts and anxieties flow through you. You are a sieve, and they are water passing through. Notice them. Name them. "Oh, that's the old stuff about my mom. There's my compulsion to always be doing something. Here's that nagging worry about money again." Don't try to stop these thoughts, just let them go by like clouds. You can invent visual ways to wave goodbye to them. Imagine writing them on a chalkboard and then erasing the whole bunch, one by one. Picture yourself surrounded by colorful empty boxes, and as stray thoughts come up, file them away in one of the boxes. Be creative. Invent a way that works for you.

Just sitting isn't as easy as it looks. It's not like becoming a limp wet noodle lolling on a chair. It's work. As Swiss artist Paul Klee said, such concentration contains an element of "dynamic repose." If this sounds like an oxymoron, it is. Dynamic repose is passionate tranquility, a merger of opposites. It's a koan, a mental riddle without an answer, that drives the conscious mind nuts! Your squirrel mind chases itself around its cage until, exhausted, it leaves you alone just to be there in peace. You can sit with the awkward, confusing, painful places. You don't have to figure them out or change them right away.

If you have great difficulty sitting still, you may want to try quieting your mind by walking. You can sit for ten or fifteen minutes and walk for five. Or you can just walk. But this isn't your usual fitness walk. It's a careful walk, an attentive walk, a mind-quieting walk. Do this kind of walking with intention and attention. Move slowly. Be aware of the way your foot touches the ground, how you step and bend, the rhythm of your movement. You can plot your own route around the block or through the woods so you can walk without having to think where you're going. Walking can be the focus of your full attention.

"Whether the earth is beautiful, fresh and green or arid and parched depends on our way of walking," said Buddhist monk and writer Thich Nhat Hanh in an interview. Walking is that important. So is sitting. So is anything you do with complete concentration, whether it's making a cup of tea, practicing archery, folding laundry or arranging daisies in a tin sprinkling can.

If you can get the scampering squirrel to sit still for a few minutes, a whole new creative way of being may open to you.

SEED THOUGHT

"Be quite still and solitary. The world will freely offer itself to you to be unmasked. It has no choice. It will roll in ecstasy at your feet."

Franz Kafka

MORE WAYS TO QUIET YOUR SQUIRREL MIND

- **Count your breaths.** Breathe slowly, in and out. Count to ten, then start over again. Or count breaths to one hundred, starting over whenever you forget the number or a thought intrudes.
- **Repeat a word aloud,** slowly, over and over. Or hum it. Sing it in a single tone. Choose something meaningful with round, beautiful sound, such as the word *rainbow*, the word *peaceful* or your own first name.
- **Watch a candle flame,** a fountain, a log fire, a flowing stream, with complete concentration.
- **Focus on an object** (a pencil, a shell, a plant, a screwdriver, a stone) for ten minutes.
- **Move to music, slowly.** Let the music take over your body and direct your motions. Or practice micro motion by touching your thumb tip with the tips of your other four fingers, in sequence, one at a time, moving so slowly it takes several minutes to do them all. Repeat ten times.
- **Listen to the sounds around you**—the patter of rain, a car shussing past on wet pavement, the thrum of the furnace or air conditioner, the chattery voices of children. Become the sounds. Sound keeps you present in the present.
- **Create atmosphere to prepare your mind for calm.** Use the same recorded music or natural sounds from a fountain or the wash of waves each time you practice. Use lavender oil, sage or scented candles to put scent to work. Make taste a trigger by sucking on a whole clove or lemon hard candy.

Explorations

❧ Describe in writing a relaxing scene geared to your own sense of what quiets your mind. Include ways in which the scene affects your senses (how the sun warms your back at the seashore, the sound of gulls chattering overhead). Continue for several pages, allowing the details of the scene to unfold as if you were really there. Write in first person, present tense: "I am lying on warm sand with the waves barely tickling my toes." Record your description by speaking it slowly into a tape recorder, or read it over until it's firm in your mind. Play the recording or reread your description as you sit quietly relaxed.

❧ Set a timer for five minutes and sit quietly. Notice what burblings come into your mind. Jot stray thoughts down as they come, then let them go.

❧ Try several of the mind-calming methods suggested in this chapter. Which ones are most comfortable and rewarding for you? Choose the method that works best, and make it your practice for ten minutes a day for a month. Write your impressions at the end of each week.

❧ What upsets, frustrates and depresses you? Make a list. What one thing stands out from the rest? Sit in silence with this thought for fifteen minutes. Let your thoughts move and change as you sit; don't try to direct them. Write about the experience. How did your thoughts change over time? Repeat this process whenever something bothersome turns up.

Experiment

❧ With another person, plan an activity in which neither of you speaks. Maintain silence as together you wash the car or each other's hair, play chess, walk through the woods. Or you can simply sit side by side or facing each other in silence for ten minutes. Afterward, write your impressions. Read aloud what you wrote. Have the other person do the same.

❧ Practice experiencing without thinking. For ten minutes, watch intently as ants build an anthill or drag a crumb along the sidewalk. Or observe goldfish snaking in and out of water plants in their tank, a spot of sun inching up a wall, the changing pattern on your computer's screen saver, animals or children at play. Pick one of these or invent your own. Be absorbed. Then write for twenty minutes.

37. The Handmade Life

Symbols for living creatively can pop up at the oddest times. When we lived in Pakistan many years ago, I was startled one morning to see our children's ayah show up dressed in an unusual outfit. What was surprising about the knee-length shift she wore over baggy white pants wasn't its design. The garment had the usual long, narrow sleeves, round neck and side slits. What riveted my attention was the fabric. It was pieced together from many items I thought I'd thrown out. Recognizable were patches from the kid's outgrown red denim coveralls, the flowered calico maternity dress I hoped I was done with for awhile, a plaid flannel shirt that had once been my cousin's and later served as a painter's smock, and remnants of a checkered tablecloth my aunt had made for my first apartment.

It was like seeing my life flash before my eyes. I realized then what a life is made of: bits and pieces sewn together with care by hand. Each piece in the patchwork has special meaning just as each person's life has special meaning. The creative, handmade life nourishes the maker and others, too, whether they know it or not.

To piece together a life of richness, meaning, satisfaction and lasting value requires an exceptional kind of creative artistry. "We must not forget that only a very few people are artists in life, that the art of life is the most distinguished and rarest of all arts," said Swiss psychiatrist Carl Jung in Jacobi and Hull's *C.G. Jung: Psychological Reflections.* It's sad that, as Jung says, so few of us are life artists. We each have the potential. No matter what our circumstances, we can be what Tina, a German photographer I know, calls a *Lebenskunstler*, a "life artist."

Learning to create an artful, handmade life means discovering how to cultivate "inner affluence." Marsha Sinetar says in her book *Do What You Love, the Money Will Follow,* "We do need inner affluence— that quality of being that enriches us in all the really important, life-affirming ways—in order to live well." Inner affluence relies on the continuing discovery of meaning and the creative expression of that meaning. In a culture that places high value on material wealth and comforts, you're not likely to meet up with anyone selling inner affluence. You have to discover it on your own.

Just as you balance your checkbook at the end of the month and tote up your earnings at tax time to assess outer affluence, you can do an accounting of inner affluence as well. I call this a deathbed inventory. Imagine you are at the end of your life, looking back. What was *really* important? What had lasting meaning? What were you most proud of? What was your life's purpose? My hunch is that looking back, even today, most of your answers don't depend on material wealth. A meaningful life can be had in a poorly heated garret in downtown Pittsburgh. It could even be had, as Anne Frank so eloquently described in *The Diary of a Young Girl,* in the back of an Amsterdam warehouse where she and her family hid for two years during Nazi occupation in World War II.

The family found meaning in small, creative ways. When electricity had to be turned off for fourteen days to conserve their ration, Anne wrote, "It's too dark to read after 4:30 so we while away the time with all kinds of crazy activities: telling riddles, doing calisthenics in the dark, speaking English and French, reviewing books." In their second year in hiding, they celebrated St. Nicholas Day as well as Hanukkah. "[W]e trooped upstairs carrying the big laundry basket which had been decorated with cutouts and bows made of pink and blue carbon paper," Anne wrote. The basket held a shoe from each person, and in each shoe was a small wrapped gift. The young girl tells of the laughter they shared on such occasions and the pleasure of small things in a life creatively lived despite terrible circumstances.

A handmade life is made, as Anne Frank demonstrated, from small things put to creative use. Carbon paper bows. Gifts hidden in a shoe. Activities to do in the dark. The handmade life is simple. That doesn't mean the handmade life is easy to live or that it doesn't take thought, care and planning.

The scramble for money and success and things, with the idea we'll take time to enjoy them someday, often stands in the way of a creative life. Creativity is more than the big invention. It's more than genius. It's more than fame and success. Creativity is a way of being. The painting, the book, the dance, the performance are not its sum. Creativity is the way you are in the world, your ease and generosity in expressing your gifts in everyday life. Creativity feeds your center and everybody else's.

"Nothing feeds the center so much as creative work, even humble kinds like cooking and sewing," says Anne Morrow Lindbergh in *Gift From the Sea*. Our idea of creativity is too lofty, too exclusive, too based on the big names. In reality, someone who creates a new recipe for ratatouille, designs a Western-theme birthday party or landscapes a backyard water garden is just as creative as Ernest Hemingway or Pablo Picasso. And maybe, because their work is more accessible, these everyday creators contribute even more to the well-lived life.

Think back. What are some of the small but significant ways your life has been creatively enriched? When have you enriched your own and other people's lives through some humble kind of creativity? We tend to overlook these ordinary expressions as unimportant, but together they make up the fabric of the handmade life.

You probably know hundreds of examples. Maybe thousands. My friend Radha welcomes the day, as women do in her native India, with rice flour stencils on her front walk. She puts the flour in a shal-

---

SEED THOUGHT

"To live our ordinary life artfully is to have this sensibility about the things in daily life, to live more intuitively and to be willing to surrender a measure of our rationality and control in return for the gifts of the soul."

Thomas Moore
Care of the Soul

low tin saucer punched with holes that make a design. When the
saucer taps the pavement, flour shakes out through the holes and
makes a pattern, usually a picture of a Hindu deity. "It's our way to creatively celebrate the day," Radha says. "The birds are fed by the flour,
and we who do it and observe it are fed by the ritual."

A woman in one of my classes tells of another way she used
creativity to express the handmade life. "We turned our family room
into a quiet room with a whole wall of shelves for books, comfy chairs
for reading and thinking, and prints of restful, natural scenes on the
wall. We even made a kind of altar where each of us—the kids, my
husband and me—could put something we made or discovered: a special stone, a handmade clay figure, a flower from the garden," she says.

My neighbor Dorothy says that her mother had a tool rack in
the garage that she embellished around each hook with curlicues and
flourishes of brightly colored enamel house paint. After many years,
the tool rack still sticks in Dorothy's memory.

Everyday creativity isn't always visible. I know a man who uses
innovative ways to help people in the business world work together
more amicably and productively. Another man I know goes out of his
way to connect people with others who can be supportive and helpful.

Native Americans recognize these humble kinds of creativity
as good medicine that enriches daily life. They have a practice of giving a basket—red and shaped like a strawberry—to a young child.
Throughout the child's life, his or her elders contribute significant
symbols to the basket: a pebble from a place they once lived, an arrow-
head, a small carved totem animal. The strawberry basket contains the
child's, later the grown person's, essence in symbolic form.

In Bangkok, Thailand, nearly every home has a spirit house in
its backyard. These elaborate, gilded and colorfully painted birdhouse-
size Thai temples on top of a tall pole provide a home for spirits. Daily
offerings of food, flowers and incense make certain that the spirits stick
around and don't wander into the house to annoy the family.

Inspired by both the Native American strawberry basket and
the Thai spirit house, I began my own creative ritual some years ago. I
began what I call a "strong box," a hand-carved teakwood box that
holds symbols of important occasions and turning points. Into it I've

put a collection of objects that include a silver pin from my reporter job on a high school newspaper, a locket with a photo of my kids, an Iranian camel bell, a broken key that once unlocked the earliest of several Hondas and a cross I had given my father when he lay dying of cancer. When I'm in need of reinforcement, I take out the strong box and go through its objects, one by one. These life symbols give me hope and strength. They remind me of what I love and have loved.

The handmade life is personal. It holds all the things we cherish. Those things can, and often do, find their way into our creative work. Pablo Picasso once said, "I put into my pictures everything I like. So much the worse for the things—they have to get along with one another."

Things you love, the innovative ways you've brightened other people's lives, the obstacles and griefs you've creatively survived all come together in the patchwork of colors and shapes and textures that compose the handmade life. Though the pieces never assemble in quite the way you planned, the work bears your individual imprint. Until the day you draw your last breath, it is a work in progress.

Explorations

❀ Make a list of ten things that contribute to your life in a deep, abiding, healthy way (people, places, a natural phenomenon, activities, creative expression, memories, events, etc.). Write about ways that some of these things can be brought into your creative life or made prominent and visible in your everyday life. Some suggestions:

> Build a shelf to hold the stones, leaves and pinecones you bring home from the woods.
> Frame snapshots of the important people in your life, and make a picture wall in a stairwell.
> Decorate a grapevine wreath with objects that symbolize what's meaningful to you.

❀ Make an identity board. Get a large piece of corrugated cardboard or foamboard. Depict your personal history and what has real meaning for you by gluing on old photos; magazine pictures; artwork; portions of letters; theater or sporting event tickets; newspaper clippings; and objects such as coins, a pencil to symbolize writing or drawing, etc. Use acrylic paint to decorate and unify the separate parts.

❀ Design your own "crazy quilt" by cutting geometric shapes from wallpaper, construction paper, junk mail, fabric or wrapping paper. Label each one with a talent, skill, interest, accomplishment, influential person or mentor. Move them around on a stiff support until they form related constellations. Glue them in place. Decorate with actual or painted-on stitches, sequins, etc.

Project

❀ Make your own version of a spirit house. It can be a clay bowl, a decoupage wooden box from a craft store or a painted birdhouse with a removable roof. Every day, put in a small, symbolic object. At the end of a week, remove the objects and write your thoughts.

Celebration

❀ Plan an artful celebration of a special holiday, a solstice, a birthday, an anniversary or a memorable event (such as a friend's new job, your spouse's first hole in one, or your own art show or successfully published article). Be creative. Use flowers, banners, posters, decorations, imaginative food, ritual, dance, music, singing. Later, write about the experience. (If such a celebration is too much to attempt right now, plan your own mini celebration, such as a tribute in art or writing to a special person, place or growing thing.)

ch 38. For the Love of Liverwurst

ALLOWING

YOUR DREAMS

TO LIVE

Chuck at the Dilly Deli once told me that bees love liverwurst. On an August scorcher, a bunch of us were melting together under outdoor umbrellas at the deli, a tiny, family-run restaurant located just across the street from where I live. The bees were on a rampage. They buzzed around our heads and dive-bombed into our potato salad. In retaliation, Chuck set out institutional-size glass bottles to capture them. There was a glob of liverwurst in the bottom of each bottle. Bees love liverwurst, Chuck pointed out. They couldn't resist. Attracted by the fragrant snack, they crawled through the narrow neck of the bottle and gorged on liverwurst. They couldn't find their way out. Trapped, the winged things fluttered helplessly inside the glass, batted repeatedly against its sides and ultimately spiraled down to land on the liverwurst, dead from exhaustion.

Without creative vision, we can get trapped in bottlenecks just like the baffled bees at the deli. We get lured in, away from our creative

direction, by the aroma of appealing distractions and the buzzing busyness of everyday life. When we're in that bottled-up space, it seems
more important to take the clothes to the dry cleaner than to glue ourselves to a chair and dig into writing the article that's been on the back
burner for months. When we allow our creative dreams to be put off
indefinitely, our muse packs her bags and hitchhikes to Wichita.

If, over time, you let too many outer demands obscure your
creative directions, you lose sight of your dreams. Creativity collapses.
It can't fly without a flight plan that keeps it in close contact with instinct and the creative source.

This close contact is what Chinese critic, writer and amateur
painter Chang Yen-Yuan in A.D. 845 called "spirit resonance." Quoted
by Thomas Munro in *Oriental Aesthetics*, he said spirit resonance "is first
active in the artist before it becomes manifest in his works." First you
have to find the dream in yourself, then it vibrates in your creative work
and the effect your work has on your audience. It's like the way the dulcimer in the corner of my living room hums when a jet flies over. The
brass book stand sings, too, and so do the windowpanes. When something finds its own vibration, everything hums in unison.

So how is it possible to discover spirit resonance? We are
pulled in too many directions—fragmented—used up by duties, other
people and our own ambitions. The world topside has our complete
attention. There's little energy left for going inside. Yet, as Ira Progoff
says in *The Dynamics of Hope*, "it is only when the level of experience has
markedly shifted from the surface to the depths that experiences of
transpersonal meaning and transpersonal affect become possible."
What Progoff is saying is that you have to go deep to get in touch with
spirit resonance. This is where you find your creative vision, your voice.

There's only one way I know of to make that connection. That
way, difficult as it may be, is to take time for solitude. Native Americans
do it when they set out on a vision quest. This kind of solitary journey
is not so much a questing after some goal as it is a state of receptiveness
toward whatever wants to come.

Counsellor Kate Lanthier tells about her quest, a trek into the
Andes where she lived among the Qero Indians in the Amazon jungles.
"I got more in touch with myself and the place where creativity

springs," she said. "It's difficult to take time out of your life to be alone. But if we don't do it, we get overly attached to our lives and to the roles we play, and that stands in the way of creativity. It doesn't mean I stop being a mother, wife or worker, but time apart gives me the opportunity to step outside of these roles for a moment. It allows me to get in touch with the deep, most essential part of myself where creativity springs. Vision grows out of this. And when we align our vision with our intention, the universe actively conspires on our behalf."

You don't have to trek to the Andes to get in touch with your vision. Jean, an organizational consultant, took part in a retreat just a few miles from his home. "It was held at a local Methodist church. Meals were prepared and served by people who had gone through the same seventy-two-hour program. We brought sleeping bags and slept on the floor." he says. It's possible, as Jean discovered, to get in touch with solitude even while being part of a group.

Whether you take time to be "alone" in a group or go off for a time by yourself, there are many good reasons to set aside a few days or a few hours for solitary coming together with yourself. A quest at any time can be valuable, but at certain times it can be absolutely essential to creative work. Some of these times are

- when your creativity has dried up or gone stale
- when you're about to begin a major project—a book, an exhibit of your work, a performance—and you need to take time to let ideas emerge and sort themselves out
- when busyness has taken over your life and has left you feeling fragmented and out of touch with your creative source
- when you're about to enter—or are already in—a life transition (a move, a divorce, a new job, recovering from illness, etc.)
- when you want to grow creatively, keep your genie fed and expand creative possibilities and ways of seeing
- when you want to clarify your creative path, direction and themes, and let ideas crystallize naturally

There are three parts to a successful vision retreat. They parallel what folklorist Joseph Campbell calls "the night sea journey." The three parts are

- making ready
- the time apart
- the return, living your dream

Possibly the most demanding step is making ready. All kinds of questions arise: Where will you go (or will you stay home)? How long? How will you take care of responsibilities while you're gone? What can you do to assure privacy?

Time apart is an opportunity to search for and strengthen your roots, your standpoint. Without such a standpoint, without knowing who you are and what you stand for, creativity would be hollow. To start out on the right foot, ask yourself, What's important? What really matters to me? Your direction will come from that place.

"I know what I do will be authentic and creative if it comes from my root place," a young woman who is part of a modern dance troupe once told me. "It's taken me a while to find that place, but the search has been worth it."

To start you off, you may find it helpful to write out your vision as you now see it. Don't make it a treatise. Just a sentence or two will do just fine. Ask yourself

> What do I want to do, creatively, more than anything else?
> How can I use my special skills, talents, experience to accomplish my vision?
> Who will benefit from my work?
> Where will I do what I do?
> What do I hope to accomplish in my lifetime?

Your written vision might go something like this:

> I would like to work at home to write self-help articles for an adult audience using my training in

SEED THOUGHT

"One must be willing to dream, and one must know how."

Baudelaire

social work and my skills with language to inspire readers to live their own possibilities.

Or this:

I want to teach art to high school students at the local recreation center using my degree in art education and experience as a teacher and painter to help students become aware of their artistic potential and the importance of visual communication in their lives and the lives of others.

When you've written a vision that sums up your creative direction, write down the first step you'd take toward your goal and when you'd take that step. Write your vision on a self-stick note, and post it a month from now in your date book to remind yourself, like a polestar that lights your path, which way you're going.

Your written vision would be a good focus for a retreat of several hours or days. See if you can translate your vision into a symbol that you could paint. Or think about writing a page or two of your creative life history and how it applies and has applied to your vision. See your vision as a growing, changing, living thing.

"I always thought I'd figure out what I wanted to do, and that would be it. I'd never have to think about it again, even to refine my direction or set off on a new track," a part-time potter and kite maker once told me. "I started out as a graphic designer and found myself drawn more and more to doing something I could hold and touch. If I hadn't been open to new possibilities, these directions could have lain dormant forever."

So you enter your time apart with eyes open. You go in with a question, a focus, a receptiveness and wait to be filled. And you wait in a place chosen just for this purpose. It can be a spot in the woods where you've cleared away debris and made a neat circle of stones to contain you and your process. It can be a particular corner in your home that you've spiffed up and decorated with cushions, flowers and artwork. You might want to make a circle of favorite objects—a collection of shells or small clay figures—on the rug, then sit in the middle. Appeal to the senses with scented candles, herbs or potpourri. Prepare yourself, too, with a ritual bath or shower (to wash away old ideas). Dress in comfortable clothes in subtle colors.

You can begin your time apart with mind-clearing practices like the ones we talked about in chapter thirty-six. Add journal writing if you like, or have your paints and pens handy to capture images that emerge. What you do during the time isn't as important as the intensity of your focus and concentration. If you provide the focusing glass and the kindling, the fire will ignite itself.

When you come out of your refuge at the end of your time apart, try to plan some way to process your experience. Get together with others to talk about your vision and get their feedback. Write about your insights. Paint your revelations. Find a way to express what you've learned from your experience. Revisit your vision statement to see if you want to make any changes.

A creative vision retreat is an opportunity to practice receptiveness. It opens you. It gives your muse a chance to speak without having to compete with the static of everyday life. Liver sausage distractions keep luring us into narrow bottlenecks where we buzz around in circles until creativity dies. Solitude broadens our vision, nourishes creativity and leads us out.

BREATHING LIFE INTO YOUR DREAMS

- What creative work gives you the greatest energy charge?
- What creative legacy do you want to leave to the world?
- What creative project have you always dreamed of doing?
- What's keeping you from doing it?
- What can you do *today* to begin to live your dream?

Explorations

✤ List five things you want to accomplish in your creative lifetime. Be bold. Write about why they're important to you. Keep the list handy in your date book or on your fridge. Revise as you need to.

✤ Using the guidelines in this chapter, create a vision statement for your creative life at the point it is right now. Post your vision someplace where you'll see it every day. Write a duplicate copy on a self-stick note and attach it to a page of your daily calendar or engagement book on a date six months from now. When that date arrives, reconsider your vision. Is the focus still appropriate? Are you on track carrying out your vision? Make any changes you need to. Write for twenty minutes about ways you've lived your vision during the past six months.

✤ How would you like to contribute creatively to the world during your lifetime? Write for a half hour about what you'd like to do and how you propose to do it.

✤ Whose work do you most admire? Why? What creative work have you done or would you like to do that reflects the values you see in the work you admire?

Project

✤ Design a coat of arms to symbolize your vision as you now see it. Draw with a black permanent marker and color in with gouache, tempera, watercolor or colored pencil.

Creative Retreat

✤ Plan a vision quest—an afternoon or several days away—using this chapter as a base to put together your own ideas. Draw and write about the images that emerge on your quest. Are any of these images powerful enough to serve as a guiding symbol for your creative life?

39. Listening to Dolphins

Someone I know, although not very well, once had a startling dream about dolphins. As a resident creative for a decidedly left-brained corporation, he's understandably shy about letting such things get out, so we'll conceal his identity and call him Robert. His name could just as well be Roberta or your name or mine, since his struggle is much like ours. The corporation Robert works for purports to value creativity, his and others'. But in practice, he's found over the years, it's another story. Each time he comes up with an original idea, no matter how valuable that idea might be, he has to fight his way through layers of corporate naysayers to get decision makers to listen and finally—*finally*—accept a new approach.

A CREATIVE

PERSON'S

RESPONSIBILITY

One night, after a long day's struggle to get the company brass to listen to a new idea, he went to sleep tired and discouraged. Then the dream began. He's standing on a pier jutting out into the ocean, and a pod of dolphins swims near. To his amazement, they start to speak. He runs off to tell his co-workers and others about the dolphins' astonishing feat. Everyone hurries to the water's edge to see firsthand. But even though the dolphins are still talking, the other people can't hear them. Disgruntled, the human onlookers shuffle away, grumbling about a hoax. When they've gone, the dolphins say to Robert, "See? We *told* you!"

The dream, Robert confides, brought a realization. Creative people try to communicate what they've heard right from the dolphin's mouth, so to speak. They try to do the undoable: translate obscure creative experience into a form other people can understand and accept.

Those stone walls are usually erected by decision makers who tend to be what Edward De Bono calls "vertical thinkers." In his decades-ago best-seller *New Think*, he says that such practical, pragmatic, linear thinking throws a wet blanket on creativity. But even so, he adds, that's to be expected. "It is a myth that those who are in a position to do something about new ideas are eagerly awaiting them. And there is no reason it should be otherwise, for it is easy enough to have a new idea, but much more difficult to put it into effect."

One writer agreed. She told me, "I wish I had a nickel for every time someone has sidled up to me at a cocktail party to suggest a book idea for me to write. They're not aware of how much grueling effort it takes to write a book and that it has to be my own idea, my own passion for the idea, that fuels momentum so I can stay the course."

Passion to stay the course despite rejection, struggle and stone walls may be the most important ingredient in creativity. Creative responsibility begins with the struggle for resolution on the inside by taming your inner critic. It ends in a battle for the life of your creative work where you hope to win the cooperation of your outer critics. Until your idea is put to work, it's not completely born.

A whole book could be written about getting your ideas accepted. This is the "90 percent perspiration" from the old adage. If you're going to be creative, you're going to run into stone walls. You have to train for the act so you can muscle through to exclaim, as Mary Tyler Moore recently did, "I'm not just a survivor, I'm a flourisher!"

Innovation is not widely accepted; that is a well-known fact. "Everyone who is creative is punished," says Henry Heimlich, M.D., inventor of the Heimlich maneuver and one of the ten best-known names in the world. The *Encyclopedia Britannica* calls him "a rebel with a cause: saving lives." He fought for over a decade to get the American Red Cross to adopt his maneuver for choking victims. He says it wasn't until a child choked on a sandwich, went into a coma and eventually died as a result of Red Cross–advocated back slaps that the tide turned. C. Everett Koop, the U.S. Surgeon General at the time, declared that the back slaps used in attempts to dislodge an object in a choking victim were "hazardous, even lethal." After ten years, the Red Cross was forced to abandon back slaps and adopt the Heimlich maneuver. "Tenacity," Heimlich says, "is the last step in creativity. If all your peers understand what you've done, you haven't been very creative."

Creativity is like learning to swim with dolphins. You dive deep for inspiration, but you don't forget to come up for air in the everyday world where you put your ideas to work. Diving too deep or staying too long can cause your work to suffer from lack of connection to reality. Spend too much time out of water and your work dries up. The dolphin way of creativity depends on a rhythm of diving and resurfacing. It's when you alternate periods of what Edward De Bono calls "creative fluidity" with periods of "developmental rigidity" that the process begins to move.

Annie Dillard describes the in-and-out creative process in *An American Childhood*:

> And still I break through the skin of awareness a
> thousand times a day, as dolphins burst through
> seas and dive again and rise and dive.

Diving and surfacing each call for a different approach. Most creative people have a knack for diving or they wouldn't be good at what they do. Where they often run into trouble is in surfacing—getting a creative work or idea out into the world. This part of the process is highly extroverted. It requires a whole new set of skills.

"Innovation is a process of swimming against resistance," says Paul Saffo, a director of the Institute for the Future. Once we recognize the truth of what he says, we can start to work on our swimming skills. "I never thought I should have to do anything with my work," a painter once told me. "I always thought someone would discover me someday and would promote what I do without any help from me. Once I wised up to the fact that I was the only one who was going to do it—that I was going to have to do it myself—I could begin to work on the skills it takes to get my paintings into the marketplace. It took a lot of doing—still does—because I'm not naturally someone who's good at promotion and countering people's resistance."

Most of us are not naturally good at this sort of thing. We have to learn the dolphin's way over time. People who have learned how to get their ideas accepted by left-brained decision makers list five things you should do:

1 **TRANSLATE YOUR IDEAS INTO LEFT-BRAINED WAYS OF THINKING.** Support your selling points with logical arguments. Use the same buzzwords that the decision-making person uses (just be sure you know how to use them). Consider models, artwork or other visual ways to make your ideas easier to comprehend.

2 **WHEN YOU WANT TO MARKET YOUR IDEAS OR CREATIVE WORK, START AT THE BEGINNING AND PROCEED STEP-BY-STEP.** Creative people tend to think in circles, and they feel comfortable jumping in at any point in that circle, figuring they'll eventually cover all the bases. Most decision makers think sequentially. First you do this, then you do this—step one, step two, step three. They want things spelled out in detail in a logical order. Honor their peculiarities by presenting your ideas accordingly.

3 **FORM A DIVERSE COALITION OF PEOPLE THE DECISION MAKER RESPECTS.** Get their input on your ideas and the way they're presented. Tell them to be completely frank and that it won't hurt your feelings (even though it probably will). Note their comments in writing so you can put them to use later.

4 **TAKE TIME TO DEVELOP, DOCUMENT AND POLISH YOUR INNOVATION.** Creative people are prone to think out loud and

expose ideas before they're completely developed. Decision makers often can't make the leap from raw inspiration to developed idea. You have to help them. Respect and account for practical considerations such as cost, manpower, time, marketability—whatever applies in your situation.

5 **NEVER GIVE UP.** Never, never, never, never give up on your creative progeny.

And one thing more. No matter how well you prepare, you are likely to meet with ferocious resistance. Such is the nature of the creative process. If you see such resistance as a challenge and not as a stop sign, you're halfway home. Let T.S. Eliot's advice be your marching song: "For most of us, this is the aim never here to be realized; who are only undefeated because we have gone on trying."

THE DOLPHIN WAY

How to Survive in a Left-Brained World
- Balance creative "deep dives" with practical resurfacing.
- Nurture creativity in yourself and other people, especially children. Do this by being more supportive than critical. Zero in on the strengths of an idea or a work.
- Encourage an environment where creativity is possible.
- Go to bat for other people's innovation, even if that innovation seems impractical at first. Point out possibilities and dwell less on impossibilities.
- Be patient with left-brained people.
- Expect resistance. See it as a test for the value of your creative ideas. The more resistance you encounter, the more likely it is that your work is truly creative.

Explorations

🌢 One of the pillars of creativity is inner strength. When have you stood up, despite opposition, for an idea or creative work you believed in? What trials have you survived so far? Are you satisfied with the outcomes? What could you or would you have done differently? Write for a half hour about your insights.

🌢 Write a case history on one creative idea or piece of work and the stages it went through before it was accepted. How did you develop the idea? Who supported you along the way? What ways did you devise to help get your idea adopted?

🌢 When have you missed an opportunity to support someone else's creativity when that person was besieged by criticism? What could you have done differently? When have you been an advocate for another person? What did you do? Explore your thoughts and feelings in writing or drawing.

Research

🌢 Give a presentation in support of an idea or creative work to a group of friends or cohorts. Note their objections and resistances as well as their enthusiasms. Using this research as a base, develop a written plan for getting your work accepted.

Assessment

🌢 Write about your strengths in the areas of (1) creative ideas and (2) getting them out into the world. Which of these two sides still needs development? How will you do it?

The Angels' Share

A Napa, California, brandy brewer practices an unusual way of giving back some of nature's creative bounty. The brewer sets aside certain vats that vent some of the brandy, in the form of steam, to the heavens. People at the brewery call this "the angels' share."

This giving back, this setting aside a portion to sustain the creative force, has been performed in dozens of ways through the ages. Ancient people slaughtered pigs and tossed them into a ditch in the earth to make sure the earth wouldn't forget to bloom again. Some primitive tribes even used blood sacrifice to pacify the gods so they would continue to look kindly upon them. From ancient times to present day, some form of sacrifice, of giving back, has always been a way to make the world more fruitful.

Creativity, too, asks for sacrifice. It whispers in your ear that it wants you to give up everything you know—empty out, surrender completely. It invites you to houseclean all your mental crannies so creativity will have an empty vessel to fill. On top of everything else, it asks you to give up control, to let it lead when you get up to dance.

After you've learned the elementary steps, creativity asks one thing more. It pesters you to share your gifts. Creativity that isn't shared, isn't communicated, is like music played to an empty room. No one benefits. Not even you.

Contributing your angels' share can be an act as simple as writing a poem for a troubled friend or figuring out how to solve an office squabble. It can be subtle, too, as when you create something beautiful in word, paint, stone or sound that other people can experience and find meaning in. Or it can be more dramatic: devising a way to address school violence or poverty or homelessness or any of the countless challenges people face today.

Creativity is not just a card trick you do to impress friends at a party. The creative act is a dance between you and your world. It's a way to contribute your angels' share to bring hope, beauty, understanding, a better way.

index